Boris Jofan, Wladimir Schtschuko, Wladimir Gelfreich: Palast der Sowjets, 415 Meter, Moskau 1931-1954 (nicht realisiert)

Capitalist Realism
Kapitalistischer Realismus

Bart Goldhoorn | Philipp Meuser

Capitalist Realism
New Architecture in Russia

Kapitalistischer Realismus
Neue Architektur in Russland

DOM
publishers

This book presents a selection of more than fifty projects built in Russia over the past ten years. Its aim is to offer a representative survey of recent trends in Russian architecture. We are aware that such an aspiration also has a problematic side. Little of what is happening in the Russian building sector at the moment is worthy of being publicised, so the projects assembled here are the exception, not the norm. Russia today is known as the Wild East – and for good reason. New construction projects often involve little input from trained architects, and it is not always the most interesting or the best planners who bring their designs to fruition. Quite apart from that, as editors we invariably have to exercise a certain restraint. By restricting our choice to designs that have actually been realised, we have had to exclude fascinating projects by such influential architects as Mikhail Filippov and Sergey Malakhov. A number of promising young architects who so far have realised their ideas mainly in the area of interior architecture will hopefully find a place in a follow-up volume on new Russian interior design which is in planning. For all these limitations, however, we are confident that the present publication will convey a distinct impression of important trends in Russian architecture.

Bart Goldhoorn
Philipp Meuser

Diese Publikation versammelt eine Auswahl von über fünfzig Projekten, die in den vergangenen zehn Jahren in Russland entstanden sind. Das Buch erhebt den Anspruch, einen repräsentativen Überblick über aktuelle Entwicklungen in der russischen Architektur zu geben. Uns ist klar, dass dieser Anspruch der Repräsentativität auch Probleme mit sich bringt. Denn das gegenwärtige Baugeschehen Russlands hat nur wenig mit veröffentlichungswürdigen Beispielen zu tun, die in dieser Eigenschaft vor allem Ausnahmen sind. Und nicht die Regel. Denn Russland wird nicht umsonst als »wilder Osten« bezeichnet. Viele Neubauten entstehen weitgehend ohne die fachliche Beteiligung von Architekten, und es sind nicht immer die interessantesten und besten Planer, die am Ende ihre Entwürfe realisieren können. Abgesehen davon, stehen wir als Herausgeber ohnehin immer unter einem Diktat der Selbstbeschränkung. Allein durch die Begrenzung der Auswahl auf realisierte Gebäude bleiben interessante Projekte von solch einflussreichen Architekten wie Michail Filippow oder Sergej Malachow unberücksichtigt; ebenso wie die Arbeiten einiger junger, viel versprechender Architekten, die ihre Ideen bislang hauptsächlich im Bereich der Innenarchitektur umsetzten. Doch ein Folgeband über junges russisches *Interior Design* ist geplant. Bei allen Einschränkungen hoffen wir jedoch, dass dieses Buch auf seine eigene, besondere Weise einen Eindruck von den wichtigen Tendenzen in der russischen Architektur vermittelt.

Bart Goldhoorn
Philipp Meuser

Contents
Inhalt

Russian Roots

Regional Russia

Post-Soviet Modernism

Russian Nostalgia

Architecture after Communism

Bart Goldhoorn

Revolutionary! New! Change! Freedom! Choice! It is not for nothing that these words are often used in commercials – they have a universal appeal. Change and revolution have positive connotations. The same was the case with the changes in Russia around 1990. The whole world was looking at the New Russia, hoping to see a miraculous economic and cultural blossoming, freed from the yoke of communism. More than fifteen years have passed. You only have to watch the news to know that the problems of Russia are more fundamental then they seemed at first glance. Architecture and urbanism are no exception. For decades to come the Russian city will bear the marks of seventy years of communism, whereas other cities with a communist past, like those in central Europe, will be able to erase this episode of history more easily. There are a number of reasons for this. Not only did industrialisation arrive much later and communism much earlier in Russia than in central Europe, the pre-revolutionary Russian city consisted largely of wooden houses (St Petersburg and Moscow excluded). So even in cities that boast a thousand years of history, scarcely any traces of the past remain. As a result the physical form of the contemporary Russian city has developed almost exclusively under communism. Communism is therefore not just a veneer that can be scraped away to reveal the real city underneath, nor can it be regarded as a historical mistake that is best forgotten as quickly as possible (as is the case in Central Europe). It is not the monuments, slogans and symbols that define the communist character of the Russian city, but the fact that it was created in a society that was ruled by communist principles: no private property, small income differences, public housing, industrialised construction.

The Fourth Revolution

The Soviet heritage that forms the basis of the Russian city is fascinating for its radical conceptuality.[1] There is no speculation, no uncontrollable market, only architecture based on ideology. Within this ideological discourse there have been three revolutions: the constructivist revolution of the 1920s and 1930s with its modernist experiments; the Stalinist revolution that replaced these with an almost baroque neoclassicism and a reversion to traditional urban design; and the Khrushchev revolution that banned any decoration and gave rise to an almost absolute form of modernism – industrialised building on a massive scale using standard prefabricated elements.[2] The fourth revolution, that of the 1990s, is no less radical than its predecessors. It is architecture's reaction to the crisis of socialism, a crisis that is certainly most vividly apparent in Russia, but also visible to a lesser extent in late-twentieth-century western Europe when the post-war social democratic planning policies were abandoned in favour of openly capitalist ones.

Paper Architecture

The essence of all of these revolutions is that they reject the previous period, and in the case of the fourth revolution this is the era of Soviet modernism initiated by Nikita Khrushchev in the 1960s. The origin of the revolt can be traced back to the 1980s, when Russian architecture had its own dissident movement that went under the name of Paper Architecture. Many young Russian architects won international competitions, most of them organised by the journal *The Japan Architect*.[3] In their work, these architects

9

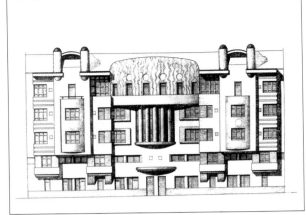

expressed their rejection of the brave new world of totalitarian modernism in favour of a romantic realm of nostalgia, ruins and metaphors. This came as a big surprise to the international architectural scene; for the first time since constructivism Russian architects were making a major contribution to the international architectural discourse, which at that time was dominated by postmodernist themes. This is the reason why, when the political situation changed drastically a decade later, many hoped for the emergence of a new architecture from the East, a renaissance comparable to that of Spanish architecture after the death of Franco. Not much of this seems to have materialised. But still, there is a place in Russia that touches on this ideal: a large industrial city four hundred kilometres east of Moscow, formerly called Gorky, known in the West primarily as the city where Soviet dissident Andrey Sakharov spent several years in exile. The new architectural school that was coming to life here embodied the principles of the fourth revolution: private initiative, plurality and freedom of expression.

The Miracle of Nizhny Novgorod

It is no coincidence that this happened in the Russian provinces. During communism, the provinces were the place where there was real repression in the field of architecture. Khrushchev's idea of industralisation and standardisation introduced a principle that most buildings (except in Moscow) had to be constructed using standard designs developed by the big institutes in the capital. Local architects were permitted to do no more than adapt the standard designs to local conditions. When this system collapsed along with the centrally controlled economy, the most ambitious took their chance to set up their own firms. A real architectural school sprung up in Nizhny Novgorod, and its leader, Aleksander Kharitonov, became the city's chief architect (head of the municipal planning authority). At the same time, the changes in the economy led to a complete reversal in the development of the city. During Soviet times, growth was concentrated in construction of large industrial complexes on the outskirts. In the capitalist economy, the city centre, neglected for decades and for a large part consisting of dilapidated wooden houses, suddenly became important as a centre for trade and communication. The necessity to reconstruct these areas combined with the demands for new housing programmes led to a genuine process of urban renewal where wooden buildings were gradually replaced by new developments. After being forced to serve a diet of concrete boxes for over thirty years, local architects now cooked up a feast of architecture: an orgy of styles expressing the creative freedom they had been denied for so long. They were helped by the prevailing economic conditions. Cheap labour, rich clients and an absence of regulation brought forth an architecture of excess in stucco, brick and paint, offering all the possibilities one could wish for. In a way it repeated nineteenth-century eclecticism, with the big difference that it referred not only to historic examples, but also to contemporary architecture. The peak of success for Nizhny Novgorod's architecture came in the second half of the 1990s, while the end of the era when the city could claim to be the architectural capital of Russia was ushered in by the tragic death of its main figure, Aleksander Kharitonov, in a car accident in 2000. Without his charismatic leadership Nizhny Novgorod's architectural achievements were soon overshadowed by developments in Moscow.[4]

Post-Soviet Moscow

If Nizhny Novgorod was the architectural capital of Russia in the 1990s, what happened in Moscow over that period? Being the economic and cultural centre of the former Soviet empire, did Moscow not present ideal conditions for the emergence of a new post-totalitarian architecture? In reality nothing of the kind happened, and paradoxically the central position of Moscow is the main reason for this. Firstly, the revolution of the 1990s led to a loss of power for the Moscow architects – in contrast with their counterparts in the provinces. In the old days they would do projects all over the Soviet Union, but now were limited to their own city. Secondly, being a relatively rich city, Moscow was able to maintain a Soviet-like planning and construction sector – large-scale and centrally controlled – whereas in many other cities such structures were replaced by small architects' offices and construction companies. As a result, in Moscow the fourth revolution progressed in a way that was quite similar to its predecessors: one diktat – modernism – was replaced with another – historicism. It is telling that the main architectural event in the capital in the 1990s was the construction of the Cathedral of Christ the Saviour, an exact copy of the cathedral built by Nicholas I in 1883 and destroyed by Stalin in 1931 to make space for the infamous Palace of the Soviets (which was never completed because of the start of the Second World War). And it was not, as one might have naively expected, the Paper Architects of the 1980s who were able to put their paper dreams into practice, but the very same design institutes that designed the Soviet concrete boxes reorienting themselves to design neo-classicist buildings. Moreover, protests by glasnost-era activists against the demolition of the historical city were coopted by the all-powerful bureaucracy, establishing a system of control designed to guarantee that new buildings in the city centre would appear historical. In fact the introduction of democracy only led to a strengthening of the bureaucratic apparatus. The real democratic content of the decision-making processes revealed by the way the so-called "social council", installed to represent the opinion of the population in general and the "creative intelligentsia" in particular on new urban developments, is in reality completely dominated by Mayor Yury Luzhkov, using the argument that because he is elected by the people, they speak through him. At the same time the municipality has an economic interest in many projects in the city. This applies not only to buildings with traditional public functions, such as theatres, museums, sports facilities etc., but also to shopping malls and residential and office developments. Many architects have to deal with a situation where the client, planning authorities and often also the construction company are part of one big municipal holding (of which the architect might also be a part): in fact a communist model, allowing ample space for arbitrary decisions resulting from economic or political interests.[5]

Private Investors – Private Studios

The situation in Russia is quite different from other countries, where public sector commissions present an ideal opportunity to realise interesting architectural projects. In fact the situation is the opposite: the closer a project is connected to the municipality, the worse its architecture. In Moscow private investors commission the best architecture.

Not all of them, of course – those who value their closeness to the city government see to it that their buildings are liked by the mayor. Closest of all is the infamous developer Don Stroy, who has just completed the Triumf Palace, the tallest residential building in Europe, designed to resemble the Stalinist skyscrapers of the 1950s. Still, there are also developers who take a different approach and mainly cater to the demand for office space for private companies and for luxury apartments for affluent New Russians. They work with a limited number of Moscow firms that have proved their ability to provide state-of-the-art architectural services. Starting from scratch in the early 1990s, these firms, such as Sergey Kiselyov and Partners, the Asadov Studio, Rezerv, ABD and Ostozhenka, managed to establish professional architecture studios. Before that all buildings were designed by municipal or national design institutes.

Interior Design

An amazing phenomenon that has had an enormous influence on the way Russian architecture has evolved over the last decade is the way all apartment buildings are built without interior layouts. This is not the result of ideological or technical considerations, but of the realities of the market. When the first apartment buildings for rich New Russians came on the market in the mid-1990s, developers found that the first thing buyers would do was demolish all the internal walls and create a ground plan to suit their specific wishes. Consequently, it was cheaper to leave the walls out in the first place. Since clients did not really know what to do with an empty space of 200–300 sqm, they started to hire interior designers. Young architects realised that they could make good money helping these clients solve their problems. For the architectural profession this brought about a split between *obemshiki* and *interiershiki*. A typical *obemshik* (literally: person who works with volumes) is an architect, aged over 40, educated in Soviet times, working within the old system, with good contacts with the authorities, designing buildings at a scale no more detailed then 1:100 and not making too much money. A typical *interiershik* is much younger, works for private clients, has good contacts with the designer furniture and interior fittings suppliers, often has his own building brigade and makes good money. In general one could say that during the 1990s the most interesting architecture was created in interior design, where the bureaucracy and the big Soviet-style construction industry had no influence. Moreover, the younger generation of architects was much better informed. They started their professional life at a time when information about foreign architecture was becoming widely available in Russia, whereas the older generation had to deal with the legacy that in the Soviet period access to information from capitalist countries had been extremely limited. This information advantage, combined with the huge budgets clients were ready to spend on their private interiors, gave the interior architects virtually unlimited possibilities. Many of the custom-made details and furniture one sees in these interiors would be simply unaffordable in western Europe.[6]

The Next Generation

Recent years have witnessed an interesting development, which can be put down to the evolution of both clients and the architects themselves. Within the profession, we see that

Car park with façade in the neo-traditional style designed by Mosproyekt 2, 2001

Parkhaus (im Hintergrund) mit neotraditioneller Fassade, Entwurf: Mosprojekt-2 (2001)

the field of the *obemshiki* is gradually being penetrated by a new generation of architects. Two groups are involved: young architects who gained experience in the big new private firms of the 1990s and then started their own architectural practices, and *interiershiki* who have gradually made their way up from interiors via private houses to residential and office buildings in the city. These architects have big advantages compared to the older generation of *obemshiki*. They are not the first to establish private architectural practices – this has been done for them already – and they have a good practical knowledge of construction because of their experience, either as assistants or project architects, or through their hands-on work as interior designers. At the same time, their skills are increasingly in demand by developers. In parallel with the architects they have gained experience, travelled abroad and understood the possibilities of architecture as a marketing tool. In Moscow, where there is a considerable reservoir of people who are ready to pay huge sums for exclusive real estate (up to $ 15,000 per sqm) every developer wants to tap into the market for luxury apartments.

Russian Architecture?

In spite of (or because of) the fact that the new generation is integrated in – or at least aware of – the international architectural context, their work is not yet articulated enough to speak of a specific approach. One of the reasons is that there has been almost no architectural debate in Russia over the last fifteen years. Everybody has been busy establishing their architectural practices under the new economic conditions. For an architecture that is outspoken and

definitely Russian we have to return to the generation of the Paper Architects. Although a big part of this generation has been absorbed into regular architectural practice, some are still developing the conceptual work they started twenty-five years ago. As before, the main theme of their work is to find a way of dealing with contemporary architecture after the disaster of Soviet prefab modernism. The fundamentalists, with Mikhail Filippov and Ilya Utkin as their main representatives, believe in the eternal value of classicism. In a way they are close to the British and American historicists like Krier and Stern, but their vision is much more melancholic and stresses the ruin-like qualities of classicism. This is at the same time their strength and weakness. Ruination may be beautifully expressed on paper, but when it is actually built it tends to lose the quality it has in the drawing. Still, these works are an expression of a genuine post-Soviet melancholy, and this why they are often more powerful than their bourgeois Western counterparts.

Secondly, there are the architects who stress the imperfection of the ruin more than its classicist aspect. They find their inspiration within communist history, but not in its official reading as a rational, logical and Taylorist system, but in a parallel world that existed alongside the official one. It is the realm of the dacha – DIY country cottages built using the left-overs of communist production, of endless discussions in the kitchen at parties, of the possibility (or necessity) of living within Soviet society but outside the Soviet system. The aesthetic of this realm is the *objet trouvé* – surrealism. It has been best researched by Sergey Malakhov, who has collected around two hundred examples of left-over buildings, presenting them as designs: with drawings, models and a story he made up to explain the *raison d'être* of the object.

Another architect inspired by this imperfection is Aleksander Yermolaev, founder of the *Theatre of Architectural Forms*. He finds this quality in the traditions of wooden architecture in the Russian north. However, the main representative of this idea is Aleksander Brodsky. His works – temporary, crude, unrefined – seem best to express the architecture of imperfection that is a critique of both Soviet modernism and the modernist architecture of Western standards. Of course this work is utterly Romantic. It does not stand the modern world's test of sustainability and economy, so over time there will almost certainly be no place for it. The same is the probable case for Russia as a whole. It will change – the question is whether it will be for the better.

1 In 1954 Khrushchev announced a modernist turn in architecture to the congress of architects and builders of the Soviet Union. An English translation of his speech may be found in "Microrayon: Post-Soviet Housing Districts", Project Russia, 2002, no. 25.

2 For a complete overview of these competitions see "Battlefield Russia: International Architectural Competitions", Project Russia, 2004, no. 29.

3 For an overview of Nizhny Novgorod architecture see "The Nizhny Novgorod School", Project Russia, 1998, no. 4.

4 An analysis of this process can be found in "Capitalist Realism", Project Russia, 2002, no. 24.

5 See "The Free Plan", Project Russia, 2001, no. 20.

6 The utopian character of communism made it impossible to be functional, and left large parts of society uncovered. In comparison with this, capitalist society is much more totalitarian – or as a St Petersburg-based architect told me: "When I first visited the West I was surprised how ideological it was. Everybody would tell you continuously what was the right thing to do."

7 See "Countryside: Between Bohemia and Bourgeoisie", Project Russia, 2001, no. 21.

Car park and shopping centre in St Petersburg, designed by Studio 44, 2005
Parkhaus und Einkaufszentrum in Sankt Petersburg, Architekten: Studio 44 (2005)

New Architecture in Russia

Philipp Meuser

Whenever Russia wanted to be modern it looked to the leading lights of European culture. Architecture, which as the most functional of all the arts always tells future generations a great deal about a society's level of development, has never been an exception to that rule. The start was made by the Russian tsar Peter the Great more than three hundred years ago. When he founded the new capital of St Petersburg he demonstrated his foresight by inviting famous architects from all over Europe to contribute. In the new Baltic metropolis architects from Italy, the Netherlands, Germany and elsewhere created an urban ensemble that to this day delights visitors from all over the world. Of course, Peter the Great's decision was motivated by considerations that were more pragmatic than architectural. But this and other political decisions by the tsar shifted his huge eastern empire much closer to Europe. And the ideas from abroad veritably fired the imagination of Russian architects. The visual language of the new capital came to be felt in every corner of the Russian Empire.[1]

The Europeanisation of St Petersburg through Baroque architectural imports exerted a lasting influence on the formal canon of Russian architecture. But it still remained an episode, and one confined to the plane of state prestige and representation. The splendour of the architecture was conspicuously symptomatic of a country that – at the time when western Europe was industrialising – was still locked into a feudal system that rested on the pillars of the tsar, the Church and the nobility, and the associated but outdated rules of power and mastery. This social system survived right through until the October Revolution of 1917.

It is worth remembering that from the outset the young Soviet Union developed between the poles of tradition and progress. For Russia the Revolution clearly meant a leap towards *European Time*, both literally – in the abolition of the Julian calendar in favour of the Gregorian that the rest of Europe had introduced in 1582 – and metaphorically through the murder of the entire Romanov family in Ekaterinburg. Both occurred in 1918, and after that there was no turning back. The revolution was to extend the Europeanisation once initiated in urban architecture by the tsars to transform the whole of society. After all, the October Revolution was a cultural revolution as well as a political one. The modern artists who rebelled against the "established understanding of art in the empire of the tsars now felt allied with those who saw the whole social system as outmoded. Communists and modernists were united by an almost fateful belief in the ability of science and technology to fundamentally reshape the human condition."[2] Enormous changes in everyday life included abolition of serfdom, forced collectivisation and a broad literacy campaign. Beyond that, industrialisation and mechanisation accompanied the building of the new political system, culminating in Lenin's famous slogan: "Communism is Soviet power plus the electrification of the whole country".

Soviet Avant-Garde: New Architecture for a New Society

One cannot overlook the enthusiasm contained in the programmatic lines written in 1929 by leading Russian constructivist El Lissitzky: "The birth of the machine signaled the onset of the technological revolution [...] Modern technology not only revolutionized social and economic developments but aesthetic ones as well. The basic elements of new architecture in Western Europe and America were deter-

Business and Cultural Complex "Riverside Towers" and Moscow International House of Music,
Architects: Yury Gnedovskiy and others, 2003
Russisches Kultur- und Geschäftszentrum »Krasnye Cholmy« in Moskau,
Architekten: Juri Gnedowskij u. a. (Genossenschaft der Theater-Architekten), 2003

mined by this revolution. October 1917 marked the beginning of the Russian Revolution and the opening of a new page in the history of human society. It is to this social revolution, rather than to the technological revolution, that the basic elements of Russian architecture are tied."[3] Through his diction we can sense the influence of the painter and art historian Kazimir Malevich, one of the leading lights of Russian modernism who forged his constructivist art as an expression of the revolutionary and technical age. It was also Malevich who persuaded El Lissitzky to join the constructivist movement. Lissitzky, who in 1919 had been teaching at the art school in Vitebsk, moved to Moscow in 1921 to head the architecture department at the state art school (VKhUTEMAS), before later spending time in western Europe. *Neues Bauen* and communism seemed a compelling logical connection, a mutually dependent pair.

Lissitzky expounded the following social brief for architecture in 1929: "Social evolution leads to the elimination of the old dichotomy between city and country. The city endeavors to draw nature right into its center and by means of industrialization to introduce a higher level of culture into the country. In these times we must be very objective, very practical, and totally unromantic, so that we can catch up with the rest of the world and overtake it."[4]

This statement echoes not only the proclamations of the Central Committee of the Soviet Communist Party, but also broadly speaking the postulates of the German avant-garde, which (albeit under conditions of much less dramatic upheaval) glimpsed the dawn of a bright new democratic society in the guise of the Weimar Republic. In their view, society had thrown off its dusty old historical mantle and appointed itself the architect of its own rebirth. Building "new housing for a new society", as Hans Scharoun put it in 1947, was what had driven the representatives of early modernism in 1920s Germany as much as it had their Russian colleagues in the young Soviet Union. Those years of social turmoil had pushed Russia to the forefront of an artistic international that now merely had to manifest itself in economic terms.

As well as guaranteeing architectural and planning support for the success of the cultural revolution, the protagonists of European – here in particular German – modernism also provided moral backing with regard to the all-decisive question of land ownership: "The worst shackle remains the immoral right to private ownership of land. Unless the land is liberated from this private slavery, it will never be possible to develop cities that are healthy, viable and economically efficient for the common good." It was neither Lenin nor Stalin who penned these words, but Walter Gropius in 1931, who went on to note: "This most central requirement has been fulfilled only, and without restriction, by the USSR, which has thus cleared the way to develop modern cities."[5] The founder of the Weimar Bauhaus made no secret that he saw the Soviet Union as a shining example and was equally open in paying tribute to "the work of Ernst May as the organiser of the construction sector and as a hands-on urban planner in Soviet Russia" in his book *Neues Bauen in der UdSSR*. So if architectural modernism was the model for revolutionary Russia – and the excuse for a steady westward stream of architectural tourists – conversely, for the representatives of New Objectivity, especially its German pioneers, Russia was a social and political trailblazer for land reform in Germany. However, the attempt to strip the politically disempowered aristocracy of its property rights by ref-

erendum failed to achieve the required support of 50 percent of the electorate. The Soviet Union – founded officially on 30 December 1922 with the Russian Socialist Federated Soviet Republic of 1918 at its core – became a playground-cum-testbed for international architects including Ernst May, Charles Édouard Jeanneret-Gris alias Le Corbusier, Bruno Taut and even Americans such as the industrial architect Albert Kahn, designer of the Ford factories. This culminated in the grotesque situation where a good part of the architectural elite of the capitalist West headed east to help build a new state whose leadership had made no secret of its goal of destroying the capitalist world. The expected swift victory of world revolution did not come, thus leading Lenin to set a course of "peaceful coexistence" and Stalin to decree "socialism in one country" as the Soviet model for the rest of the world to follow, but the question was never if but when the time would come for world revolution and just war against "European imperialism" (Lenin).

At home, the most urgent task for economic development was to catch up with the technical standards of the Western world. The Soviet Union's tool for tackling this economic exertion was the New Economic Policy (NEP), which stood for the industrialisation and mechanisation of all economic life from the production line to the fields. It is in that vein that *Bauwelt* quotes Ernst May, then a council official in Frankfurt, before he set off to find new challenges in the east: "New cities must be built, others remodelled. The most interesting and difficult task will be to create completely new cities. First and foremost these cities will be home to a new iron and steel industry, to be set up from scratch."[6] May set off for Moscow on 1 September 1930 with a team of twenty-one.

Socialist Realism: New Cities in Familiar Format

Ernst May had taken part in a competition for the design of the heavy industrial complex of Magnitogorsk, whose place in the first Five-Year Plan (1929–33) was to serve as a model city and pattern for the many other towns to come from the drawing board. Magnitogorsk was in principle a Western-style company town, but blown up to gigantic dimensions; a pioneer settlement on the eastern flanks of the southern Urals. The second challenge was to expand the existing cities, transforming the impoverished agglomerations of the industrial proletariat into secure accommodation and preparing the conurbations for completely new population influxes. Moscow was a model here and at the latest after the inauguration of the metro in 1935 it ranked as the capital of the socialist world.

At the same time, from 1931 on, the limits of the "world political experiment", as May termed the building of the Soviet Union, became ever clearer in the field of urban planning. Lazar Moiseyevich Kaganovich – Stalin's favourite city planner and right-hand man in the Central Committee – called for "the old cities to be reconstructed and the new – like Magnitogorsk – to be moderately modern."[7] Here Kaganovich outlined the marching route for Soviet urban planning that was to lead directly to Andrey Zhdanov's 1934 directive proclaiming "Socialist Realism" to be the patriotic Soviet taste. This marked the end of freedom of creative spirit in the sphere of culture, and with it also the end of any effective room for manoeuvre for the modern avant-garde, whose architects had hardly even begun to make their mark due to the political exigencies.

Triumf Palace Residential High-rise Building, by developer Don Stroy, 2006 (left) Triumf Astana Residential Building in Astana/Kazakhstan by developer Baziz-A, 2006 (right)
Wohngebäude »Triumf Palas« in Moskau, Projektentwickler: Don Stroi, 2006 (links)
Wohngebäude »Triumf Astana« in Astana/Kasachstan, Projektentwickler: Baziz-A, 2006 (rechts)

Like in Germany, the protagonists of early modernism succeeded in realising relatively little measured against their high-flying ideals. Most of it remained castles in the air. The brief social and cultural intermezzo enjoyed by modernism in Russia was even shorter-lived than in Germany. Like in the Stalinist Soviet Union, in Nazi Germany too the basic principles of modernism became blended with traditions of a so-called *Heimatstil* (native style) and assembled using traditional town planning theories to form a heroic whole, following the principle of rationality in use of materials, but taste and grandness in appearance. Here too, the parallels between Stalinism and Hitlerism are – contrary to the theses of the German "Historians' Quarrel" of the 1980s that National Socialism and communism were polar opposites – most perplexing. Comparing Stalinist plans for occupied Berlin with Albert Speer's concepts for turning the city into the Nazi world capital, Germania, reveals remarkable similarities in gesture and statement right through to the ideological definition of architecture itself. In this respect it is simply a fact that the Soviet Union under Stalin succeeded to a great extent in realising the socialist city project, and after the Second World War even exported it to the very borders of the Warsaw Pact. Karl-Marx-Allee in Berlin – Germany's longest architectural monument – represents both a bricks-and-mortar monument to that era, and a fragment of the largely unrealised Stalinist planning for the East German capital.

The reasons for hostility towards functional neutrality are obvious. Modernist architecture in its pure form and its "urban expression of a bourgeois society atomised into economically and intellectually independent individuals" contradicted the social realities of the Soviet Union and was declared by the new nomenklatura – who had adopted the principles of power of the tsarist empire, merely exchanging the double-headed eagle and crown for hammer, sickle and red star – to be incompatible with the self-image of the new state. From that perspective communist Russia was comparable with a company that rebrands itself and reorders its staff hierarchy, while retaining an authoritarian management style. The Soviet Union now pursued a course of aggressive state capitalism.

"Socialist Realism" was the secular substitute for all the certainties the nation had lost by that point – including the religious. Artists were told to see themselves as "engineers of the human soul" (Stalin). The influential author and publicist Anatoly Lunacharsky, who was largely responsible for Soviet cultural policy, coined the popular slogan "Do not disdain the masters of the past!" to justify the new line. Bruno Taut captures the mood of the times in his observations on the state of architecture in Russia in 1929: "It is the purpose of art to express the invisible breath of the father in a tactile and visible manner [...] In Russia the search for fundamentals takes on dramatic forms. There, as anywhere else, human weaknesses become part of the struggle as manifested in competition work and its results, where over and over again we can see the conflict between design for a functional purpose as opposed to the quest for beauty." As an example Taut cites the competition for the Lenin Library in Moscow, where the jury chose a traditional building rather than a glass structure in order to symbolise "the work of the academician" and had had to make "corresponding sacrifices of functional clarity in the layout."[8]

Astonishingly for a proponent of New Objectivity, Taut postulates: "The task of Russian architecture will be to bring the

21

new insights into harmony with the existing down-to-earthness of the Russian national character." That is exactly what the Central Committee commissars of taste were thinking of when they came up with the idea of "Socialist Realism". The Frankfurt magazine *Die Neue Stadt* mocked the ensuing architectural tightrope act in an article published in 1933: "They pay tribute to the classical, justify classicism (Lunacharsky) but at the same time do not want to entirely do without Le Corbusier, the poet of constructivism. Plus economy and standardisation at all costs! They want one thing and are compelled to satisfy the other; the result is generalised uncertainty."[9] The apparent contradiction reveals a dialectic that nonetheless found its (admittedly strange) synthesis in the artistic doctrine of Socialist Realism. Moderate modernism in architecture meant, for example, that Ernst May[10] drew up the overall development plan for the new industrial city of Magnitogorsk and the American industrial architect Kahn designed the buildings.

Reconstruction meant that a traditionally minded urban planner like Cologne communist Kurt Meyer took the plans for Cologne he had drawn up under Mayor Konrad Adenauer and generalised them for socialist Moscow. Meyer, who was a member of the German Communist Party, left Cologne in 1930 after Adenauer had made it clear that if he took on the post of city architect he would have to pipe down politically.[11] Hans Schmidt describes the situation of the modernists in Soviet Russia in 1932, after the modernist entries in the competition for the Moscow Palace of the Soviets had been rejected by the jury: "It does not even come as a surprise when the same young architects who spent years flogging their idol Le Corbusier to death on Whatman paper with glass façades and roof gardens today design façades of

classical beauty on the same Whatman paper under the guidance of the old masters of architecture."[12] An understandable reaction on the part of those involved, who saw themselves as the artistic vanguard of a political avant-garde but recognised that they were no longer needed. The authoritarian party doctrine of the young Soviet Union had pulled the rug out under the rising ambitions of modernism. On the other side of the equation, the new artistic doctrine invigorated the creative energies of the older native architects from the tsarist era.

Stalin's rule actually gave rise to buildings that – regardless of whether they made economic sense – represented milestones of moderate modernism. To this day the contribution of Stalinist architecture to the international debate has rarely been taken seriously. Through simple ignorance the assessment rarely goes any deeper than mockery ("wedding-cake style") or dismissal ("dictatorial crimes against good taste"). We are still waiting for a serious assessment of Socialist Realism's place in the architectural history of the twentieth century, even if Harald Bodenschatz and Christiane Post have made a very promising start with their standard work *Städtebau im Schatten Stalins*, published in 2003. In their foreword the authors point out that Western architectural historians simply do not know enough to do justice to the significance of Stalinist architecture for the urban environment. The same applies to the development of the architecture itself. In fact, one could propose the provocative thesis that the way today's Russian architecture draws on its Soviet heritage makes it the most traditionally grounded architecture in Europe.

Cold War: Between Prefab Reality and Hand-Drawn Visions

In a sense, the Russian Bauhaus offshoot of constructivism and Soviet functionalism as the USSR's post-war strain of Western modernism (which came to the fore in the mid-1950s under Nikita Khrushchev's motto of "higher quality with lower costs") could both be seen as failed developments that were superseded by Stalinism and neo-Russian regionalism respectively. But that would not do justice to either. Soviet functionalism was a spartan version of constructivism – a socialist variety of the West's International Style, with the pragmatic purpose of creating as much housing as possible as economically as possible, and at the same time, as an artistic form of expression, reinforcing the country's internal cultural unity. From Minsk in the west to Vladivostok in the east almost identical buildings went up, their permits issued in Moscow and each given a centralised serial number. In the Soviet Union rationalisation of planning and construction – the spirit of the age in West and East alike – led to the disappearance of the building trades. When the West returned to conventional building methods, partly for reasons of economy, prefabrication in the Soviet Union had become the prisoner of its own success. Outwardly too, architecture had become a means of artistic self-representation in the struggle for control over a world that had been paralysed by the Cold War but under the pressure of globalisation was growing together at breakneck speed with scant regard for political divisions. Suddenly modernism with its thoroughly familiar themes – from rational construction through to industrial mass production of architecture – came to be seen as the ally of the state, for which its reputation fell just as hard as it had in the West. Russia, as the

heartland of a political hemisphere had yet again taken the West as its model. During the Brezhnev era the post-Stalinist Soviet Union torpefied into sober functionalism which "surpassed even the Western disaster of container architecture",[13] only to complete an about-turn in 1991, now doing everything possible to fast-forward through all the Western cultural phases the Russians felt they had missed. This psychological profile of a nation that believes it arrived too late on the scene and is always chasing its tail is not foreign to us Germans either. After the collapse of the Soviet Union it is now a form of neo-traditionalism that can be identified as one of the main currents of contemporary Russian architecture. There are several reasons for this.

The political explosion of glasnost and perestroika (openness and restructuring) announced by Mikhail Gorbachev encouraged architects who had for years realised their utopias and fantasies only on paper to build their ideas in reality. Their "inner emigration" had been a reaction to the creative impasse and a protest against a "politically paralysed state and a correspondingly paralysed architecture, whose liaison was confirmed on a daily basis by firmly entrenched party architects". A kind of bureaucratic cronyism had come into being, guaranteeing one assignment after another for architects who toed the official line, while simultaneously wiping out every last shred of human imagination.

Those who had been prevented from practising, or were unable to work under the suspicion of "opposition to progress" rebelled, either leaving the country or retreating into the creative backrooms and niches of society. Freed of all bureaucratic control, creative imagination blossomed and spawned sometimes bizarre images of buildings and

the city. The only taboo restraining these architects was that there was no taboo. Everything was possible and so it came to a meeting of the drawn architectures of Russian constructivism of the 1920s, sixteenth-century classicism à la Giovanni Battista Piranesi, the Prussian classicism of Schinkel and his ilk, and the early modernism of people like Adolf Loos. Epochs touched and interlocked as if they always had. At the same time, contradictions and opposites anchored in the theory revealed themselves to be organic lines of development. Suddenly it became apparent that although associated with preconceived images, the different stylistic epochs did have much in common.

In the fantasies of the Paper Architects these elements blurred into a new whole or adopted unadulterated contemporary forms. The pictures and designs of N. Bronzova, M. Filippov and V. Petrenko suggest primarily influences from the stylistic catalogue and utopias of the Italian Renaissance, while M. Labazov and A. Cheltsov, on the other hand, melded Cubism with Oriental patterns. Others supplied designs for real sites, for example Mikhail Belov, who yearned for a reconstruction of Moscow's Shchusev Street in the manner of Italian Renaissance architecture, under the title of "The Architect's Street". Often the medieval models were themselves a bit like "paper architecture". At least when they painted and lived out their architectural ideas in the motifs, as demonstrated by Raphael's *The School of Athens* in the Stanza della Segnatura fresco in the Vatican. With the Russian Paper Architects this freedom of imagination sometimes led to the brink of the most frivolous kitsch – even to eyes that have become accustomed to the visual catalogue of postmodernist cuteness.

If we are to understand what is unique about the Paper Architecture of the kind produced by the NER group in the 1960s, which worked solely for the purpose of theoretical investigation, we have to distinguish between utopia and fantasy. According to Russian architectural historian Alexander Rappaport: "The utopian idea that had developed in the theory and practice of European architecture in the nineteenth and twentieth century and in the construction industry of the USSR rejected pluralism." Since a utopian project aims to improve the world, he says, it always contains the will to put it into practice. "Fantasy also contains a possible vision of the world, but unlike a utopia it makes no claim to its vision really being a key to solving urgent human problems",[14] Rappaport concludes. That is precisely the difference between the Paper Architects of the 1980s and the early-twentieth-century constructivists. As utopians, the latter saw the Bolshevist revolution as an opportunity to create a fitting artistic backdrop for the new society. The constructivists fought against anything that contradicted their definition of taste. The European modernist camp was no different. Understandably in view of the nervousness of the times, the spirit of totalitarian architecture reared its head even there, and actually it was only waiting for a political seal of approval. It found its guarantor in the shape of the Weimar Republic, though it actually had no need of state patronage. Even in the corrupted political culture of the Kaiser's Germany on the eve of the First World War creative dynamism and more convincing ideas – ones that were more up-to-date – meant that change was possible to a greater degree than has generally been realised. In fact, the idea of implementing a utopia in a totally planned environment already existed in the eighteenth century, but "not until the twenti-

Residential and office building in Samara, designed by Alexey Morgun, 1996 (left)
Office and commercial building in Perm, designed by Oleg Goryunov, 2001 (right)
Wohn- und Geschäftshaus in Samara, Architekt: Alexej Morgun, 1996 (links)
Büro- und Geschäftshaus in Perm, Architekt: Oleg Gorjunow, 2001 (rechts)

eth century were the technical and political preconditions created" (Rappaport). The Paper Architects of the 1980s had long since emancipated themselves from ideas of that kind. The fact is, they were thwarted architects, one and all, although that was to change dramatically for many after 1991. Since then Aleksander Brodsky and Mikhail Belov have been among those who have suddenly started designing to build and have thus moved from the conceptual "anything is possible" to the constructional. Shopping centres with façades that look like models from the Bauhaus repertoire and elegant functional buildings stand alongside ornate constructions whose reinforced concrete façades often mimic the authentic old ones that were bulldozed to make way for them.

Capitalist Realism: Architecture in the New Russia

"Historic buildings are disappearing even more quickly than in Soviet times", complains Nikolay Malinin, to be replaced, he says, by "new buildings with a whiff of history. Reconstruction gave way to restoration" – following the motto "demolition followed by rebuilding" – right down the line and had, he says, consequently transgressed its brief, which can only relate to places where previously nothing or only unfitting buildings stood.[15] But these days the authority to decide what is fitting and what is not no longer lies with the Central Committee but with local authorities, which in this respect act like little feudal lords or political commissars. One such figure is Yury Luzhkov, mayor of Moscow, who has built up a gigantic property empire (officially run by his wife), and dictates the appearance of major development sites. "Always present in person at meetings of the public city planning council, he speaks his mind on almost every project and is a proponent of pretty clear aesthetic principles: in the centre we only build historically, glass only in the suburbs, and no smooth façades."[16] That is not of itself objectionable, but the authoritarian personal directive that has replaced the ruling party's edict has sharpened to the point of censorship and at the same time become intertwined with corruption, because "the architect has to pay for every innovation (from the client's wallet of course)", and then there is suddenly a little room for manoeuvre outside the decrees of personal taste, which incidentally also come to substitute for an urban development plan.

This development took a different course elsewhere, in Berlin for example. Here, according to Moscow architecture critic Irina Shipova, the master plan for "long-term urban development" drawn up by Josef Paul Kleihues in the course of the Internationale Bauausstellung laid the foundations for successfully bringing together the two halves of the city astonishingly quickly and harmoniously after the fall of the Berlin Wall in 1989. Whereas Berlin succeeded in turning the aesthetic of the solitary building into the architecture of the city, she says, urban planning is nowhere to be seen in post-Soviet Moscow. Construction follows the principle of intuition and if it works out that is more a matter of chance than anything else. According to Shipova, in contrast to Soviet times, there are now not even the rudiments of an idea of how the city should function as a civilised organism. Therein, she says, lies the ambivalence of the eager efforts to use architectural ornateness to generate some feeling of cosiness at the level of planning detail. The individual building is overriding, the greater whole more a matter of chance. Architecture usurps urban planning. And here Moscow has

been leading the way since 1991. This also includes setting unmistakable optical landmarks in an urban economy controlled by the laws of the market, where even the aesthetic has been rationalised. One tile in this mosaic is church-building. One of the most conspicuous examples of the ecclesiastical reconstruction programme is the rebuilding of the Cathedral of Christ the Savior in 1997 for the city of Moscow's 850th anniversary celebrations. On the prominent site originally earmarked for the Palace of the Soviets but ultimately occupied by a swimming pool, Mayor Luzhkov had a copy of the former cathedral constructed. Now it stands there as ever, as if the place of worship had never been among the 80 percent of Russia's ecclesiastical buildings that were torn down on Stalin's orders. Although the shape of the building is deceptively authentic, it features a lucratively marketed underground car park in the basement. In Russia, as Malinin pointedly notes, as far as building is concerned, planning, aesthetic judgement and decision-making are all governed by the law of lucre.

That the Cathedral of Christ the Savior was not unanimously welcomed by public opinion has more to do with the obscure machinations of the property trade than with the tastes and sensibilities of the population. Alongside the raw materials business, property is one of the most lucrative sectors of the new Russian economy. And has remained so even though a study by an international firm of auditors shows that the average annual return on the Moscow property market has fallen since the economic crisis of the late 1990s to a level of 30 percent in 2004. Although the property market has become jittery it is still a crock of gold compared with conditions in the rest of Europe, where for a good while investors have had to make do with annual

returns of 4 or 5 percent. The enormous profits in the Russian property market do not necessarily lead to good quality of the buildings. This is due to three factors: the investors themselves, a general mistrust of architects and the naivety of flat buyers. "Clients in Moscow are penny-pinching, cowardly and unostentatious. They save on everything: building materials, technology, building workers, architects. Most investors mistrust their architects, they favour those who get all the formalities dealt with fastest." But this trend is disappearing along with the cartel of banks, politicians and estate agents; the normalising "collapse" of profitability is probably the best proof of this.

In the meantime Malinin too sees signs of a turn to more quality, to more imaginative architecture with up-to-date language in the place of adaptations of classicism, Art Nouveau and the stylistic excesses of a twenty-year-delayed European postmodernism. In the end, after the crash of 1998, a new "class of investors formed who understood that money" should be invested "not just in floor space but also in architecture". Also, says Malinin, the Paper Architects did not manage to convincingly translate their creative flights of fancy into buildings of substance. Malinin, an equally sharp and sharp-tongued observer of his city, Moscow, claims to see evidence of a qualitative turn in the choice of building materials and growing influence of the new generation of architects in their thirties; in view of the fact that "there has only been architecture here for the past fifteen years" and consequently the "profession of architect is difficult to inherit", that is definitely astonishing. Another sign according to Malinin are the increasing numbers of foreign architects winning competitions in Russia. The evidence on the ground for this modernist turn include Sergey Skuratov's Copper

House and the high-tech Stolnik building by the firm A-B (Andrey Savin, Mikhail Labazov, Andrey Cheltsov).

One could certainly discuss endlessly about the truth of that observation, especially given that the author makes it equally clear that architecture responds to social needs: "While the average Muscovite loves the old Moscow, he absolutely rejects new architecture." Malinin sees the reasons for this as lying in history, and in the way the many decades of new architecture have disfigured the city, as well as the resentments of ordinary citizens who register that the well-heeled hide behind walls of fine functional architecture, with the result that modernism has come to represent the style of the bourgeoisie. On the other hand there is also a yearning for a sense of calm, order and stability.

In the field of prominent public buildings nobody satisfies this public sentiment and taste more reliably than the Russian Orthodox Church with its unchallenged visual tradition going back centuries. Even after decades of Soviet repression, it possesses a familiar, recognised and unmistakable artistic repertoire that can easily be called on without prejudice in the service of national identity and reassurance. For all the controversy over the Cathedral of Christ the Saviour in Moscow, it is nevertheless a milestone of the New Russian Architecture, and at the same time reconstructing a building that had been absent from the city for more than fifty years is truly a symbol of political and architectural freedom. The ecclesiastical buildings are principally about superficial appearances. The few exceptions merely confirm the rule. More than 90 percent of new Russian Orthodox churches follow the stylistic canon of the tsarist era. Whether in Moscow, Ekaterinburg, Samara or somewhere in Siberia, the new churches would be almost indistinguishable from

their historic predecessors were it not for the modern façade materials and the plastic window frames. The astonishing thing here is that the architects who fall back on the historical typologies for today's church designs are generally the very same who did very well for themselves in Soviet times designing massive functionalist buildings. In other words, today we have a similar phenomenon to the situation following the proclamation of the doctrine of Socialist Realism in 1934, when tsarist architects did ornamentation for the Soviet Union.

Another phenomenon is the renaissance of Stalinist architecture, which also gives a splendid response to the needs described above and finds a political counterpart in the re-election of Vladimir Putin, who held a leading position in the foreign service of the Soviet KGB and now leads the New Russia under the emblem of the tsarist double eagle. With Putin's approval, the "neo-stalinist style" has undergone a revival in the Russian capital without it being possible to construe a direct link between the architectural style and centralisation of power. In Moscow, which is unmistakably defined by Stalin's architecture, the renaissance of this style comes as no great surprise. In fact there is actually an inherent planning logic if the intention is to recreate unity in the city's visual appearance. The "eighth sister" of the Stalinist tower blocks went up in 2005 close to the city centre. This residential tower designed by project developer Don Stroy is named Triumf Palace and is the tallest of its kind in Europe – and is built in the Neo-Stalinist style. Transposed to Berlin that would be roughly the same as extending the former Stalinallee eastwards – but as a highly exclusive residential complex for a new moneyed elite rather than the collective workers' palace for the political elite. But Triumf Palace tells

The Kul Sharif Mosque in Kazan, built by developer Tadinvestgrazhdanproyekt, 2004 (left)
The Patriarch's House, designed by Vladimir Markov, next to the Cathedral-on-the-Blood, by Grigory Masayev, 2003 (right)
Kul Sharif Moschee in Kasan, Projektentwickler: Tadinvest-graschdanprojekt, 2004 (links)
Haus des Patriarchen (Architekt: Wladimir Markow, 2004) vor der Kathedrale »Erlöser auf dem Blut«, Architekt: Griogori Masajew, 2003 (rechts)

a lot about a society where what people have in their heads – not just simple folk, but also the purchasers of luxury apartments – is the Stalin-era apartment block with its high ceilings, wide windows, spacious rooms, balconies and balustrades. Everybody knew what it meant to live in such places and to this day many Russians are firmly convinced that they are still the best place to live.

Additionally, many Russian property developers, especially in the housing sector, satisfy the demands of the market by catering to popular taste. And in post-Soviet Russia, where more than three-quarters of the population still lives in mass-produced prefab blocks, that means ornate forms and not abstract simplicity. Only where young architects buck the mainstream trend and – after training in Europe or intensive study of international journals – design purist buildings inspired by Swiss or Spanish schools do we find designs that do without bay windows, mouldings and ornamentation. But these next-generation projects are still the exception. A tendency to stick to what is familiar and time-tested is typical for a society that has otherwise only known upheaval and uncertainty. After all, Russia's urban planning and architecture have never again seen the kind of quality they enjoyed under Stalin. In that respect Stalinist architecture is something like a mixture of Schinkel imitation and the early modernism that Germans still regard as sturdy yet also aesthetic, and thus definitely comparable with the trends where architects like Hans Kollhoff draw accolades such as dignified, stone-like and elegant for his rationally expressionist brick architecture in Berlin.

But the trend for reconstruction is not a Muscovite peculiarity. In St Petersburg too, which has an almost intact Baroque and classicist city centre, the new architecture slots incon-

spicuously into the existing structure. That is to say, the planners urge architects building at sensitive sites in the centre to take a softly-softly approach to the question of old and new. For example the Russian Central Bank building on the Fontanka Canal (by architects Vladimir Grigoryev, Vadim Ponomarev, Pavel Vasilyev, Yekaterina Zhelezni), which was completed in 2004, features a front façade with structuring mouldings, protruding bay windows and floral ornaments that is almost indistinguishable from the almost century-old neighbouring buildings. But the façade on the side street is anything but neo-traditional in its cool steel and glass expanse. Indeed, this represents an attempt at architectural revolution. Thus the choice in early 2003 of Dominique Perrault's crystal-like glass building for the extension of the Mariinsky Theatre is little else than the exception that proves the rule.

When we look at the wealth of projects that have gone up in the New Russia, the wheat is quickly separated from the chaff. Returning to Moscow, we have the Patriarch Residential Complex, which was completed in 2002 to plans by Sergey Tkachenko. This building, constructed for the new moneyed elite, stands at the edge of the Patriarch's Pond, in a central residential quarter that was already des-res in Soviet times. With its pronounced diversity of colours and forms it represents an unparalleled mixture of styles. The ornate façade towers its way skyward to end in a peerless multi-tiered structure. A symbolic reference provides the finishing touch – above the top floor a reduced-size copy of Tatlin's never-realised tower protrudes into the Moscow skyline. Neither the architects nor the residents seem to care that this incunabulum from the early years of constructivism was originally supposed to be several hundred metres high. Nor

that the respective architectural roots of the richly ornamented façade and the utopian steel structure are as different as can be.

In this respect, Russia reflects a phenomenon that can be observed all over the world and regularly entangles the profession in heated discussions under ever-changing labels. Whether it is New Urbanism in North America or its European offshoots (now organising in associations), or the Chinese desire for European identity in housing and town planning – everywhere the new traditionalists are quoting tried-and-tested forms and recipes, rising up against the anonymous architectural language spoken by globalisation. At the same time Russia is also trying to develop an artistic profile of its own to distinguish it from the other states of the former Soviet Union, which themselves are revisiting traditional forms of architectural expression in a technically standardised world. So it is only now, in the course of cultural regionalisation of the former Soviet Union, that we can really properly speak of a Russian regionalism.

The extremes found in Moscow are unknown in the regions. To examine the new Russian regionalism in its pure form it is worth taking a trip to the Volga region. In places like Nizhny Novgorod, Perm and Samara there are new urban residential and office buildings that seek stylistic references to Art Nouveau or Art Deco. These buildings fit naturally into their urban settings and give a little identity back to cities that in places were grossly disfigured during the Soviet era. Russian architecture has produced its most expressive examples precisely in the regions. The most outstanding buildings here include the Garantiya Bank in Nizhny Novgorod, which was completed back in 1995 by the duo of architects Yevgeny Pestov and Aleksander Kharitonov (see page 122). The

plaster façade on the street side features oval windows and fine ceramic details that recall the art deco age of the closing years of the tsarist dynasty. A residential and commercial building in Perm by Mendel Futlik (see page 130) and in Samara Leonid Kuderov's "Dom Mukha" (Mouse House) both also date from the mid-1990s. Both quote Art Deco motifs without batting an eyelid and blend them with the functionalist language of modern architecture.

Whereas a certain pluralism of international styles and currents predominates in Moscow, the diversity in the regional centres is restricted to these neo-traditional forms, as well as those cold and soulless boxes – unfortunately to be found everywhere in the world – behind whose ornate or mirrored façades we find hotels, shopping malls and business centres. Also in terms of regionalism, Russian architecture can be counted among the European avant-garde. But above all the neo-traditionalists must gauge their place in the international discourse by the extent to which the New Russian Architecture can contribute to the ideological renewal of society by focusing sharply on stylistic questions and marketing considerations. The demand for new buildings has not yet been satisfied. But as soon as the market is characterised by competing offers, architectural quality will turn out to be the marketing trump card. Then the astronomical prices – sometimes over Euro 10,000 per sqm on the Moscow housing market – will adjust to the European level. Until then we will continue to see the extreme side of post-communist capitalism. In a country like Russia, which must still be considered one of the transition states despite its endless wealth of natural resources, the search for identity is far from over.

The Garantiya Bank Building in Nizhny Novgorod by Yevgeny Pestov and Alexander Kharitonov, 1995 (left)
The National Bank in Nizhny Novgorod by architect Vladimir Pokrovsky, 1913 (right)
Bankgebäude »Garantija« in Nischni Nowgorod, Architekten: Jewgeni Pestow und Alexander Charitonow, 1995 (links)
Nationalbank in Nischni Nowgorod, Architekt: Wladimir A. Pokrowski, 1913 (rechts)

*Triumf Palace residential
building in Moscow,
developer: Don Stroy, 2006
Wohngebäude »Triumf Palas«
in Moskau, Projektentwickler:
Don Stroi, 2006*

1   Kristin Feireiss and Hans-Jürgen Commerell (eds), B.A.U.
    Berliner Architektur Union, exh. cat. (Berlin and Moscow,
    2003). Also Philipp Meuser, "Russischer Regionalismus",
    Baumeister, August 2004.

2   Translated from Jan Pehrke, "Der Künstler-Ingenieur", Jungle
    World, 13 January 1999.

3   El Lissitzky, "Basic Premises", in El Lissitzky, Russia: An
    Architecture for World Revolution [1930], trans. Eric Dluhosch
    (Cambridge, Mass., 1986 [1970]), 27.

4   El Lissitzky: "The New City", in El Lissitzky, Architecture for
    World Revolution (see note 3), 59.

5   El Lissitzky: "The Future and Utopia", in El Lissitzky, Architec-
    ture for World Revolution (see note 3).

6   Translated from Walter Gropius, "Was erhoffen wir vom russi-
    schen Städtebau?", in Walter Gropius, Ausgewählte Schriften,
    ed. by Hartmut Probst and Christian Schädlich (Berlin, 1988).

7   Translated from "Stadtrat Mays Russlandpläne", Bauwelt,
    1930, no. 36.

8   Translated from Harald Bodenschatz and Christiane Post (eds),
    Städtebau im Schatten Stalins: Die internationale Suche nach
    der sozialistischen Stadt in der Sowjetunion 1929-1935 (Berlin,
    2003).

9   Bruno Taut, "Russia's Architectural Situation", in El Lissitzky,
    Architecture for World Revolution (see note 3), pp. 167, 171.

10 Translated from "Zu den Auseinandersetzungen über
    Rußland", Die neue Stadt, 1933, no. 12.

11 Ernst May left the Soviet Union again in 1933 after completion
    of the first Five-Year Plan and worked as a farmer and
    architect in Kenya from 1934 to 1954, leaving evidence of
    his modern architecture in Nairobi. In 1954 he returned
    to Germany, where he worked as a town planner on the
    reconstruction and redevelopment of German cities

    (Mainz, Wiesbaden, Bremerhaven). Until 1961 he was also
    head planner of the Neue Heimat housing association
    (including the Neue Vahr development in Bremen).

12 Kurt Meyer initially rose quickly through the Soviet hierarchies
    as a town planner, but was arrested at the end of the 1930s
    during the great purge of party cadres and murdered in 1944
    in a gulag. See also Susanne Schattenberg, Stalins Ingenieure:
    Lebenswelten zwischen Technik und Terror in den 1930er-
    Jahren (Munich, 2002).

13 Translated from Hans Schmidt, "Die Sowjetunion und das
    neue Bauen", Die neue Stadt, 1932, no. 6/7.

14 Translated from Heinrich Klotz (ed.), Papierarchitektur: Neue
    Projekte aus der Sowjetunion, exh. cat. (Frankfurt am Main,
    1989).

15 Translated from Heinrich Klotz (ed.), Papierarchitektur
    (see note 14).

16 Translated from Alexander G. Rappaport, "Sprache und
    Architektur des 'Post-Totalitarismus'", in Heinrich Klotz (ed.):
    Papierarchitektur (see note 14).

17 Translated from Nikolay Malinin, "Eine Hauptstadt ohne
    Gesicht", in Moskau-Berlin: 1950-2000: Architektur, exh. cat
    (Moscow, 2004).

18 Translated from Irina Shipowa, "Das geteilte Berlin: Kampf
    und Einheit der Gegensätze", in Moskau-Berlin: 1950-2000:
    Architektur, exh. cat (Moscow, 2004).

Murmansk

Arkhangelsk

Khanty-Mansiysk

St. Petersburg

Perm

Nishny Novgorod

Ekaterinburg

Moscow

Kazan

Ufa

Chelyabinsk

Berlin

Tolyatti

Samara

Magnitogorsk

Kiev

Saratov

Astana

Rostov

Volgograd

Astrakhan

International Style in Russia

Residential Complex in Moscow
Wohngebäude in Moskau

Sergey Skuratov
2005

This project involves two neighbouring residential buildings which, despite their different appearances, were actually designed by one and the same architect. The piano nobile of the house with the rounded corner is clad in red brick, while its plinth and staircase are faced with Jura limestone. This contrasts clearly with the materials and design of the adjacent building with its three malachite elements jutting out above the ground floor. The brick-clad building offers a smooth and yet distinctive visual transition within the five-storey residential complex. Its style reflects the tenets of what is known as contextual architecture, where the relationship between buildings and their environment plays an important role. A characteristic feature of the contextual approach to architecture is the neutral style of its buildings. Judging by its appearance, No. 5 could just as well be an office building as a residential building. Its quality does not derive from its architectural style, but from the way it is firmly anchored in its surroundings. The main contextual theme addressed here is the contrast between the old and the new Ostozhenka, between Jura limestone (a bow to the building across the street) and dark brick (a nod to the district's red brick houses). Copper House, in turn, manifests an entirely different approach focused not on the environment, but on the building's essential character. The new generation of elite buildings seeks not to emulate but to impress, and architecture becomes an important way of creating value. The gentle curve of the building, the projecting corbels, the use of pre-patinated copper and the building's glassed-in corners all highlight the exclusiveness of this residential building.

Bei diesem Projekt handelt es sich um zwei benachbarte Wohngebäude, die in ihrer Erscheinung unterschiedlich sind, jedoch aus der Feder desselben Architekten stammen. Das Haus mit der abgerundeten Ecke bildet nicht nur aufgrund der ziegelsteinernen Außenhaut seiner Beletage und dem hellen Jurakalkstein an Treppenhaus und Sockel einen Kontrast zu den drei über dem Erdgeschoss auskragenden Malachit-Elementen seines Nachbarn. Das mit Ziegelstein verkleidete Haus stellt einen fließenden Kontrast, einen optischen Übergang innerhalb der fünfstöckigen Wohnanlage dar. Charakteristisch für diesen kontextuellen Zugang zur Architektur ist der neutrale Duktus der Gebäude. Von seinem Äußeren her betrachtet kann Haus Nummer 5 sowohl ein Geschäftshaus als auch ein Wohngebäude sein: Seine Qualität begründet sich nicht im Baustil, sondern in seiner Unverrückbarkeit aus seiner Umgebung. Kontextuelles Hauptthema ist hier der Kontrast zwischen der alten und der neuen Ostoschenka: hier die Verwendung von Jurakalkstein – eine Verbeugung vor dem gegenüber liegenden Haus – dort dunkle Ziegel als Reminiszenz an die roten Ziegelhäuser dieses Viertels. Das »Copper House« zeigt eine gegenteilige Auffassung: Hier ist nicht die Umgebung, sondern der Gebäudecharakter die Hauptsache. Doch die neue Generation der Elite-Häuser möchte nicht nachahmen, sondern beeindrucken. Architektur ist hierfür eines der wesentlichen Mittel zur Erhöhung des Mehrwertes. Der stark geschwungene Baukörper, die vorspringenden Konsolen, das patinierte Kupfer, die verglasten Gebäudekanten – hier soll alles von der Exklusivität des Wohngebäudes zeugen.

This ensemble is part of a larger development on Moscow's Molochny Lane. The five buildings surround a new quadrant discreetly open to the road. These town houses each have a distinct character of their own and offer a palpable example of a new Muscovite architecture that eschews superfluous embellishment.

Dieses Gebäude ist Teil eines Ensembles in der Moskauer Molotschni-Gasse. Die insgesamt fünf Bauten bilden ein neues Karree, das sich zur Straße hin dezent öffnet. Die Stadthäuser mit ihrer unverwechselbaren Note sind der greifbare Beleg für schnörkellose Wohnkultur im neuen Moskau.

Committed to design outside and inside: Functional elegance characterises both forecourt and foyer. Even the severely-styled swimming pool gives an impression of elitist hauteur.

Gestalterisch konsequent von der Außenhaut bis ins Innenleben: funktional-ästhetische Eleganz als Visitenkarte sowohl am Stadtplatz als auch im Foyer. Selbst das Schwimmbad versucht durch seine Strenge elitäre Distanz zu formulieren.

Residential Building in Moscow
Wohngebäude in Moskau

Projekt Meganom
2002

This residential complex consists of two buildings: a four-storey multiple dwelling, which faces concavely onto the park at the fork of Butikovsky and Molochny Lane, and, to the rear, the older private villa Ostozhenka, to which the quarter owes its name. This is an outstanding area in the south-west of Moscow's city centre within sight of the Kremlin's towers and close to the Christ-the-Saviour Cathedral. The Pushkin Museum of Fine Arts and the Supreme Court form the cusp of an array of state buildings spreading out from the Kremlin within the former course of the early sixteenth-century city walls. A glazed ground floor facing the park is followed by a three-storey piano nobile clad in natural stone, which is topped with a recessed single-storey penthouse. The builder modestly describes the complex as a property which follows the principle of »good architecture attuned to the demands of the market«. It seems architects are not afraid to speak again of such lofty ideas as »good architecture«, as nowadays the defining factor is the future buyer – both the architect and the builder oriented themselves towards a personality free of Soviet complexes and prejudices. This example refreshingly casts aside the cliché that exclusive living in Russia is synonymous with wasteful embellishments. European standards have set new benchmarks which include such evidently sound criteria as convenience of location, comfort and market liquidity. Instead of the claustrophobic »My home is my castle,« the private sphere has become more open and in this case includes a foyer, lift, indoor swimming pool, gym and courtyard together with a garden.

Der Wohnkomplex besteht aus zwei Gebäuden: einem viergeschossigen Mehrfamilienhaus, das konkav zum Park an der Gabelung der Butikowski- und Molotschni-Gasse liegt und der rückwärtig gelegenen Privatvilla »Ostoschenka«. Das Quartier im südwestlichen Stadtkern Moskaus gilt als exklusiver Ort. Die Türme des Kreml sind in Sichtweite und die neue Christus-Erlöserkirche in nächster Nachbarschaft. Das Puschkin-Musuem für Bildende Kunst und der Oberste Gerichtshof sind hier innerhalb des ehemaligen Verlaufs der Stadtmauer des frühen 16. Jahrhunderts der Zipfel einer Ansammlung staatstragender Einrichtungen. Über einem dem Park zugewandten gläsernen Parterre folgt die mit Naturstein verkleidete dreistöckige Beletage und ein zurückgesetztes einstöckiges Dachgeschoss. Der Bauherr bezeichnet den Komplex bescheiden als eine Immobilie, welche den Prinzipien der »guten, den Erfordernissen des Marktes entsprechenden Architektur« folge. Die Architekten sprechen wiederum ihrer Kunst folgend unpathetisch von »guter Architektur«. Der bestimmende Faktor ist der zukünftige Käufer: Bauherr und Architekten orientierten sich an einer von sowjetischen Komplexen und Vorurteilen freien Persönlichkeit. Dieses Beispiel widerlegt zudem ein Klischee: Exklusives Wohnen in Russland ist nicht identisch mit verschwenderischem Schnörkel. Neue Maßstäbe setzen auch die europäischen Standards, die eine günstige Lage, Komfort und Marktliquidität einschließen. Entgegen dem klaustrophilen Motto »My home is my castle« versteht sich das neue Private öffentlich: auch Vorhalle, Aufzug, Schwimmhalle, Fitnessstudio oder der Innenhof samt Garten gehören dazu.

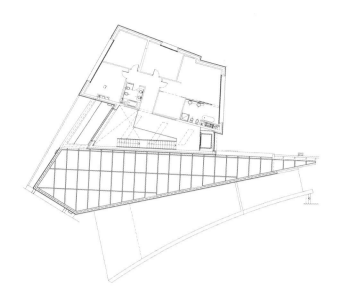

This residential complex is one of those new buildings in Moscow that confidently combine cool sobriety and an urban aesthetic. The eye-catching concave front faces a square in the elegant Ostozhenka quarter.
A villa of asymmetric design is to be found in the back garden. At night the building's unostentatious, functional coolness makes way for the intriguing aura conveyed by cunning illumination.

Das Haus gehört zu den Neubauten in Moskau, die kühle Sachlichkeit in stadträumlicher Ästhetik souverän vereinen. Das Haus ist der konkave Blickfang eines Platzes im großbürgerlichen Ostoschenka-Quartier. Im rückwärtigen Garten steht eine asymmetrische Villa. Ein tagsüber eher unspektakulärer Körper mit funkional-ästhetischer Kühle verwandelt sich abends mit Hilfe einer geheimnisvollen Lichtinszenierung.

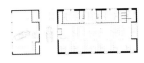

Office Building in Chelobityevo
Bürogebäude in Tschelobitjewo

Yevgeny Ass
2004

In a dull village marred by disparate development within the commuter belt of the Russian capital, a small firm has proven with its straightforward office building that good, functional architecture does not inevitably have to be faceless and joyless. On a stream in leafy, park-like surroundings, the architects have set an elongated flat building that is reminiscent of a warehouse in its simplicity. The client desired a new building which would include garages for company vehicles as well as offices, reception and recreation areas. Accordingly, the building was divided into three zones. The employee offices can be found in the southern area, separated by the garages and utility rooms. The central section, which includes the main entrance, was designed to serve as reception and communication area. In addition to the reception there is a cafeteria, a club with fireplace and bar and a smoking lounge. The modern solid-wood furniture in this section was designed by the architect. The northern section of the building is reserved for the management. The building's external design is the most captivating aspect of this compact, one-storey gabled construction: the brickwork that covers the roof and the entire length of the building on both sides contains a diagonal coloured pattern which lends the simple structure a dynamic feel and ensures the building's individuality. The painstakingly fashioned, paved outdoor areas as well as a terrace situated beside the stream give both visitors and employees the impression that the company works with the greatest care and the strictest attention to details.

In einem tristen, mit disparater Bebauung verstellten Dorf nahe Moskau hat eine kleine Firma mit ihrem einfachen Bürogebäude gezeigt, dass gute, zweckmäßige Architektur nicht zwangsläufig gesichts- und freudlos daherkommen muss. In eine parkartige Umgebung setzte der Architekt ein langgestrecktes, flaches Gebäude, das in seiner Schlichtheit zunächst an eine Lagerhalle erinnert. Vorgegeben war ein Neubau, der sowohl Garagen für die Firmenfahrzeuge als auch Büros, Aufenthalts- und Empfangsbereich sowie Räumlichkeiten für den Vorstand beherbergt. Entsprechend wurde der Bau in drei Zonen gegliedert. Im südlichen Bereich befinden sich, abgetrennt von vier Garagen und Technikräumen, die Büros der Mitarbeiter, während der zentrale Trakt mit Haupteingang als Empfangs- und Kommunikationszone eingerichtet wurde. Hier gibt es neben einer Rezeption auch eine Cafeteria, einen Club mit Kamin und Bar sowie eine Raucherlounge. Die Massivholzmöbel in diesem Teil wurden vom Architekten geplant. Der nördliche Gebäudeteil ist dem Vorstand vorbehalten. Der kompakte, eingeschossige Giebelbau besticht vor allem durch seine äußere Gestaltung: Die komplette, das Dach sowie die Längsfronten umfassende Ziegelverkleidung wurde mit einem diagonal verlaufenden farblichen Muster versehen, das der einfachen Hülle Dynamik verleiht und Unverwechselbarkeit garantiert. Die sorgfältig gestalteten Außenbereiche sowie eine am Bachlauf platzierte Terrasse vermitteln Besuchern den Eindruck, dass hier mit Sorgfalt und Sinn für Details gearbeitet wird.

Far more than just a garage: This polychrome structure near Moscow combines parking, working and chilling out in one multi-functional entity. The diagonal swathes of colour give the plain shell a sense of dynamism and individuality.

Von einer reinen Garage kann hier keine Rede sein. Vielmehr lässt sich die bunte Architektur im Moskauer Umland als kombinierte Einheit aus Parken, Arbeiten und Chill-Out verstehen. Die diagonal verlaufenden Farbmuster verleihen der einfachen Hülle Dynamik und Individualität.

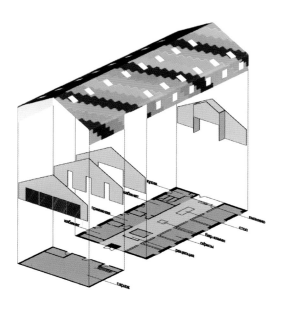

Country House in Gorky-2
Landhaus in Gorki-2

Projekt Meganom
2000

This property, which has quite an unusual ground plan, is situated on the edge of a country-home settlement outside of Moscow. The building's main façade with its many windows faces the forest rather than the street, thus harking back to the traditional wooden house, the *izbushka*, of Russian fairy tales. There are no people here to disturb the fantastic view. The floor plan consists of a staggered succession of shrinking prisms. The façade is accentuated by a high cornice supported by wooden columns whose form is a continuation of the pitch of the roof. A part of the building recedes to allow space for a generous terrace which complements the garden area terraced with quarried stone. The quarried-stone masonry not only forms the plinth of the house, which is situated on a slope, but in some sections reaches the level of the ceiling on the ground floor. The house is equipped with a sauna, a small swimming pool as well as a »relaxation zone«, which balance out the open-plan living area. As much as the house contrasts with the typical buildings constructed in Russia in recent years, everything seems so tidy in this model-house-like villa with pent roof and porch. Perhaps it is also unusual because it resembles European-style holiday homes, at least in terms of basic set-up and comfort. In Moscow, this style has triggered an explosive construction boom of villas for the New Russians in the last green spaces untouched by urban sprawl, thereby thwarting the inner-city renewal plan of Mayor Yury Luzhkov.

Das Grundstück, das einen außergewöhnlich geschnittenen Grundriss aufweist, liegt am Rande einer Landhaussiedlung außerhalb Moskaus. Das Gebäude ist mit seinen vielen Fenstern nicht zur Straße, sondern zum Wald hin ausgerichtet und erinnert so an das traditionelle Holzhaus aus den russischen Märchen, die *Isbuschka*. Hier stören keine Menschen die fantastische Aussicht. Der Grundriss besteht aus einer gestaffelten Abfolge aus sich verkleinernden Prismen. Die Fassade wird durch ein hohes, von Holzpfeilern gestütztes Gesims akzentuiert, dessen Form die Neigung des Daches fortsetzt. Ein Teil des Gebäudekörpers tritt zurück und bildet Raum für eine großzügige Terrasse, der eine mit Bruchsteinen terrassierte Gartenanlage entspricht. Das Bruchsteingemäuer bildet nicht nur den Sockel des Hauses an der Hanglage, sondern greift abschnittsweise bis in Deckenhöhe des Erdgeschosses. Das Haus ist mit einer Sauna, einem kleinen Swimmingpool sowie einer so genannten Erholungszone ausgestattet, die einen Ausgleich zur durchgehenden Wohnfläche schafft. So sehr sich das Haus von seinen in den vergangenen Jahren in Russland gebauten Typenbauten auch abheben mag, wirkt doch auch hier alles in seiner Weise aufgeräumt: das Musterhaus in Form einer Villa mit Pultdach. Ungewöhnlich vielleicht auch deshalb, weil sich unweigerlich Assoziationen zu europäischen Ferienhäusern aufdrängen, die nun mit Hilfe der »Neuen Russen« die letzten nicht zersiedelten Grünflächen Moskaus erobern.

Country House near Moscow
Landhaus bei Moskau

Projekt Meganom
2003

A new type of residential house should be included in the typology of modern villa construction: the forest house. After all, almost every second dacha built in the environs of Moscow in recent years is surrounded by thick woods. The architects were anxious to preserve the pines on the site and incorporate them into the design. The house and property are arranged quite functionally. The two-storey, three-winged bungalow is surrounded by a wooden fence which denotes the outline of the property. A paved footpath running through the middle of a well-kept green space leads directly to the main entrance. The three sections of the building – a sleeping area on the first floor, guest rooms and living area on the ground floor and connecting wing – provide for a flexible and, most of all, generous spatial arrangement due to the strict composition of the interior. The wood-clad first-floor section, which contains the bedrooms, rises above a concrete plinth. The form and arrangement of the windows repeats the arrangement of the beams on the wooden façade. Sometimes horizontal, sometimes vertical, they suggest a right-angled pattern. The transparent façade of the hall contrasts with the wooden cladding of the first floor and the concrete base. The elongated structure is connected to a transverse wing which is again connected to a shorter offset horizontal wing, hinting at a horseshoe-shaped courtyard. A swimming pool and other amenities are situated here.

In die Typologie des modernen russischen Villenbaus sollte ein neuer Wohnhaustyp eingeführt werden: das Waldhaus – schließlich ist fast jede zweite in den vergangenen Jahren entstandene Datscha in der Umgebung von Moskau mit dichtem Baumbestand umgeben. Die Architekten waren bestrebt, den Bestand der Kiefernbäume auf dem Grundstück weitgehend zu erhalten und in den Entwurf einzubinden. Der zweigeschossige und dreiflügelige Bungalow ist von einem Holzzaun umgeben, der die Linienführung des Grundstücks markiert. Ein gepflasterter Fußweg inmitten einer Grünanlage führt direkt zum Haupteingang. Die drei Gebäudeabschnitte – ein Schlaftrakt im ersten Obergeschoss, Gästezimmer und Wohnraum im Erdgeschoss sowie ein Verbindungstrakt – gewährleisten gerade wegen der strengen Komposition im Innern eine flexible und vor allem großzügige Raumgestaltung. Über einem Betonsockel erhebt sich der komplett mit Holz verkleidete Trakt des ersten Obergeschosses. Form und Anordnung der Fenster wiederholen die Anordnung der Balken der Holzfassade und ergeben mal in horizontaler, mal in vertikaler Stellung ein rechtwinkliges Muster in der Fassade. Die transparente Fassade der Halle kontrastiert sowohl die Holzverkleidung als auch den Betonsockel. An den vorderen Längsbau schließen sich zwei Flügel um einen hufeisenförmigen Innenhof an. Hier befindet sich auch der Swimmingpool.

Sober elegance is the mark of this country house in the woods near Moscow. The windows provide a clear structuring element. They endow the elongated façade with a geometric rhythm taken up in the three staggered wings of the house. The result is a subtle harmony of light.

Sachliche Eleganz strahlt auch diese Villa in den Wäldern vor Moskau aus. Gestaltendes Element sind zweifelsohne die Fenster. Sie ordnen und strukturieren in geometrischer Rhythmik die längliche Eingangsfront. Die drei zueinander versetzten Baukörper der Villa nehmen diesen Akkord auf und schaffen harmonische Lichtverhältnisse.

54

Country House near Moscow
Landhaus bei Moskau

Eduard Zabuga
2000

Three structural elements, each different in form and consisting of copper, wood and stone, have been fitted together like the pieces of a jigsaw puzzle. Together they make up a two-storey residential house complete with swimming pool, spacious living room and an accessible roof. As the property is located in the immediate vicinity of a colony of villas, parts of existing foundations were used in the construction. The architects' main concern was to create a house which reveals little of its interior yet remains open to its natural surroundings – to sun and air. The street side of the house has only two small windows in its rusticated façade. Sunlight comes in through a large window above a pent roof, through the glass ceiling over the swimming pool and through the glazed access to the roof. The ground floor has an elongated living area with windows on both sides. Two flights of stairs lead to the first floor with its private areas and children's room. The owner, a sculptor, has his studio in a separate part of the building. Laid out intriguingly in the shape of a quadrant, the studio is marked by huge windows and provides fitting surroundings for the artist's sculptures.

Drei in ihrer Form unterschiedlich ausgeprägte und aus Kupfer, Stein und Holz entwickelte Baukörper sind wie Teile eines Puzzles ineinander gesteckt worden. In der Summe ergeben sie ein zweigeschossiges Wohnhaus, das mit Swimmingpool, geräumigem Wohnraum und einem begehbaren Dach ausgestattet ist. Hauptanliegen der Architekten war die Konstruktion eines Hauses, das von seinem Inneren wenig nach außen preisgibt und dennoch offen für die natürliche Umgebung ist. Zur Straße hin hat das Haus lediglich zwei kleine Fenster in der Rustikafassade. Das nötige Tageslicht fällt durch ein großes Fenster über einem Pultdach, durch das Glasdach über dem Swimmingpool sowie durch einen gläsernen Zugang zum Dach. Ein langgestreckter Wohnraum prägt das Erdgeschoss. Zwei Treppen führen in das Obergeschoss zu den Privaträumen und einem Kinderzimmer. In einem separaten Gebäudeteil befindet sich das Atelier des Hausbesitzers, der als Bildhauer tätig ist. Es zeichnet sich durch riesige Fenster sowie einen interessanten, viertelkreisförmigen Schnitt aus und bietet so eine passende Umrahmung für die hier entstehenden Skulpturen.

Guardhouse in Gorky-10
Wachschutzgebäude in Gorki-10

Alexey Kozyr/Arch-4
2003

This guardhouse in Gorky-10 is a rather unusual project in the oeuvre of the architect Alexey Kozyr, who has drawn attention to himself in recent years mainly through his experiments with black concrete. Due to its unconventional appearance as well as its numerous technical finesses, the building was among the favourites at Russia's most important architecture fair, the ARCH Moskva, in 2002. To be exact, this structure is not a house but rather an embodiment of the function for which it was created. The security aspect is reflected in the strict arrangement of the building and its hidden symmetry: a simple, charcoal-grey cube, like a giant Lego block perched upon white columns. Its façade is interrupted solely by narrow vertical window-slits. A perron leads up to the door. These are only the visible parts of the building. A second cube, containing the transformers, is hidden in the ground. To the right is the owner's bungalow. The double rings around the windows make its front façade look like a bespectacled face through which the owner can see if the guard is really guarding – or sleeping.

Das Wachschutzhaus in Gorki-10 ist ein eher ungewöhnliches Projekt im Œuvre des Architekten Alexej Kosyr, der in den vergangenen Jahren vorwiegend durch Experimente mit schwarzem Beton in Erscheinung getreten ist. Im Prinzip ist dieser Baukörper kein Haus. Er verkörpert lediglich die Funktion, für die er geschaffen wurde. Der Sicherheitsaspekt spiegelt sich in der strengen Gebäudegliederung und seiner versteckten Symmetrie wider. Der schlichte, anthrazitfarbene Kubus, dessen Fassade lediglich durch schmale senkrechte Fensterschlitze unterbrochen wird, und die Tür, zu der eine Freitreppe hinaufführt, sind nur der sichtbare Teil des gesamten Gebäudes. Ein weiterer Kubus, in dem Transformatoren untergebracht sind, ist im Boden versteckt. Das Häuschen wirkt wie aus einem Steckbaukasten zusammengesetzt. Rechts daneben befindet sich der Bungalow des Hausherren, mit einer Frontfassade, die mit den Doppelringen um die Fenster wie ein bebrilltes Gesicht aussieht. Durch die Fenster kann der Besitzer kontrollieren, ob der Wachschutz auch wirklich wacht – oder schläft.

Shopping Centre in Moscow
Einkaufszentrum in Moskau

Sergey Kiselyov and Partners
DNK Architects
2003

This building is located next to the Aeroport metro station on Leningradsky Prospekt, one of Moscow's major arterial roads. This new shopping centre in the city's inner north-west was to provide not only an architectural solution but also contribute to the urban development. Whereas the right side of the street leading out of town is lined with residential buildings from the Stalinist era, large building complexes from the era of state-directed progress and gymnastic fervour extend along the left side of the street. These include the airport for the former state airline Aeroflot (hence the name of the metro station), and various sports complexes. The angled ground plan of the complex, consisting of several modular structures, takes in Ernst Thälmann Square. A particular gesture is formed by the propped-up, streamlined transverse wing which reaches almost to the edge of the street and transforms the urban function of the square into a visual focal point. Light brown brick alternates with matt green glass surfaces and metal giving the entire ensemble a tidy appearance. The horizontally encompassing metal bands form a visual element which unites the various buildings, like a collection of geometric figures, into a single ensemble which now provides a worthy backdrop for the statue of Ernst Thälmann, an illustrious figure regardless of political upheavals, granting him a guaranteed place even in post-Soviet Russia. Just as the square lends the statue a sense of dignity, it in turn transfers the idea of a classless society, which is anchored in the collective consciousness, to the commercial structure: all are equal when shopping, even if no one notices.

Das Gebäude befindet sich neben der U-Bahnstation »Aeroport« am Leningrad-Prospekt, einer der großen Ausfallstraßen. Hier im Nordwesten der Innenstadt war mit dem neuen Einkaufszentrum sowohl eine architektonische als auch eine städtebauliche Lösung gefragt. Während die Straße stadtauswärts gesehen rechter Hand von fünf- bis neunstöckigen Wohnbauten vor allem aus der stalinistischen Ära gesäumt ist, erstrecken sich linker Hand die Großbauten aus den Zeiten des staatsdirigierten Fortschritts und der Körperertüchtigung. Der alte Flughafen der ehedem staatlichen Gesellschaft Aeroflot, an den die Metro-Station erinnert sowie diverse Sportkomplexe. Der aus mehreren Körpern baukastenartig zusammengesteckte Bau fasst räumlich in seinem winkligen Grundriss den Ernst-Thälmann-Platz. Eine besondere Geste ist der aufgeständerte, windschnittige Querflügel, der fast bis an die Straßenkante reicht und zu der städtebaulich ordnenden Funktion des Platzes es einen Blickfang addiert. Hellbrauner Backstein wechselt mit grün mattierten Glasflächen und Metall ab. Optisch verbindendes Element der verschiedenen Baukörper sind horizontal umlaufende Metallbänder. Vor dieser Kulisse erhebt sich die Skulptur des über alle ideologischen Umbrüche erhabenen Ernst Thälmann, die damit eine würdige Bühne und somit auch im postsowjetischen Russland eine gewisse Bestandsgarantie erhalten hat. Denn so wie der Platz dem Standbild seine Würde verleiht, so überträgt die Statue eine im kollektiven Bewusstsein verankerte Botschaft von der klassenlosen Gesellschaft auf den Kommerzbau: Beim Einkauf sind alle gleich, ohne dass es einer merkt.

This house is as fast as its surroundings. The horizontal lines of the façade emphasise an exterior and interior dynamism matching the high-speed context. And who is that waving to us? A statue of German communist Ernst Thälmann, no less.

Ein Haus, so schnell wie seine Umgebung: Die horizontalen Linien der Gebäudefront unterstreichen die äußere und innere Dynamik des Gebäudes als Teil seiner bewegten Umgebung – und mittendrin grüßt der deutsche Kommunist Ernst Thälmann auf dem Sockel.

Office Building in Moscow
Bürogebäude in Moskau

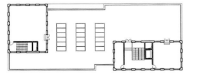

DNK Architects
2005

No, no one would expect a miracle of urban development in this part of Moscow. Just what should happen between huge apartment blocks and industrial buildings? Yet here on an abandoned lot containing the ruins of an old kindergarten, a first-class office building has been built, which can lend the paralysed, lifeless area on Vavilov Street a lease of hope for a new beginning. In this sense the new building on this spot is something of an epiphany. At first the design makes a respectful bow to the conservative business architecture of Berlin-based Hans Kollhoff. The fact that this clear reference does not come across as exotic or degenerate into a cheap triumph is due to the markedly objective and reserved implementation of these forms in the Moscow context. The building's eave line is clearly lower than that of the other buildings in the neighbourhood, and only the reddish, iridescent brick façade allows the building to break away from the mud-coloured buildings in the surrounding area. The altogether docile appearance of the elongated structure is balanced out by its outer form: the rhythmically uniform façade with its long horizontal rows of windows achieves a sense of plasticity through use of robust pilaster strips; the sculptural character of the cube is accentuated by generous cut-out balconies on the edges and façade setbacks. The penthouse contains the building's prestigious office space. Its internal structure is dictated most of all by the down-to-earth criteria of efficiency. The building possesses flexible floor plans, rational building services and a pragmatic division of space in accordance with contemporary demands. This office building allows capitalism to present itself in Moscow in a classical guise.

Nein, städtebauliche Wunder würde in diesem Teil Moskaus wohl niemand erwarten. Was soll zwischen Großplattenbauten und Industriehallen schon Bemerkenswertes passieren? Doch hier, auf einer verwahrlosten Brache mit den Ruinen eines alten Kindergartens, entstand ein Bürogebäude der A-Klasse, das dem erstarrten, leblosen Stadtraum an der Wawilov-Straße tatsächlich einen Hauch von Aufbruch zu geben vermag. Insofern ist dieser Neubau an dieser Stelle so etwas wie eine Epiphanie. Der Entwurf reflektiert zunächst eine respektvolle Verbeugung vor der konservativen Geschäftshausarchitektur eines Hans Kollhoff. Dass dieser deutliche Bezug hier nicht exotisch wirkt oder zum billigen Triumph gerät, ist der ausgesprochen sachlichen und zurückhaltenden Übersetzung der entsprechenden Formen in den Moskauer Kontext zu verdanken. Die Traufkante des Hauses bleibt deutlich unter den Gebäudehöhen der Nachbarschaft, und nur seine rötlich changierende Klinkerfassade setzt sich von der schlammfarbenen Bebauung der Umgebung belebend ab. Der insgesamt fügsame Auftritt des lang gestreckten Baukörpers wird allerdings durch seine äußere Gestaltung aufgewogen. Die gleichmäßig rhythmisierte Fassade mit ihren langen, horizontalen Fensterreihen gewinnt durch kräftige Lisenen Plastizität, der skulpturale Charakter des Kubus wird durch großzügig ausgeschnittene Balkonflächen an den Kanten sowie Fassadenrücksprünge betont. Den zeitgemäßen Anforderungen entsprechend verfügt das Gebäude über flexible Grundrisse, rationale Haustechnik und pragmatische Raumaufteilungen. Mit diesem außerwöhnlichen Bürohaus zeigt sich der Kapitalismus in Moskau im klassischen Gewand – wenn man es findet.

64

Restaurant on Klyazma River
Restaurant an der Kljasma

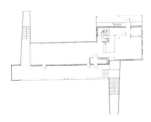

Totan Kuzembayev
2004

A long stretch of beach on a lake near Moscow is dominated by this new restaurant building and connecting guest house. The small individual buildings in the area are united by the gravitational pull of this expressive architecture. The squat body of the restaurant also denotes the border between the existing beach on the one side and the large marina and riding hall, designed by Yevgeny Ass, to be built on the other. With its classical beach-house architecture – a wooden superstructure resting on slender stilts – Kuzembayev's expressionistic building resembles Alexander Brodsky's nostalgically inspired 95 Degrees Restaurant. On sunny days the sight of the bright red building set on a clear lake, a wide blue sky, the yellow sand and the green treetops is reminiscent of a Cubist colour study. This charm is no accident. The stylistic details found in the architecture clearly allude to the Russian avant-garde and its bold constructivism. The central role of the large restaurant is accentuated by the subordination of the smaller buildings. The composition's dynamism draws on the open confrontation of opposing elements: the right-angled front of the restaurant against the zigzagging diagonal stilts and posts, or upward-pointing roofs against deep-set entrances and verandas. The structures of the architecture rise effortlessly above the solid ground and at the same time seek a solid footing. We are left suspended somewhere between heaven and earth.

Das neue Restaurant mit angeschlossenem Gästehaustrakt dominiert einen längeren Strandabschnitt an einem See bei Moskau und entfaltet mit seiner ausdrucksstarken Architektur ein Gravitationsfeld, das die versprengt stehenden kleinen Einzelbauten der Umgebung in einen Zusammenhang zwingt. Der stämmige Baukörper des Restaurants markiert auch die Grenze zwischen dem Badestrand auf der einen Seite und einem Yachthafen auf der anderen Seite. An sonnigen Tagen wirkt der Anblick des signalroten Baus vor dem klaren See, einem hohen blauen Himmel, dem gelben Sand und den grünen Baumwipfeln wie eine kubistische Farbstudie. Die Architektur bezieht sich in einigen stilistischen Details ganz offen auf die Russische Avantgarde und ihren kühnen Konstruktivismus. Die zentrale Rolle des großen Restaurantflügels wird durch die gefügige Unterordnung der kleinen Häuser betont. Die Dynamik der architektonischen Komposition beruht auf der offenen Konfrontation der Gegensätze: die rechtwinklige Front des Restaurants gegen die in Zickzack-Linien verlaufenden diagonalen Stäbe und Stützpfeiler, in den Himmel ragende Dächer gegen tief nach unten gezogene Eingänge und Veranden. Die Strukturen dieser Architektur erheben sich mit Leichtigkeit über den festen Grund und suchen gleichzeitig nach verlässlicher Bodenhaftung. Was bleibt, ist ein merkwürdiger Zustand irgendwo zwischen Himmel und Erde.

Clubhouse near Moscow
Klubhaus bei Moskau

Architecture Studio XYZ
2003

This building belongs to a shooting range and is located at the edge of a sandpit. The sand heaps and the clear waters of a lake help create the illusion of a unique mountainous landscape. The Lisya Nova Clubhouse is an idiosyncratic gateway to this hidden world. The complex includes offices for the personnel, technical services for the shooting range, public areas, shops and a restaurant. Three blocks are brought together on one side by an open terrace. Glazed passageways connect the bright-red wooden structures with one another. The visually uniform façade of the divergently styled buildings, which continues outwards from both sides of the single-storey central section, also underscores the functional unity of the wooden structures. The middle section, the linchpin of the obtusely-angled complex, is defined by a covered veranda which can be reached by an open stairway – here one finds the restaurant. This emphasises the role of the middle section as the visual focal point of the composition.

Das Gebäude gehört zu einem Schießgelände und befindet sich an einer Sandgrube, die eine natürliche Landschaft bildet. Das Klubhaus »Lisja Nowa« ist ein eigenartiges Tor in diese geschlossene Welt. Die Anlage beherbergt Büros für das Personal, technische Dienste des Schießplatzes, Öffentlichkeitsräume, Geschäfte und ein Restaurant. Drei Blöcke werden mit einer Fläche der geöffneten Terrasse vereinigt. Verglaste Übergänge verbinden die grellrot gestrichenen Gebäudekörper aus Holz miteinander. Die optisch einheitliche Fassade der unterschiedlich gestalteten Bauten, die sich links und rechts des einstöckigen Mitteltraktes fortsetzt, unterstreicht auch die funktionale Zusammengehörigkeit des Holzbaus. Der Mitteltrakt, der die im Grundriss stumpfwinklige Anlage zusammenhält, wird von einer überdachten Veranda geprägt, die über eine Freitreppe zu erreichen ist. Hier oben befindet sich das Restaurant. So wird der Mitteltrakt als optischer Blickfang des Arrangements auch inhaltlich hervorgehoben.

Russian Roots

Concrete Villa near Novosibirsk
Plattenbauvilla bei Nowosibirsk

Anatoly Andryushchenko
1995

Retired helicopter pilot Anatoly Andryushchenko built himself a five-storey villa from prefabricated concrete elements in the district town of Ordynskoye near Novosibirsk. For this, the active pensioner set up his own small "pre-cast concrete factory" in his workshop. The house is a distinct oddity, not just in the choice of material but also in design. Its shape could be taken to resemble a fortified border castle with a chapel (indicated by the apse). Above all, however, the concrete slab segments show just how closely the ornamental design of mass-produced modules – and the very model of a modern building – is related to works of traditional craftsmanship. Standing amidst farms and silos, the villa looks all the more bizarre, like an alien body from another world. The building's most notable feature is the natural way in which it combines industrial and do-it-yourself construction methods. Andryushchenko, who basically had no previous building experience, simply copied industrial methods of prefabricating concrete parts, or rather what he thought those methods to be. Using a single mould that was adapted by adding or omitting certain details, he succeeded in producing more than two dozen different pre-cast elements, a wealth of shapes that normal pre-cast concrete factories and design institutes can only dream of. He calculated the dimensions and weight of the prefabricated elements so that installation and assembly required no lifting or transportation devices – only sheer muscle power.

Der pensionierte Hubschrauberpilot Anatoli Andrjuschtschenko baute sich in der Kreishauptstadt Ordynskoje bei Nowosibirsk eine fünfgeschossige Villa aus vorgefertigten Betonelementen. Hierzu richtete der geschäftige Rentner ein eigenes kleines »Plattenbaukombinat« in seiner Werkstatt ein. Das Haus ist nicht nur in der Materialwahl, sondern auch in seinem Aufbau eine Groteske sondergleichen. Seine Form erinnert an eine Art Grenzburg mit Kapelle. Die Apsis wäre hier die »Burgkapelle«. Vor allem aber zeigen die einzelnen Plattenbausegmente, wie nah sich die Ornamentik massenhaft fabrizierter Bauteile, ja der moderne Bau an sich, und das traditionelle Handwerk sind. Inmitten von Bauernhöfen und Speichergebäuden wirkt die Villa im fernen Sibirien umso absonderlicher. Bemerkenswert ist der Bau vor allem wegen der Kombination von Industriebauweise mit Heimwerkermethoden. Andrjuschtschenko, der zuvor keine Bauerfahrung hatte, imitierte einfach die Verfahrensweise der in den ehemaligen sowjetischen Plattenbaukombinaten verwendeten Methoden der Betonfertigteilproduktion – beziehungsweise das, was er dafür hielt. Der Eigenheimbauer schaffte es, mit einer einzigen Matrize, die durch Hinzufügen oder Weglassen von Details variiert wurde, mehr als zwei Dutzend verschiedener Fertigelemente zu erzeugen. Maße und Gewicht der Fertigelemente wurden von ihm so berechnet, dass für Einbau und Montage nur seine Muskelkraft nötig war.

72

73

Summer School in Oshevensk
Sommerschule in Oschewensk

Studio TAF
2000

The summer school in Oshevensk in the Archangel region was established for future designers, architects and painters, who come here during the brief summer season to study the genius loci, a genuine traditional popular culture that survives in landscapes, buildings, everyday objects and clothing. For the students, the building has to resemble a textbook. It must concentrate within itself the characteristics typical of buildings of the past. It must be functional and display familiarity with modern architectural traditions while simultaneously looking as if it had always been there. The main design themes fall within three parameters. First is the sketchiness of the architectural process at every stage. This began with informal planning, with no conventional plan of execution. Next, decisions on the location of individual tree trunks were taken only on site and, last but not least, timber was processed to fashion the interior and the windows. Without a tremendous capacity for innovation, the project would not have been possible. The second planning parameter limited the building to small window openings while making maximum use of natural light in the interior. The third design feature is the asymmetrical ground plan, which follows the bend in the river and makes the house look as if it originated more than two hundred years ago and had lived through as many changes of season. No one here would understand a modern architectural language with materials atypical of the region anyway, nor would it survive the hard winter, which can last to up to six months.

Die Sommerschule in Oschewensk im Archangelsker Gebiet – knapp eineinhalb Flugstunden nördlich von Moskau – wurde für auszubildende Designer, Architekten und Maler gegründet. Für die Studierenden sollte das Gebäude inmitten des nordrussischen Städtchens einem Lehrbuch ähnlich sein. Es sollte Eigenschaften in sich vereinen, die für Bauten der Vergangenheit typisch sind, gleichzeitig aber in der Tradition der Moderne stehen und eine hohe Funktionalität aufweisen. Die Hauptthemen der Gestaltung lassen sich auf drei Parameter eingrenzen. Zum einen zeigt sich die Architektur auf allen Ebenen skizzenhaft. Die Planung erfolgte ohne herkömmlichen Ausführungszeichnung. Erst auf der Baustelle wurde die Verortung der einzelnen Baumstämme entschieden. Nicht zuletzt wurde hier das Holz zur Fertigung des Interieurs und der Fenster bearbeitet. Ohne großes Improvisationsvermögen wäre das Projekt nicht möglich gewesen. Der zweite Parameter ist die Beschränkung auf kleine Fensteröffnungen bei maximaler Ausnutzung natürlichen Lichts im Innenraum. Das dritte Gestaltungsmerkmal ist der asymmetrische Grundriss, der sich an der Biegung des Flusses orientiert und den Eindruck vermittelt, als sei das Haus schon vor über 200 Jahren entstanden und habe ebenso viele Jahreszeitenwechsel erlebt. Eine moderne Architektursprache mit Materialien, die in dieser Gegend untypisch sind, würde hier auf wenig Verständnis stoßen. Solches würde auch der strenge Winter nicht tolerieren, der hier manchmal länger als ein halbes Jahr das Alltagsleben regiert.

74

What better place to commune with the spirit of Russian folk culture than this stylish log cabin? It dwells in the surrounding village and is wakened by the contrast of rough walls and fine design characterising the cabin's outside and its inside, where the Vassily Chair is juxtaposed with a chunk of wood serving as a table.

Wahrscheinlich eine der schönsten Designer-Blockhütten, um mit dem Genius Loci der russischen Volkskultur in direkten Kontakt zu treten. Dieser hat in der Umgebung die Gestalt einfacher Dorfhäuser angenommen. Der Gegensatz von rauher Wand und feinem Design setzt sich im Interieur fort: Neben Wassily-Stuhl stehen klotzige Holzblöcke, die als Tische dienen.

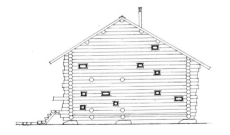

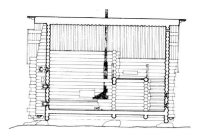

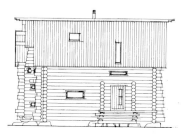

Cocoon Club in Moscow
Klub »Kokon« in Moskau

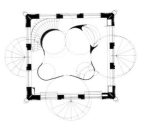

Vladimir Kuzmin
Vlad Savinkin
2002

The Cocoon Club boasts one of the most unusual interiors created in Moscow in recent years. The name is programmatic for the architecture. The discotheque on Prospekt Mira is hidden in a three-storey pavilion whose postmodern façade with its polished granite, stainless steel and glass looks somewhat cool and distant. This style has long been passé in a progressive city like Moscow. Circular windows riddle the cuboid building like a Swiss cheese, disclosing views of the interior. Elongated, contorted and ovate openings permeate the outer biomorphic shell, directing curiosity towards an interior shaped even more strongly by the natural elements wind and water. Entrances and passageways that, as in natural caves, make circular and wavelike incisions in fluently protruding sections of wall, and niches that look as if nature had worked away at them for centuries to turn them into cosy spaces for lovers to retreat to for a while in the evenings while the Cocoon is grooving fit to burst. The discotheque's biological shape and in particular the moulded timber from Bioinjektor provide a shell for special, yet contrasting, arrangements. There is the obligatory chill-out zone with cylindrical wooden tables and lamps on soft imitation grass whose understated elegance cannot but stand out against ice-cube-shaped tables and chairs on a high-gloss floor. A sequence of highly contrasting rooms and dance floors with rest areas winds its way from basement to first floor. They all have one thing in common – the apparently hand-fashioned wooden shell.

Zu den ungewöhnlichsten Innenräumen, die in den vergangenen Jahren in Moskau entstanden sind, gehört der Klub »Kokon«. Der Name ist architektonisches Programm. Die Diskothek am Prospekt Mira versteckt sich in einem dreigeschossigen Pavillon, dessen postmoderne Fassade aus poliertem Granit, Edelstahl und Glas eher kühl und abweisend wirkt. Kreisrunde Fenster durchlöchern den Kubus wie einen Schweizer Käse und eröffnen Blicke in den Innenraum. Langgestreckte, verzogene und eiförmige Öffnungen lenken den Blick auf die äußere biomorphe Hülle und die Neugierde auf ein von den Naturelementen Wind und Wasser noch stärker geformtes Inneres. Zugänge und Durchgänge, die wie in natürlichen Höhlen kreisrunde und wellenförmige Einschnitte in fließend auskragenden Wandpartien und Nischen hinterlassen, wirken so, als hätte Jahrhunderte lang die Natur an ihnen gearbeitet. Nun dienen sie als lauschige Räume für Verliebte, die sich hier abends zurückziehen. Währenddessen will der Kokon vor lauter Lebensfreude fast platzen. Ganz oben liegt die obligatorische Chill-out-Zone mit hölzernen Zylindertischen und mit Lampen auf flauschigem Gras-Imitat, die sich mit sachlicher Eleganz gegen Tische und Stühle in Gestalt von Eiswürfeln auf glänzendem Boden behaupten muss. Vom Keller bis zum ersten Stockwerk reihen sich unterschiedliche Räume, Tanzflächen samt Ruhezonen, die gegensätzlicher nicht sein könnten und nur eines gemeinsam haben: ihre wie von Hand geknetete hölzerne Hülle.

Organic shapes and futuristic furnishings: functional, sensual and exciting, that is the motto.
Geformt wie von der Natur und ausgestattet mit futuristischen Finessen, ganz nach der Devise: funktional, sinnlich und aufregend.

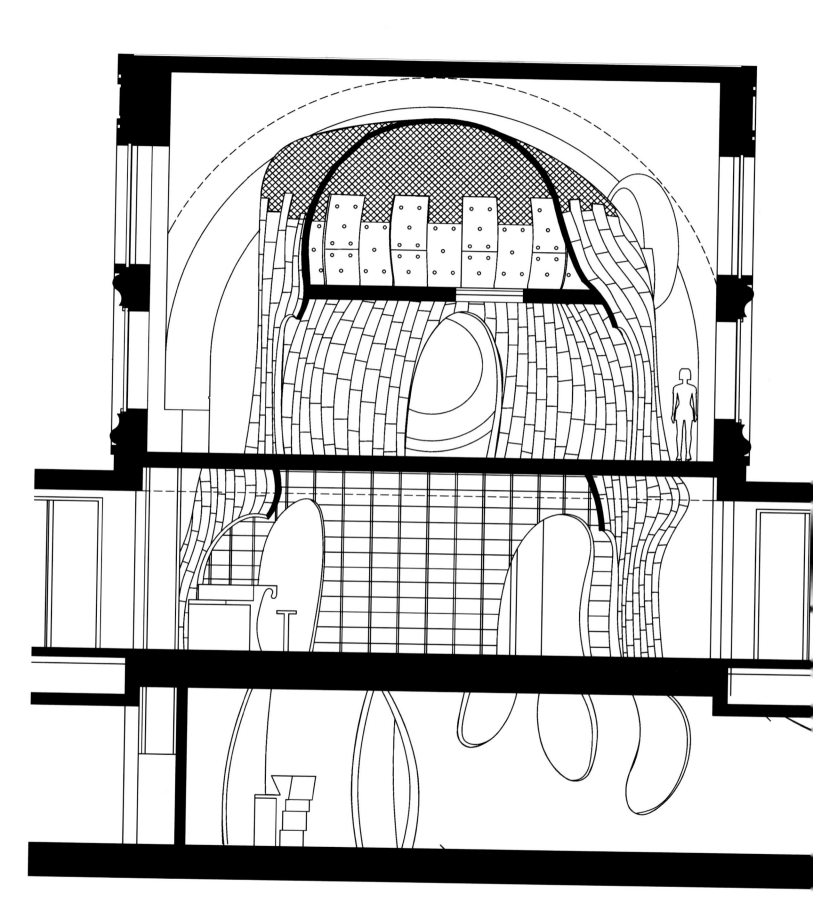

Residential Building in Vnukovo
Wohngebäude in Wnukowo

Vladimir Kuzmin
Vlad Savinkin
2003

To attribute the aesthetics of this country house to the architects' fondness for traditional timber construction alone would be to exaggerate. When Kuzmin and Savinkin began designing this building, several log cabins were already in the vicinity of the site, which is in the catchment area of Vnukovo regional airport southwest of Moscow. Their building material was the remains of a disused school and several houses imported from the Republic of Mari-El (an autonomous republic in the Volga region). The architects wanted the building's design to reflect its owner's character. A dynamic, energetic businessman, he prefers unusual solutions in his private life, as well as in his work. This in turn gave the architects design leeway. They created an unusual construct by placing several complete log cabins on metal and concrete piers, as it were, and slotting them together. This assembly is broken by flights of stairs and skylights. At the same time, the architects took account of the past life of the building fragments by highlighting various nuances in the surface of the timber and recombining different grains. This did not prevent them from employing additional "industrial" elements such as galvanised steel and metal braces or corrugated steel fencing. The spatial diversity that is a typical element of traditional Russian timber houses is thus achieved not only by playing with perspective, but also by layering transparent and widely differing materials one upon another.

Es wäre eine Übertreibung, die Ästhetik dieses Landhauses nur auf die Vorliebe der Architekten für die traditionelle Holzbauweise zurückzuführen. Als Kusmin und Sawinkin mit dem Entwurf begannen, gab es schon einige Blockhäuser in der näheren Umgebung des Grundstücks, das sich im Einzugsbereich des Regionalflughafens Wnukowo im Südwesten der Hauptstadt befindet. Als Baumaterial verwendeten sie die Reste einer ausgedienten Schule sowie einiger Häuser, die aus der Republik Mari-El (einer autonomen Republik in der Wolga-Region) importiert wurden. In der Konstruktion des Hauses sollte sich nach Wunsch der Architekten auch das Wesen seines Besitzers widerspiegeln. Sie schufen eine ungewöhnliche Konstruktion, indem sie mehrere komplette Blockhütten quasi auf Metall- und Betonpfeilern platzierten und ineinander verschoben. Durchbrochen wird diese Komposition durch Treppen und Oberlichter. Die Architekten berücksichtigten jedoch auch das »Vorleben« der von ihnen verwendeten Hausfragmente, indem sie unterschiedliche Nuancen in der Holzoberfläche besonders betont und verschiedene Maserungen neu miteinander kombiniert haben. Die räumliche Vielfalt, ein typisches Element des traditionellen russischen Holzhauses, wird so nicht nur durch das Spiel mit der Perspektive, sondern auch durch Übereinanderschichten von transparenten und äußerst unterschiedlichen Materialien erzielt.

Think of Russia's wide lands, and timber houses will rise to your mind's eye. This country house, however, defies all clichés. It combines the remains of several older buildings. *Wer an Russlands Weiten denkt, hat Bilder von Holzhäusern vor Augen. Aber dieses Landhaus – konstruiert aus dem Vorleben anderer Bauten – stellt alle gängigen Vorstellungen auf den Kopf.*

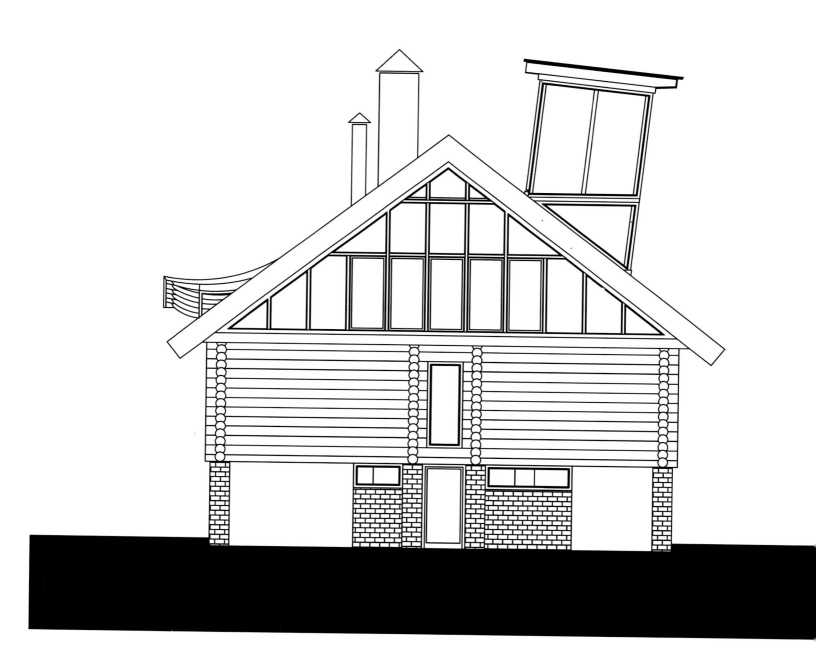

Museum of the Floating Arts near Moscow
Museum der »Schwimmenden Künste« bei Moskau

Art-Blya (A-B)
2002

The surreal-looking floating elements are miniature water craft made by children at the studio of artist Mikhail Labazov. However, these colourful works of art cannot be compared with ordinary boats. For about a year the small craft were housed on the ground floor of the 95 Degrees Restaurant designed by architect Alexander Brodsky on the neighbouring jetty. Mikhail Labazov designed this timber structure on the bank of the Klyazma River in order to display them to better advantage. The new Museum of Floating Arts reproduces the eternal subject matter of museum buildings on a small scale. The art itself is informal, but the design of an exhibition building must be formalised and categorised. The museum's austere, elegant timber structure forms an exciting contrast with the playful little boats. The exhibition space is divided into tiers, making the presentation appear very rational. The exhibits, some suspended, some standing, are protected by a canopy that juts out over the river, linking architecture and nature, art and water.

Die surrealistisch anmutenden Schwimmelemente sind Mini-Wasserfahrzeuge, die Kinder im Atelier des Künstlers Michail Labasow selbst angefertigt haben. Diese bunten Kunstwerke sind jedoch nicht mit gewöhnlichen Booten vergleichbar. Etwa ein Jahr waren die kleinen Wasserfahrzeuge im Erdgeschoss eines an der benachbarten Anlegestelle gelegenen Restaurants untergebracht. Um sie besser zur Geltung zu bringen, entwarf Labasow diese Holzkonstruktion am Ufer des Flusses Kljasma. Das neue »Museum der Schwimmenden Kunst« wiederholt im Kleinformat die ewige Thematik von Museumsbauten: Die Kunst selbst ist informell, die Konstruktion eines Ausstellungsgebäudes muss formalisiert und kategorisiert werden. Die Aufteilung des Ausstellungsraumes in Ränge lässt die Präsentation rationell wirken. Geschützt werden die teilweise hängenden, teilweise stehenden Exponate durch ein über das Wasser auskragendes Vordach, das auf diese Weise Architektur und Natur, Kunst und Wasser wie selbstverständlich miteinander verbindet.

The Carrot Country House near Moscow
Landhaus »Karotte« bei Moskau

Art-Blya (A-B)
2004

This country house near Moscow – dubbed "The Carrot" by its architects – is hard to classify and must be characterised as an architectural oddity. It does not fit into the existing framework of typologies and styles and falls outside the context of conventional planning. Yet when the Carrot House is seen as part of the overall work of the Art-Blya group of architects, its design becomes more than intelligible. The identity of this edifice is to be found not in the framework of the architecture itself but within the logic of the architects. Within the parameters of this identification, three basic principles are discernible: architecture as an act of art, the act of art as a process in time, and the process as the creation of a synthetic product in space. In this case, art is not an aesthetic category but a method of form-finding. Architecture is treated as a collective activity of the people involved. In this type of concept the client becomes a co-author who experiences not only the pain of the economic decision but also the pain of artistic creation. Characteristically, architects of the Art-Blya practice are reluctant to release detailed plans for publication. They see that as the lot of the builders. With the client and with colleagues they customarily communicate in the language of pictures and sketches. Ceramic artist Yevgeny Rybin, known for his experiments with colour and materials, designed the column capital, but building workers pieced together the endless tile jigsaw puzzles on site.

Das Landhaus, das bei Moskau errichtet und von den Architekten »Karotte« getauft wurde, ist als architektonischer Sonderling schwer zu klassifizieren. Unmöglich, es in die vorhandenen Rahmen der Typologien und Stile einzuordnen. Das Gebäude fällt aus dem Kontext einer konventionellen Planung. Betrachtet man das »Karottenhaus« jedoch als Teil des Gesamtwerkes der Moskauer Architektengruppe Art-Blja, wird dieser Entwurf durchaus verständlich. Drei Grundprinzipien betimmen den Entwurf: Sie unterstreichen die Architektur als Kunstakt, den Kunstakt als einen in der Zeit dauernden Prozess und den Prozess als Schaffung des synthetischen Produktes im Raum. Die Kunst ist in diesem Fall aber keine ästhetische Kategorie, sondern eine Methode der Formfindung. Architektur wird als kollektive Tätigkeit der Akteure verstanden. Bei einer solchen Auffassung wird der Auftraggeber zum Mitautor, der nicht nur die Qual der wirtschaftlichen Entscheidung, sondern auch die Qual des künstlerischen Schaffens erlebt. Es ist charakteristisch, dass die Architekten des Büros Art-Blya nur ungern Detailpläne zur Veröffentlichung freigeben – Ausführungspläne und Werkzeichnungen sind für sie das Los der Bauarbeiter. Mit dem Auftraggeber und mit den Kollegen kommuniziert man in der Sprache der Bilder und Skizzen. In dieser Haltung spiegelt sich vor allem auch der künstlerische Ansatz der Architekten.

It is to the pillars that this unusual house owes its nickname. The Carrot House, with its colourful clinker façade and oval ground plan, gleams in the sunlight like a fairy-tale castle.

Die Pfeiler geben diesem eigenwilligen Bau seinen Namen: Karotte. Die bunten Klinkersteine lassen das Haus mit dem ovalen Grundriss im Sonnenlicht wie ein Märchenschloss schimmern.

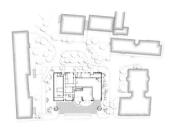

Stolnik Apartment House in Moscow
Appartmenthaus »Stolnik« in Moskau

Art-Blya (A-B)
2003

Is that an apartment building? Truly, this new building on Maly Lyovshinsky Lane does not accord with traditional Moscow ideas of a respectable middle-class home in the city centre. From the outset, it has been the target of numerous criticisms invariably ignited by its self-confident differentness and leading to the conclusion that this was not what a normal apartment building in Moscow should look like. The critics are right. The Stolnik apartment complex in the middle of the historic centre of the Russian capital, close to the legendary Arbat, is like a glistening UFO amid upmarket, late-nineteenth-century Art Nouveau villas and apartment blocks, individual high-rise buildings and drearily austere tenements built in the Soviet era. Its expressionistic shapes and smooth, cool materials, and the dreamy air with which it occupies the urban space are without a doubt a novelty. Its architects deliberately refrained from historical borrowings and realised a fantasy that is most closely comparable with the architecture of Frank Gehry or Hans Hollein. So much for the theory: in practice, the building obediently complies with the usual local standards for urban development. The eaves height is customary for Moscow and the site itself is only of average size. Together with the five-storey post-war apartment house opposite, the building forms a self-contained ensemble that emphasises the introverted character of narrow Maly Lyovshinsky Lane. With its elegant façade and large interior courtyard, the building also follows the urban development principles that defined residential building in Moscow during the last decade.

Das soll ein Wohnhaus sein? Der Neubau in der Mali-Lewschinski-Gasse entspricht tatsächlich nicht den herkömmlichen Moskauer Vorstellungen von einer bürgerlichen Adresse mitten im Stadtzentrum. Von Anfang an sah sich das Gebäude heftiger Kritik ausgesetzt. Das Wohnhaus »Stolnik«, mitten im historischen Zentrum der russischen Hauptstadt in der Nähe des legendären Arbat gelegen, wirkt zwischen den vornehmen Jugendstilvillen und Mietshäusern aus dem späten 19. Jahrhundert sowie einzelnen Hochhäusern und schlicht-traurigen Wohnblocks aus Sowjetzeiten in der Tat wie ein gleißendes Ufo. Seine expressionistischen Formen, die glatten, kühlen Materialien und der traumtänzerische Gestus, mit dem es sich im Stadtraum platziert, sind ohne Zweifel ein Novum. Die Architekten verzichteten bewusst auf historische Anleihen und haben eine Phantasie verwirklicht, die sich am ehesten mit der Architektur Frank Gehrys oder Hans Holleins vergleichen lässt. Soweit die Theorie. Praktisch jedoch gehorcht das Haus brav dem städtebaulichen Maßstab. Seine Traufhöhe entspricht den ortsüblichen Maßen, und auch die Parzelle ist nur durchschnittlich dimensioniert. Das Gebäude bildet zusammen mit dem gegenüberliegenden, fünfgeschossigen Wohnhaus aus der Nachkriegszeit ein geschlossenes Ensemble, das den introvertierten Charakter der Gasse betont. Das Haus selbst entspricht mit seiner urbanen Fassadenfront und einem großen, dem öffentlichen Raum entrückten Hof im Blockinneren auch den städtebaulichen Prinzipien, die im vergangenen Jahrzehnt den Wohnungsbau in Moskau bestimmten.

The massive, granite-clad plinth is firmly anchored in a sea of buildings. The delicate tops, however, standing tall, open the view to the roofs of Moscow.

Der massive Sockel – mit Granit verkleidet – liegt schwer im Häusermeer. Nur die filigrane Spitze ragt hervor und eröffnet den Blick auf die Dächer von Moskau.

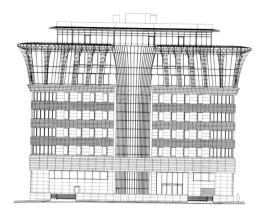

The façade details look a bit chunky and suggest an office building. However, the forbidding structure topped with a metal crown is in fact an apartment house.

Die Fassadendetails wirken etwas grob und erinnern eher an einen Bürobau. In der Gasse wirkt das Appartmenthaus mit seiner Metallkrone fast unnahbar.

94

A closer look reveals the theme of this architecture: the classical capital recurs on the sign at the door, in the lobby and in the overall shape.

Bei näherer Betrachtung rückt das gestalterische Motiv der Architektur in den Fokus: das klassische Kapitell. Die Architekten variieren es auf dem Eingangsschild, in der Lobby und in der Gesamtform.

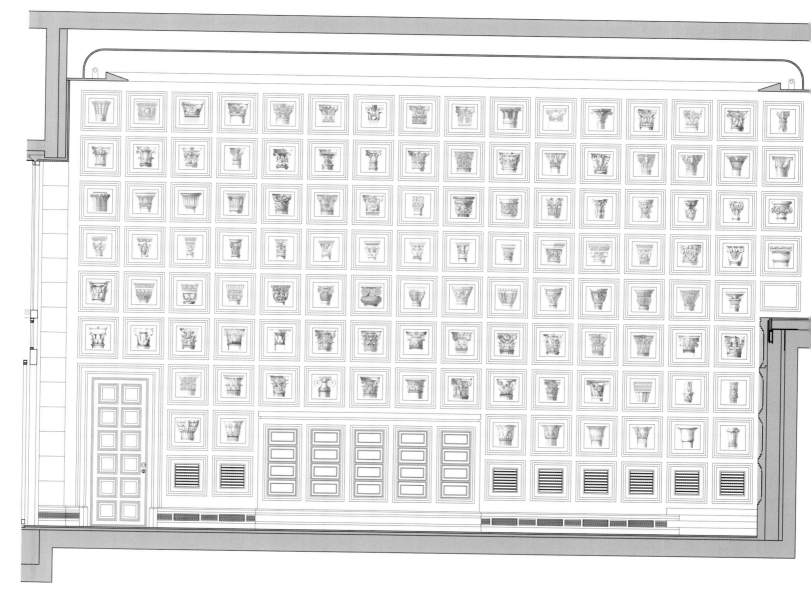

95 Degrees Restaurant near Moscow
Restaurant »95 Grad« bei Moskau

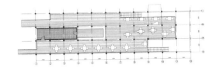

Alexander Brodsky
2000

Not far from the Museum of the Floating Arts is the 95 Degrees Restaurant, a simple timber construction that imitates the shape of a jetty. The name is symbolic: the vertical members are placed at an angle of exactly 95 degrees. The arrangement of rooms in the building, which is more than two thirds transparent, recalls the inside of a ship. The area where food is served, an elevated deck house, dominates the entire structure with its russet brown colour scheme. The kitchen on the tween deck is separate from the main area and panelled in corrugated metal. It has an impressive, lattice-patterned glass front that defines the appearance of the river-bank elevation. At the same time, its transparency opens up the lower level towards the water, establishing a link between nature and architecture. This motif is continued in the irregular roof covering, which is additionally protected by a transparent plastic sheet. Details such as companionways and mast-like beams lend further emphasis to the nautical theme.

Nur unweit vom »Museum der Schwimmenden Kunst« entfernt befindet sich das Restaurant »95 Grad«. Die einfache Holzkonstruktion, welche die Form einer Anlegestelle nachahmt, trägt einen symbolischen Namen: Genau 95 Grad beträgt der Winkel der Vertikalen. Die Raumabfolge in dem zu mehr als zwei Dritteln transparenten Baukörper erinnert an das Innere eines Schiffes. Der Speisesaal dominiert die gesamte Konstruktion durch seine Farbgebung: ein hoch gelegenes »Deck House« in rostbraun. Die vom Hauptraum abgetrennte und mit Wellblech verkleidete Küche »im Zwischendeck« ist mit einer eindrucksvollen, gitterförmig gerasterten Glasfront versehen. Gleichzeitig öffnet sich die untere Ebene durch diese Transparenz zum Wasser und verbindet Natur und Architektur. Dieses Motiv setzt sich auch in der unregelmäßigen Dachdeckung fort, die zusätzlich durch eine transparente Plastikplane geschützt ist. Der nautische Charakter wird durch Details wie die Leitertreppen oder die mastartigen Stützbalken noch zusätzlich betont.

Vodka Pavilion near Moscow
Wodka-Pavillon bei Moskau

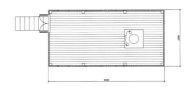

Alexander Brodsky
2003

Alexander Brodsky long dreamed of building a pavilion for vodka ceremonies. Two factors enabled him to make this dream come true. One was the demolition of the Butikovsky factory in Ostozhenka and the other was the annual Klyazma festival of arts. The festival organisers placed a piece of land at the edge of the forest at Brodsky's disposal and the old factory supplied him with unique material in the form of pre-1917 window frames. In the architect's hands, the frames became a universal building element, forming both load-bearing structure and cladding. The extensive glazed areas do not detract at all from the intimacy of the vodka ceremony because an old coat of white paint renders the windows fully opaque. During the daytime, light filters through the matt windows. When evening falls, candles are lit in the small building and a warm glow starts to emanate. This attracts all devotees of the vodka ceremony, which is very simple and yet ritualistic. Two people stand, drink and feel in complete harmony with themselves and each other. Dispensing with the traditional third participant further enhances the intimacy of this ceremony. One can certainly tell the architect's attitude towards the ritual from the pavilion's external appearance. Standing in a slightly elevated position, it points not toward hell, but in the direction of heaven.

Lange hegte Alexander Brodski den Wunsch, einen Pavillon für Wodka-Zeremonien zu realisieren. Der Abriss der Butikowski-Fabrik im Moskauer Ostoschenka-Viertel und das jährlich stattfindende Kunstfestival »Art Kljasma« machten dies möglich. Die Organisatoren des Festivals stellten Brodsky ein Grundstück am Waldrand zur Verfügung, die abzureißende Fabrik versorgte ihn mit einzigartigem Material: Fensterrahmen aus der Zeit vor 1917, die sowohl die Tragkonstruktion als auch die Verkleidung bilden. Trotz der großflächigen Verglasung wird die Intimität der Wodka-Zeremonie jedoch keineswegs beeinträchtigt – die Fenster sind aufgrund einer alten weißen Farbschicht völlig blind. Am Tag dringt das Licht durch die matten Fenster, am Abend werden innen Kerzen angezündet. Dieses Licht zieht alle Liebhaber der Wodka-Zeremonie an. Diese ist sehr einfach und dennoch feierlich: Zwei Menschen trinken stehend und befinden sich im vollen Einklang mit sich selbst und miteinander. Die Intimität der Zeremonie wird noch zusätzlich betont durch den Verzicht auf den traditionellen dritten Teilnehmer. Die Einstellung des Architekten zu dem Ritual kann man durchaus an der äußeren Erscheinung des Pavillons ablesen: Leicht erhöht stehend, weist er nicht zur Hölle – sondern in Richtung Himmel.

Bathhouse on Klyazma Reservoir
Badehaus am Kljasma-Reservoir

Alexander Brodsky
Yaroslav Kovalchuk
2002

The bathhouse on the bank of the Klyazma Reservoir does not particularly resemble a Russian *banya*, which traditionally has to be small, dark and very hot. Nor would it meet the goals of the client, who wanted to build an exclusive recreation centre on this artificial lake in the south of Moscow. Its clientele comes from the nearby dachas and villas that shape the landscape in this area. The building was designed by Brodsky and Kovalchuk and, unlike their neighbouring restaurant 95 Degrees, stands firmly on the ground. The timber structure is made from rectangular cross-section logs and is surrounded by openwork verandas. Despite their transitory nature, verandas play a role as a structural element by linking together various elements of the façade. The verandas' slender vertical supports and horizontal braces create a rigid network of rods to enclose the main body of the building. This outer framework makes it possible to dispense with otherwise customary structural elements of a traditional timber building. Since the body of the building bears "inwards", it does not look solid and heavy, even though its dimensions would actually require it to be so. Only one section of the building, on the first floor, was built monolithically. It houses the cloakroom, toilet, steam bath and shower. The project's centrepiece is without a doubt the glazed bay with the round bathing tub. It appears to float above the artificial lake, lending the *banya* an almost meditative character.

Das Badehaus am Ufer des Kliasma-Reservoirs ist der russischen Banja, die traditionell klein, dunkel und sehr heiß sein muss, nicht besonders ähnlich. Das würde den Zielen des Auftraggebers auch nicht gerecht werden, der an dem künstlichen See im Süden von Moskau einen Klub als Erholungszentrum errichten wollte. Die Klientel der Besucher findet sich in den benachbarten Datschen und Villen. Das Holzbauwerk besteht aus in ihrem Querschnitt rechteckigen Holzstämmen und wird mit einer filigranen Galerie umgürtet. Trotz ihrer Vergänglichkeit spielen die Galerien eine Rolle als Konstruktionselement, da sie verschiedene Elemente der Fassade miteinander verbinden. Die senkrechten, dünnen Stützen und die waagerechten Klammern der Galerien schaffen ein in sich steifes Stabwerk. Aufgrund dieses äußeren Gerüstes ist es möglich, auf die üblichen Konstruktionselemente eines klassischen Holzbaus zu verzichten. Dank der Gliederung des Gebäudevolumens »nach innen« sieht das Gebäude nicht massiv und schwer aus, obwohl seine Ausmaße dies eigentlich erfordern würden. Nur ein Bauteil im ersten Obergeschoss wurde monolithisch ausgeführt und beherbergt Garderobe, Toilette, Dampfbad und Dusche. Herzstück des Projektes ist zweifelsohne der verglaste Erker mit der runden Schwimmbeckentonne. Sie scheint über dem künstlichen Teich zu schweben und verleiht der Banja einen nahezu meditativen Charakter.

Scaffold Construction near Moscow
Kunstinstallation bei Moskau

Iced Architects
2000

The authors of this Scaffold Construction in the Forest, the members of the Iced Architects group, came up with the idea for this project in 1999 after seeing an old poplar that had grown into the window grille of the House of Journalists on Suvorovsky Boulevard. They found that the interplay of nature and artificial objects (in this case an architectural monument) was not antagonistic. Rather, the young architects concluded, the different elements achieved equality by pervading each other's space. This idea was successfully put into practice during the Festival of Modern Art held in August 2000 in the grounds of the health resort by the Klyazma Reservoir. The fifteen-metre metal structure encompassing an entire treetop was installed in a birch forest situated on a hill and bounded by the reservoir's sandy beach. The result was a dynamic composition, the changes in which depend on the natural cycle of the trees and the weather. At night, the structure was illuminated. Dozens of electric lights in the metal tubing lent the unusual construction an almost mythical quality. The idea was for the trees to engulf the three-dimensional metal framework as time went on, allowing an organic symbiosis to emerge – a unique mixed forest of birch trees and scaffolding.

Die Idee des Projektes »Baugerüste im Wald« entstand im Jahre 1999 bei dem Quartett »Iced Architects«, nachdem die Mitglieder der Gruppe eine alte Pappel gesehen hatten, die in das Fenstergitter des Journalistenhauses am Suworowski Boulevard eingewachsen war. Die Architekten stellten fest, dass die Wechselwirkung der Natur mit den künstlichen Objekten (in jenem Fall einem Architekturdenkmal) harmonisch funktioniert. Auf der Basis der gegenseitigen Durchdringung werde sogar eine Gleichberechtigung der Elemente erreicht, wie die jungen Architekten schlussfolgerten. Diese Idee wurde im Rahmen des Festivals der Modernen Kunst auf dem Territorium des Pensionates am Kljasma-Reservoir im Sommer 2000 erfolgreich verwirklicht. In einem Birkenwald, der auf einem Hügel liegt, und von dem der Sandstrand des Reservoirs begrenzt wird, wurde die Metallkonstruktion errichtet, die mit ihren 15 Metern die gesamte Baumkrone umfasst. Es entstand eine dynamische Komposition, deren Veränderungen vom natürlichen Zyklus der Bäume und der Witterung abhängen. Nachts wurde die Konstruktion beleuchtet. Dutzende von Leuchten in den Metallröhren verliehen der ungewöhnlichen Installation nahezu mythische Qualität.

Regional Russia

Lukoil Office Building in Nizhny Novgorod
Bürogebäude »Lukoil« in Nischni Nowgorod

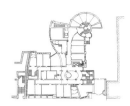

Valery Nikishin
2000

If you want to see Russian architecture beyond Moscow, go to Nizhny Novgorod. Formerly known as Gorky, this is the third-biggest city in Russia. When it finally opened its gates to foreign visitors, new ideas and theories came in, and in the early 1990s the city became a veritable hub of architecture. And it is still thriving. Architects know Nizhny Novgorod as a place of pluralism. Different approaches to architecture coexist – or shall we say cohabit – in domestic harmony. The architectural scene is lively and attracts interest all over the world. However, Nizhny Novgorod is also beset by the problems typical of a provincial capital: the office building constructed for oil giant Lukoil is a case in point. While projects in Moscow are outlined overnight and need just a few months to take shape in the cityscape, Valery Nikishin had to wait six long years before his design was realised, all the while exposed to critical crossfire. For his task was not an easy one. Flanked by constructivist and modernist façades, the street elevation was restricted to three storeys. To generate the space he needed, the architect shifted five floors to the courtyard. With its striking façade ornaments, projections and niches, combined with easily recognisable references to architectural history (the staircase, for example, features a Melnikov façade), the office building fits harmoniously into its architectural context.

Die Öffnung des ehemaligen Gorki und der damit ermöglichte äußere Einfluss auf das Baugeschehen haben Nischni Nowgorod zu Beginn der Neunzigerjahre den Rang einer »Hauptstadt der Architektur« eingebracht. In der Fachwelt gilt die Stadt als Ort des Pluralismus, in dem verschiedene Architekturauffassungen parallel existieren. Außerdem verfügt die drittgrößte Stadt Russlands über eine Architekturszene, die sich weit über Russland hinaus Gehör verschafft hat. Allerdings hat sie – und dafür steht das Bürogebäude des Öl-Imperiums von Lukoil stellvertretend – auch mit den Problemen einer Provinzhauptstadt zu kämpfen. Während in Moskau Projekte über Nacht geboren und binnen weniger Monate im Straßenbild sichtbar werden, musste Valeri Nikischin immerhin sechs lange Jahre warten, bis sein Entwurf in der Grunsinskaja-Straße realisiert wurde. In dieser Zeit hatte er eine schwierige Aufgabe zu lösen: flankiert von Bauten des Konstruktivismus und der Moderne durfte die Straßenfront drei Geschosse nicht übersteigen. Um das Raumprogramm unterzubringen, verlegte Nikischin fünf Geschosse in den Hof. Durch die auffällige Dekoration der Fassade, den zahlreichen Vor- und Rücksprüngen sowie durch bekannte Zitate aus der Architekturgeschichte – etwa das Treppenhaus mit Melnikow-Fassade – ist es jedoch gelungen, das Bürogebäude sensibel in die Nachbarschaft zu integrieren.

Apartment Building in Nizhny Novgorod
Wohngebäude in Nischni Nowgorod

Alexander Kharitonov
Yevgeny Pestov
1999

The Jumble House is situated close to the football stadium in the city formerly known as Gorky in an area of eighteenth-century housing with some single-storey dwellings. The English name with its overtones of confusion and disorder does not do justice to this street-corner development, which ranges from four to seven storeys in height. True, it plays along with what seems to be a favourite game in modern Russian architecture – to be in some way original. But it was developed along strictly linear, well-ordered and comprehensible lines. The ground floor with its dark render and ornamental bands of masonry has a copper roof all round. Above it is a four-storey residential block, which is lent structure only by a regular arrangement of windows. On top of this is a one- to three-storey structure featuring protrusions, recesses, bays and bands of red and light grey brick that runs in this guise through the rear of the building, in some places down to the ground floor. One building is made up of two. The upper structure with its varying roof heights and sequence of independent family town houses makes it look as if a suburb had landed on the building. This complex obviously includes a series of postmodern references, and a little Mario Botta never does any harm, especially when the aim is to bring together the aesthetic contrasts of an area in a single work of architecture. In this building, the architects tried to bridge the contrast between the plain 1970s developments in this neighbourhood and the architecture of the eighteenth and nineteenth centuries, which, though artistically likewise simple, was more contemplative.

Auf Englisch heißt dieses Wohnhaus »Jumble House« – Gewirr oder Durcheinander. Ein Attribut, das dem vier- bis siebenstöckigen Eckhaus in Nachbarschaft zum Fußballstadion und zur eingeschossigen Bebauung aus dem 18. Jahrhunderts nicht unbedingt gerecht wird. Hier manifestiert sich vielmehr das architektonische Streben nach Originalität. Diese Andersartigkeit entfaltet sich hier sehr streng linear in wohl geordneten und nachvollziehbaren Bahnen. Einem mit dunkel verputzten und mit Mauerbändern verzierten Erdgeschoss mit umlaufendem Kupferdach folgt ein weiß verputzter vierstöckiger Wohntrakt. Dieser wird allein durch die gleichmäßige Anordnung der Fenster strukturiert. Darüber befindet sich ein mit Auskragungen, Einschnitten, Erkern sowie mit roten und hellgrauen Ziegelbändern gestaltetes Penthouse, dessen Muster den rückwärtigen Teil des Gebäudes teilweise bis in das Erdgeschoss prägt. Das »Jumble House« besteht gewissermaßen aus zwei Gebäuden, wobei das Penthouse durch die tanzenden Baukörper fast wie eine Reihung eigenständiger Stadthäuser erscheint – so als sei auf dem Haus eine Vorstadt gelandet. Die Zitatreihe der Postmoderne ist offenkundig – ein wenig Mario Botta schadet nie. Zumal dann nicht, wenn es darum geht, die ästhetischen Gegensätze eines Ortes in der Architektur zusammenzuführen. Mit dem Entwurf versuchten die Autoren den Kontrast einer schlichten Bebauung aus den Siebzigerjahren mit einer künstlerisch zweifellos einfachen, wenngleich maßstäblicheren Architektur der vergangenen zwei Jahrhunderte zu betonen.

Nomen est omen.
An alien settlement seems to have lost its bearings right on top of the white main wing of Jumble House. Or is that a different building in the background? The illusory effect is certainly intriguing.

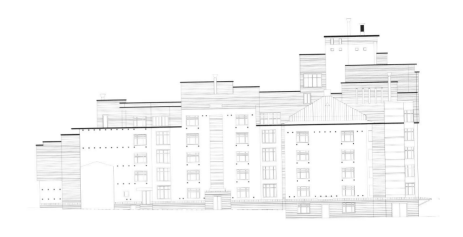

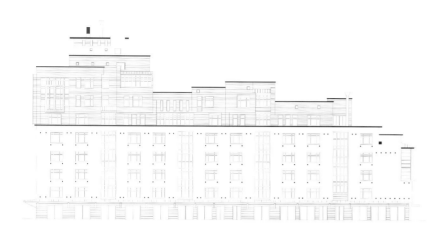

»Haufen« – Nomen est Omen. Auf dem weißen Haupttrakt scheint sich eine fremde Siedlung verirrt zu haben. Oder befindet sich doch ein anderes Gebäude im Hintergrund? Die Sinnestäuschung ist zumindest verblüffend.

Etazhi Shopping Centre in Nizhny Novgorod
Einkaufszentrum »Etaschi« in Nischni Nowgorod

Viktor Bikov
2003

Until recently, apart from two earlier exceptions, major shopping facilities in Nizhny Novgorod were housed in former apartment buildings, hotels or sports complexes that had been remodelled to serve new commercial purposes. The exceptions were two department stores built in the 1930s in this city of roughly 1.4 million people, which was named after its native son, the writer Maxim Gorky, in 1932 and reverted to its traditional name in 1990. Since then, consumer requirements have also changed in this historic city. Once a fourteenth-century princely capital, it is now a centre of the automotive industry – the Russian Volga motorcar is produced here. The Etazhi Shopping Centre is both a response to this change and characteristic of new commercial architecture. It stands on the corner of Belinsky and Izhorskaya Street in a line with old wine depots and the opera house. Yet this five-storey building with its eye-catching glass show front sets its own accents. The glass façade provides views of the building's inner workings, including escalators and a panorama lift. The circular annex follows up the horizontal white steel braces on the main façade with narrow bands of fenestration that continue in the adjacent three-storey side wing in the form of narrow white lines and partly continuous, partly broken lines of fenestration. The visual design framework of the main façade is formed by bands of fenestration that are somewhat evocative of the Bauhaus in Dessau and consequently of the formal patterns of early modernism, to which visible tribute is paid here.

Bis vor kurzem wurden in Nischni Nowgorod, abgesehen von zwei frühen Ausnahmen, größere Einkaufsmöglichkeiten in ehemaligen Wohnhäusern, Hotels oder Sportanlagen geschaffen, die für die neuen kommerziellen Zwecke umgestaltet wurden. Die Ausnahmen bilden zwei Kaufhäuser, die in den Dreißigerjahren in der rund 1,4 Millionen Einwohner zählenden Stadt errichtet wurden, die 1932 nach dem hier geborenen Schriftsteller Maxim Gorki umbenannt wurde und nach 1990 wieder ihren angestammten Namen angenommen hat. Seither haben sich auch die Konsumbedürfnisse in der alten fürstlichen Residenzstadt des 14. Jahrhunderts und heutigen Fahrzeugindustriestadt – unter anderem wird hier der Wolga gebaut – geändert. Das Einkaufszentrum »Etaschi« ist ein Beleg dafür und zugleich kennzeichnend für eine neue Kommerzarchitektur. Das fünfstöckige Gebäude sorgt mit seiner auffälligen gläsernen Schaufassade jedoch für eine eigene stilistische Note. Die Glasfassade gibt Einblicke in das funktionale Innenleben des Hauses. Der runde Anbau nimmt in Form von schmalen Fensterbändern die weißen horizontalen Stahlverstrebungen der Hauptfassade auf, um sie dann wieder im angrenzenden dreistöckigen Seitenflügel als schmale weiße Linien und in Gestalt der teils geschlossenen, teils unterbrochenen Fensterbänder fortzuführen. Den optischen Konstruktionsrahmen der Hauptfassade bilden Fensterbänder, die ein wenig an das Bauhaus in Dessau und somit an Gestaltungsmuster der hier sichtlich geschätzten Frühmoderne erinnern.

114

115

City Shopping Centre in Nizhny Novgorod
Einkaufszentrum »City« in Nischni Nowgorod

Alexander Kharitonov
Yevgeny Pestov
2000

Since Nizhny Novgorod became a regional architectural capital in the late 1980s, the new Russian architecture here has shown a strong penchant for the stylistic forms of the turn of the last century and early modernism. The shopping centre in Kanavino, a district in the Lower City, is further testimony to this. Like the Etazhi Shopping Centre, it formed part of an urban regeneration programme that in this case involved developing the area between Meshchera and Beryozka and filling in gaps between buildings as far as Kavinsky Market. Following reconstruction of the market the commercial space filled up with shops. Retailers moved into the ground floors of existing buildings, enlivening the surroundings but initially doing nothing to alter the area's ambience. The shopping centre has changed that. Its core is an old jeweller's shop above a pedestrian underpass. The new shopping mall was built above this shop. The goal was to erect a solid building with a clearly structured façade that could take an advertising billboard, with overhead lighting and possibly also a glazed roof and a forecourt that could be used on market days. The result is a building that, at first sight, does not reveal its internal function as a shopping mall, looking more like a conventional department store. This is mainly due to the row of shop windows on the ground floor. Above them is a self-contained, abstract cube with recesses and openings outlined by steel structures. The cut-out sections are then found on the roof in the form of glazed top sections with bands of fenestration. This restrained play with geometrical shapes continues in the Mondrian-style façade.

Seit Nischni Nowgorod Architekturhauptstadt der Region ist, zeigt sich im Zuge der neuen russischen Architektur vor allem eine Vorliebe für die Stilformen der letzten Jahrhundertwende und der Frühmoderne. Das Einkaufszentrum, das in Kanawino, einem Viertel in der Unterstadt errichtet wurde, ist ein weiterer Beleg für diesen Trend. Wie das Einkaufszentrum »Etaschi« ist auch dieser Bau Teil einer städtebaulichen Neugestaltung. Nach der Wiederbelebung des Kawinski-Marktes füllten sich die Handelsflächen mit Geschäften. Der Handel ließ sich in den Erdgeschossen bestehender Gebäude nieder, belebte die Umgebung, änderte aber zunächst nichts am Milieu der Gegend. Das hat sich nun mit dem Einkaufszentrum geändert, dessen Kern ein alter Juwelierladen ist. Über diesem Geschäft wurde das neue Gebäude errichtet. Ziel war es, einen massiven Baukörper zu schaffen, mit einer klar strukturierten Fassade, die auch eine Reklametafel verträgt – einen Bau mit Oberbeleuchtung, eventuell auch einem verglasten Dach und einem Vorplatz, der nicht nur an Markttagen genutzt werden kann. Das Ergebnis ist ein Gebäude, das auf den ersten Blick nicht auf seine innere Funktion als *Shopping Mall* rückschließen lässt, sondern wie ein ganz herkömmliches Kaufhaus anmutet. Dazu trägt vor allem die Schaufensterzeile im Parterre bei. Darüber erhebt sich ein geschlossener abstrakter Kubus, mit Einschnitten und Hohlräumen, deren Ausschnitte sich als mit Fensterbändern verglaste Aufsätze auf dem Dach wiederfinden. Das zurückhaltende Spiel mit geometrischen Formen setzt sich in der im Stil Mondrians gestalteten Fassade fort.

117

Loudspeaker Office Building in Nizhny Novgorod
Bürogebäude »Lautsprecher« in Nischni Nowgorod

Alexander Kharitonov
Yevgeny Pestov
1995

"That's what I call real architecture!" the German historian Karl Schlögel is said to have exclaimed on seeing the Loudspeaker Tower. It is, at least, clearly recognisable as an Art Nouveau building, so it may have evoked Schlögel's mental pictures of contemporary buildings by Albert Gessner, Paul Geldner in the area of domestic architecture, or Otto Kaufmann. That speaks for the genuine quality of this complex, in which the architects drew on the entire spectrum of that epoch at the transition from historicism to functional modernism to close a gaping wound in the historic built environment with no fewer than four buildings. The eye-catching feature is the corner tower with its oval window at the sweeping transition from smooth façade to coffered pattern and rather ornate roof hood. It is said to be shaped like a loudspeaker. A more apt description, to use the language of tableware, might be to compare it with the lid of a coffee pot in this style, which covered all fields of life, including fashion. The loudspeaker comparison is definitely far-fetched and somewhat limp in the face of architecture that, after more than a century, proves impressively in its own organic calm that it has lost none of its style-setting dynamic of rebelliousness against everything imposed. Art Nouveau is and will continue to be poetry and an attitude to life. Asymmetrical ornamentation and floral contours make the transition to the neighbouring round tower in the interior courtyard with its vertical bands of fenestration, and from it to the next building, so fluently light and agile. This building at the street's edge picks up the façade motif in a somewhat modified form and merges into the adjacent building with its gabled roof.

»Da ist sie – eine echte Architektur!«, soll der deutsche Historiker Karl Schlögel angesichtig des »Lautsprecherturms« ausgerufen haben. Das Gebäude ist zumindest eindeutig als Haus des Jugendstils zu erkennen und mag in Schlögels Gedächtnis sofort die gespeicherte Bildergalerie zeitgenössischer Bauten eines Albert Gessner, Paul Geldner oder eines Otto Kaufmann abgerufen haben. Das alles spricht für die Echtheit dieses Gebäudes, für das die Architekten die Palette dieser Epoche am Übergang von Historismus und sachlicher Moderne abrufen, um mit gleich vier Baukörpern eine klaffende Wunde in der historischen Bebauung zu schließen. *Point de vue* ist dabei der Eckturm, der mit seinem ovalen Fenster am geschwungenen Übergang von der glatten Fassade zum Kassettenmuster mit der eher blumigen Dachhaube einen Lautsprecher nachformt. Verglichen mit den Tischservices einer alle Lebensbereiche durchdringenden Stilepoche läge ein Vergleich mit der Haube einer Kaffeekanne näher. Die Analogie zum Lautsprecher aber ist allemal bemüht und zeigt sich eher hilflos gegenüber einer Architektur, die an dieser Stelle nach über einhundert Jahren eindrucksvoll beweist, dass sie sichtlich nichts von ihrer stilbildenden Dynamik in der Aufsässigkeit verloren hat. Jugendstil ist und bleibt Poesie und Lebensgefühl. Fließend ist der Übergang zwischen den Baukörpern. Dies garantieren die asymmetrische Ornamentik einerseits und die floralen Konturen andererseits. Die Architekten haben ihre Aufgabe mit wohlproportionierter Formgebung gelöst – und mit dem »Lautsprecher« eine außerordentliche Komposition im Stadtbild von Nischni Nowgorod geschaffen.

No doubt about it:
Art Nouveau and Russian
traditionalism are two
styles that go well together, as is evident from the
harmonious ensemble
that gives this street its
character.

Jugendstil und russischer
Traditionalismus sind
offenbar zwei Stilformen,
die bestens miteinander
harmonieren und hier ein
stimmiges Straßenbild
prägendes Ensemble
hinterlassen haben.

Garantiya Bank in Nizhny Nowgorod
Bank »Garantija« in Nischni Nowgorod

Alexander Kharitonov
Yevgeny Pestov
1995

The head office of the Garantiya Bank pension fund also expresses its self-image as a capital fountain of youth with the architectural energy of Art Nouveau. The horizontal bands at the base are the dominant stylistic element uniting all parts of the building. What really catches the eye, however, is the portico with its oval windows, angular profiles that seem to flow along the bands across the wall, and what looks like a solidified river of concrete running from the fascia in the shape of a twin-pillared archway with an oval window. The other dominant element is the lateral tower with its fluid shapes. The entire complex looks like poetry shaped from dough. Only the sign "Bankomat" brings it back to earth. Inside, there is little to see of the floral lushness of the elevation facing the street. In the building to the rear, this has already given way to a very austere, regular façade.

Der Verwaltungssitz des Pensionsfonds der Bank »Garantija« bringt sein Selbstverständnis als kapitaler Jungbrunnen in der architektonischen Energie des *Art Nouveau* zum Ausdruck. Stilprägendes Element sind die Fassadenbänder im Sockelgeschoss. Blickfang ist der Portikus mit seinen ovalen Fenstern, den eckigen Mauerprofilen, die entlang der Bänder über die Wand zu fließen scheinen und der sich von der Dachkante in einer Form erstarrt scheinende Zementfluss in Gestalt eines Torbogens mit zwei Säulen und einem ovalen Fenster. Ein anderes prägendes Element ist der seitliche Turm mit seinen fließenden Formen. Der gesamte Komplex wirkt wie aus Teig geronnene Poesie, die allein das Hinweisschild »Bankomat« wieder auf den Boden der Tatsachen zurückbringt. Allerdings ist von der floralen Üppigkeit der Fassade im Innern nicht mehr viel zu sehen.

One bank, three styles.
The front facing the forecourt bubbles over with
creative joy, while the
façade along the side
street meekly conforms
to its surroundings.
Eine Bank, drei Stile:
Zum Vorplatz hin
sprudelt die Gestaltungs-
freude geradezu über,
während sich die Front
zur Seitenstraße in Reih'
und Glied fügt.

125

Chess Apartment Building in Nizhny Novgorod
Wohngebäude »Karo« in Nischni Nowgorod

Yevgeny Pestov
2004

This office and apartment building rounds off a neighbourhood in the historic part of the city. When planning this building, architects Alexander Kharitonov and Yevgeny Pestov, who also designed the other new buildings in this section, faced the task of linking the historic city with Soviet-era buildings while simultaneously giving direction to the foreseeable widening and lengthening of the street. The contemporary use of shapes in the building at the corner of Studyonaya and Gorky Street is also a tactical game with the ghosts of the past. Its clear geometrical simplicity and unadorned rationalism fall within the architectural parameters of Soviet architecture. However, they break with the box aesthetics of that era in their exaggeration and abstraction. A two-storey base with narrow, embrasure-like window openings and an entrance countersunk into the corner defines the street space and looks like a terrace in front of the building's distinct lattice pattern. The actual façade is a composition of overlying geometrical structures. These diamond-like structures of black brick, red clinker and white cross-hatching lend it not only vivacity but also a three-dimensional quality. The surprising visuals are further emphasised by slightly offset windows in the façade openings, two diagonal bands of fenestration and a brash penthouse breaking through the overhanging fascia. The elevation on Gorky Street is dominated by a prism-shaped loggia that juts out over the street.

Das Büro- und Wohngebäude rundet ein Quartier im historischen Teil der Stadt städtebaulich ab. Alexander Charitonow und Jewgeni Pestow sahen sich bei der Planung des Hauses vor die Aufgabe gestellt, die historische Altstadt mit der sowjetischen Bebauung zu verknüpfen und gleichzeitig der absehbaren Ausweitung und Verlängerung der Straße eine Richtung zu weisen. Die zeitgenössische Formensprache des Gebäudes ist auch ein taktisches Spiel mit den Geistern der Vergangenheit. Seine geometrisch klare Schlichtheit und die schmucklose, rationale Anmutung entsprechen den architektonischen Parametern des sowjetischen Bauens; sie brechen mit der Kasten-Ästhetik dieser Ära jedoch in ihrer Überhöhung und Abstraktion. Ein zweigeschossiger, umlaufender Sockel mit schmalen, schießschartenartigen Fensterausschnitten und einem in die Ecke gefrästen Eingangsbereich definiert den Straßenraum und wirkt vor dem klar gerasterten Gebäuderiegel wie eine Terrasse. Die Hausfassade selbst ist eine Komposition aus sich überlagernden geometrischen Strukturen. Die wie ein Karo gezeichneten Strukturen aus schwarzen Ziegeln, roten Klinkern und einem weißen Gitternetz verleihen der Fassade nicht nur Lebendigkeit, sondern auch eine plastische Qualität. Die überraschende Optik wird noch betont durch die leicht verrückten Fenster in den Fassadenöffnungen, zwei über Eck laufende Fensterbänder sowie ein freches Penthouse.

126

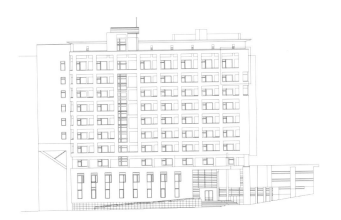

Strict order and severity on Gorky Street, riot and ruckus on the façade along Studyonaya Street. This house has two faces. The plinth is dominated by a prism-shaped loggia that juts out over the street.

Ordnung und Strenge zur Gorki-Straße, Unruhe und Wildwuchs dagegen an der Fassade zur kreuzenden Studjonaja-Straße. Das Haus präsentiert sich mit zwei Gesichtern. Der Sockel wird von einem prismaförmigen Loggia-Anbau beherrscht, der in den Straßenraum ragt.

Residential Building in Perm
Wohngebäude in Perm

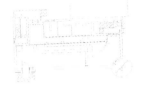

Mendel Futlik
1996

This building, which follows Art Nouveau both in its structure and its decorative use of shapes, is basically a foreign body in this area, one that is forced onto this street corner like a consignment of the wrong material and, not fitting, fails to fill the gap. The result is a gaping hole between this corner building and one of the adjacent tenements. On the other hand, this was evidently the only way of drawing attention to this intersection in an area that is stylistically coherent and therefore monotonous. That is important in a city that owes its existence to metal processing and, since its establishment in 1723 as one huge workers' housing estate, has never become anything more than a city where people earn their bread by the sweat of their brows. Above all, Perm is a city without a centre. Where space is scant, a building like this sets important accents. This four-storey building with its corner shaped by semi-circular balconies, its bands of green and grey tiles, its stucco floral motifs and its wall profiles certainly does that. The anodised aluminium windows and the black marble-clad ground floor also contribute to the building's harmonious look. Everything here is in tune, not least the pleasantly high ceilings and the elegant design of the stairwells. The only thing missing is some finishing touch on the corner tower, which recalls a metal reducer profile. Instead of an artistic, backlit staff of Aesculapius, trailing power cables await a meaningful use for the niche. This may point to the fact that this building, originally designed to house offices or doctors' surgeries, is now an apartment block.

Im Grunde ist der Bau, der sich im Aufbau wie in seiner zierenden Formensprache am Jugendstil orientiert, ein Fremdkörper in dieser Gegend. Denn zwischen diesem Eckhaus und einem der nachfolgenden Stadthäuser klafft eine Lücke. Andererseits ließ sich offenbar nur so in dieser zwar stilistisch stimmigen, aber eben auch einförmigen Gegend Aufmerksamkeit erzielen. Genau das braucht eine Stadt, die ihre Existenz der Metallverarbeitung verdankt und seit 1723 eine Arbeitersiedlung ist, deren Bewohner im Schweiße des Angesichts ihr Brot verdienen. Vor allem aber ist Perm eine Stadt ohne Mitte. Wo der Raum fehlt, setzt ein solches Haus schon bedeutende Akzente, wie im Falle dieses vierstöckigen Gebäudes mit seiner von halbrunden Balkonen geprägten Ecke, den grünen und grauen Kachelbändern, den floralen Stuckmotiven und Wandprofilen. Zur harmonischen Gesichtskosmetik des Hauses tragen darüber hinaus die stilgetreu strukturierten Fenster aus eloxierten Aluminiumprofilen und das mit schwarzem Marmor verkleidete Parterre bei. Alles stimmt hier, nicht zuletzt auch die wohltuend hohen Räume und die feine Gestaltung der Treppenhäuser mit ihren bullaugenförmigen Oberfenstern. Nur der krönende Abschluss am Eckturm, der an ein metallisches Gleitprofil erinnert, ist leer geblieben. Statt eines kunstvollen und hinterleuchteten Äskulapstabes, warten lose hängende Stromanschlusskabel auf eine sinnvolle Bestimmung. Möglicherweise ein Hinweis darauf, dass das Wohnhaus zunächst als Ärztehaus bestimmt war.

Context matters, but this Art Nouveau *building* defies its Stalinist surroundings and sets an important accent. Unfortunately, the staff of Aesculapius originally intended to adorn the corner tower was not realised.

Wie die Straße, so auch die Bebauung. Mitten in dieser stalinistischen Architekturumgebung setzt dieses Jugendstil-Haus provokant seinen eigenen Akzent: leider ohne den ursprünglich geplanten schmückenden Äskulapstab im Eckturm.

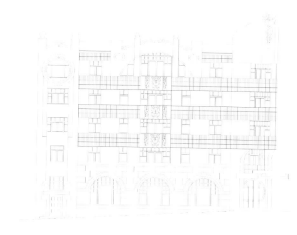

131

Shopping Centre in Perm
Einkaufszentrum in Perm

Viktor Tarasenko
Eugene Kolchanov
2001

The new shopping centre in this industrial city at the southern tip of the Kama Reservoir in the Kamskaya Taiga region in the western foothills of the Urals is razor-sharp. At first sight this steel structure with a glass skin that emanates a bright light at night, turning it into a showcase visible from afar, looks more like a local railway station than a department store. Its other confusing feature is the steel girder construction and the associated urban development functions that the building fulfils. Most shops and offices in this 550-square-metre building are on the ground floor, which is mounted on steel girders slightly above street level, above the entrances to a pedestrian underpass. This provides convenient, weatherproof access to the pedestrian underpass from the shopping centre. From the north, visitor access is via a ramp leading to the first floor of this small mall. From the south, staircases lead from outside to the main shopping centre entrance. Moreover, the southern section of the building is designed to serve simultaneously as a covered waiting area for public transport passengers. At *Arkhitektura 2001* in Moscow, this shopping centre won the prize for Best Architectural Work of the year.

Die Stahlkonstruktion mit der gläsernen Haut, die nachts von innen hell erleuchtet, zum weithin sichtbaren Schaukasten wird, lässt auf den ersten Blick eher auf eine Bahnhofsstation des städtischen Schienenverkehrs schließen als auf ein Kaufhaus. Ebefalls irreführend ist die Stahlträgerkonstruktion und die damit verknüpften städtebaulichen Funktionen. Die meisten Laden- und Büroräume des insgesamt 550 Quadratmeter großen Gebäudes befinden sich im Erdgeschoss, das vom Straßenniveau etwas erhöht auf Stahlträgern über den Zugängen zu einer Fußgängerunterführung steht. Von dem Einkaufszentrum ist der Fußgängertunnel also bequem und direkt zu erreichen. Das Einkaufszentrum selbst hat zwei Zugänge. Von Norden her gelangen Besucher über eine Rampe in die erste Etage der kleinen Mall. Von Süden her führen Treppen von außen zum Haupteingang des Shopping-Centers. Der südliche Teil des Gebäudes ist ferner so konstruiert, dass er gleichzeitig als Haltestellenüberdachung für die auf die Verkehrsmittel wartenden Fahrgäste dient. Auf der *Architectura 2001* in Moskau wurde dieses außergewöhnliche Einkaufszentrum als beste architektonische Arbeit des Jahres ausgezeichnet.

Post-Soviet Modernism

Lokomotiv Stadium in Moscow
Stadion »Lokomotive« in Moskau

MNIIP Mosproyekt-4
2002

The new thirty-thousand seat Lokomotiv Stadium, belonging to the football club of the same name, was built according to the guidelines of the Union of European Football Associations (UEFA) and the International Federation of Football Associations (FIFA) and meets all international standards. It has six levels with three tiers for the stands. The lower tier consists of twenty rows of seats, while the upper tier has seventeen. Between the two tiers is a narrow, glazed restaurant level with sixty private boxes. Radiant heaters mounted on the drop ceiling ensure a temperature of fifteen degrees for the comfort of all the other spectators. Even the pitch is heated and aerated. Financed by the Moscow railways and displaying many similarities with the Amsterdam stadium, it is Russia's most exclusive stadium, where one can find world-class comfort. The conventional tiers are divided into four sectors at the ends and five sectors along the sides of the stadium, each with separate entrances. This ensures an overview of the crowd as well as additional security. A six-metre-wide and three-metre-deep trench, railings and additional security strip encircle the pitch, creating an eight-metre-wide gap between spectators and pitch. The entrances to the stadium are located at each of the arena's four rounded corners which, with their steel and glass roof construction and pitched canopy on the long sides, lend the stadium the appearance of an oyster – particularly when the stadium illumination accentuates the structure's contours at night. The roof construction is supported by steel cables which are connected to an axial strut attached to two L-shaped supports fastened to the exterior. The roof rests on the stadium like a raised cloth, without casting shadows or darkening the interior, since the 230,000-square-metre cloth, reinforced with titanium wire, is almost 90 percent translucent.

Das dem gleichnamigen Klub gehörende neue Stadion »Lokomotive« für 30.000 Zuschauer wurde nach den Richtlinien der Europäischen Fußballunion (UEFA) und des Internationalen Fußballverbandes (FIFA) errichtet. Es hat sechs Etagen mit drei Rängen für die Tribünen. Auf den unteren Rang entfallen 20 Sitzreihen; auf den obersten Rang 17 Sitzreihen. Dazwischen befindet sich eine schmale, verglaste Restauranttribüne mit 60 Firmenlogen. Auf allen anderen Plätzen sorgen an der Zwischendecke montierte Heizstrahler für angenehme 15 Grad. Selbst der Rasen wird beheizt und gelüftet. In Russlands vornehmsten Stadion, das viele Ähnlichkeiten mit der Amsterdamer Arena aufweist und von der Moskauer Eisenbahn finanziert wurde, herrscht Komfort von Weltklasseniveau. Die konventionellen Ränge sind an den Querseiten in vier Sektoren und an den Längsseiten in fünf Sektoren mit jeweils separaten Zugängen aufgeteilt. Das schafft Übersicht in der Masse und zusätzlich Sicherheit. Ein sechs Meter breiter und drei Meter tiefer umlaufender Graben, Geländer und ein ebenfalls umlaufender Sicherheitsstreifen zwischen Tribüne und eigentlichem Spielfeld sorgen für einen acht Meter breiten Abstand. Die Zugänge zum Spielraum befinden sich an den vier abgerundeten Ecken der Fußballarena, die mit ihrer Stahlglas-Dachkonstruktion und dem aufgeschlagenen Vordach an den Längsseiten das Erscheinungsbild einer Auster hat – besonders, wenn das illuminierte Stadion seine Konturen in die Dunkelheit zeichnet. Gehalten wird die Dachkonstruktion von Drahtseilen, die alle mit einer an zwei L-förmigen Trägern an den Außenseiten befestigten Längsverstrebung verknüpft sind. Wie ein angehobenes Tuch präsentiert sich das Stadiondach, das auf 230.000 Quadratmeter aus Titanfäden gestaltet und zu fast 90 Prozent lichtdurchlässig ist.

Russia's first football stadium to meet all international standards may resemble a mollusc, but inside it is warm and dry.
Die erste Fußballarena in Russland von Weltklasseniveau nach Weltklassenorm sieht aus wie ein Weichtier und ist auch im Innern ganz warm.

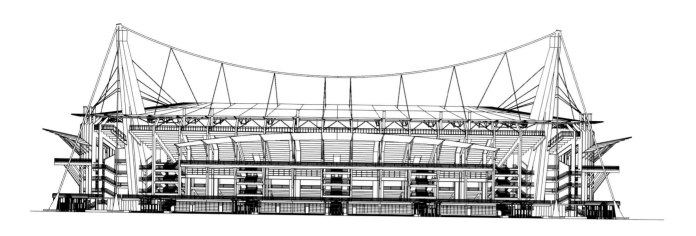

139

Ice stadium in Krylatskoye
Eissport-Stadion in Krylatskoje

MNIIP Mosprojekt-4
2004

For years the Russian ice-skating team trained abroad – in Germany, for example. The new ice stadium has made this athletic jet-set lifestyle superfluous. Although it is located on the edge of the city, the district of Krylatskoye was chosen from among several potential locations. Krylatskoye, with a metro station bearing the same name, is a large residential estate marked by the mass apartment blocks of the 1980s located in the west of Moscow on the edge of the Fili Recreational Park. The area was also a sports venue for the 1980 Summer Olympic Games. Near the meandering Moskva River are the archery arena and the course for the rowing regatta as well as the cycling racetrack and the oyster-shaped cycling arena, the Velotrek. The ice stadium introduces organic architectural forms to the athletic village. Further structures are to follow. As in the football stadium, a hanging construction was chosen for the ice stadium, which lends an appropriately crustacean-like form to this sports venue located near the river. The roof spans the arena, 117 metres wide, and covers a total area of 297,000 square metres. It rests solely on the external walls of the stadium and is supported by steel cables emanating from a steel support, thus forming a cut cylinder. Seen from a distance the structure resembles a suspension bridge. Under the immense roof is a 12,000 square metre ice surface designed for ice hockey and speedskating with a 400 metre and 250 metre ice rink, in addition to the stands and the service area. The functional arrangement of the ice surface allows for up to 300 athletes to train in their disciplines side by side.

Lange Zeit hat die russische Eislaufauswahl im Ausland trainiert, beispielsweise in Deutschland. Das neue Eissportstadion macht dieses sportive Jetset-Leben überflüssig. Unter den zahlreichen möglichen Plätzen wurde trotz seiner Randlage der Stadtteil Krylatskoje als Standort ausgewählt. Krylatskoje mit gleichnamigem Metroanschluss liegt im Westen Moskaus am Rande des Erholungsparks Fili und ist eine vom Massenwohnungsbau der Achtzigerjahre geprägte Großsiedlung. Aber die Gegend war eben auch schon ein Standort für die Olympischen Sommerspiele von 1980. Unweit der mäandernden Moskwa befinden sich die Sporthalle für die Bogenschützen und die Rennstrecke für die Ruderregatta sowie die Radrennstrecke und die austernförmige Radsporthalle, das Velotrek. Wie beim Lokomotive-Fußballstadion wurde auch beim Eisstadion eine hängende Konstruktion gewählt, die dieser Sportstätte, entsprechend zur Flussnähe, die einem Schalentier ähnliche Bauform verleiht. Das Hallendach überspannt die Arena mit den Tribünen in einer Breite von 117 Metern und bedeckt damit eine Fläche von insgesamt 297.000 Quadratmetern. Es liegt nur auf den Außenwänden des Stadions auf und wird zusätzlich von Stahlseilen gehalten, die von einem Stahlträger aus einen geschnittenen Zylinder beschreiben. Von weitem wirkt die Konstruktion wie eine Hängebrücke. Unter diesem riesigen Dach befinden sich neben Tribünen und Logistik eine Eisfläche von 12.000 Quadratmetern mit einer 400 Meter und 250 Meter langen Eislaufbahn. Bis zu 300 Sportler können hier ungestört nebeneinander trainieren.

Auch technisch ist das Stadion eine ebenso gewagte wie ausgereifte Konstruktion. Von der Ruderregattastrecke im Vordergrund aus gesehen gewinnt der Betrachter den Eindruck, die Abspannseile einer Hängebrücke der nahe gelegenen Moskwa zu sehen.

Technically, too, the stadium is a bold and well-engineered construction. Looking across from the course for the rowing regatta, one might think one is looking at the cables of a suspension bridge across the nearby Moskva River.

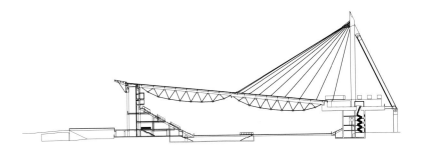

Organic shapes charac-
terise Russia's new sport-
ing venues. No matter
what the season is, the
Ice Stadium fits perfectly
into the landscape, as if it
had always been here.
*Biomorphe Formen zeich-
nen die neue Sportarchi-
tektur Russlands aus.
Das Eisstadion fügt sich in
die üppige Landschaft zu
jeder Jahreszeit ein, so als
sei es schon immer ein
Teil von ihr.*

Sports and Amusement Complex in Yasenyevo
Sportanlage mit Aqua-Park in Jasenewo

Sergey Kiselyov
2002
(destroyed in 2004)

Visitors had to drive quite far to reach the new amusement arena in the district of Yasenyevo in the outer south-west of the capital. Yasenyevo is a satellite city characterized by nine- to twenty-three-storey prefabricated high-rises and forests on the motorway ring in the Moscow municipal area. It can also be reached by metro. The amusement arena is located on the border between high-rise buildings and forest and includes an athletic swimming pool, a South-Pacific style recreational pool, saunas, a bowling alley, a gym, a roller-skating rink and a number of chain restaurants. The aqua-park's glass shell rises above foundations clad in natural stone. The hall with the ribbed glass front and curved roof is wedged between the two- to three-storey buildings which contain the sport and restaurant areas. A barrel-shaped tower set before the backdrop of high-rise buildings shows the way to the sport and recreation mall from afar. At night the illuminated inner life of the shell draws attention to the complex. Sergey Kiselyov reacted to the location on the threshold between city and countryside with brick exteriors and a light, transparent shell, leaving it unclear whether the building is still part of the city or already part of nature. However, the discussion has become pointless after the shell collapsed in the spring of 2004 for reasons as yet unknown, burying several visitors beneath it.

Besucher mussten sehr weit fahren, um zum neuen Entertainment-Park im äußeren Südwesten Moskaus zu gelangen. Der Stadtteil Jasenewo ist eine am Autobahnring gelegene Trabantenstadt. An dieser Schwelle zwischen Hochhäusern und Wald entstand 2002 eine Vergnügungsarena mit Schwimmhalle, Südsee-Spaßbad, Saunen, Bowlingbahn, Fitnessstudio, Rollschuhbahn und einer Anzahl von Gastronomieketten. Auf einem mit Naturstein verkleideten Unterbau erhob sich die gläserne Muschel des Aquaparks. Die Halle mit der gerippten Glasfront und dem geschwungenen Dach fügte sich keilartig zwischen die im rechten Winkel stehenden ein- bis dreistöckigen gruppierten Bauten, in denen der Sport- und Gastronomiebereich untergebracht war. Ein Turm in Form eines Fasses wies vor der Kulisse des Hochhausgebirges auch von weitem sichtbar auf die sportive Vergnügungs-Mall. Bei Dunkelheit machte die Muschel mit ihrem illuminierten Innenleben auf sich aufmerksam. Mit einer Konstruktion aus backsteinernen Umbauten und der leichten und transparenten Muschel reagierte Sergei Kiselew auf die Lage an der Schwelle zwischen Stadt und Landschaft. Es war unklar, ob das Gebäude noch Teil der Stadt oder ein schon Teil der Natur war. Im Frühjahr 2004 stürzte die Konstruktion aus bislang ungeklärter Ursache ein und begrub zahlreiche Besucher unter sich.

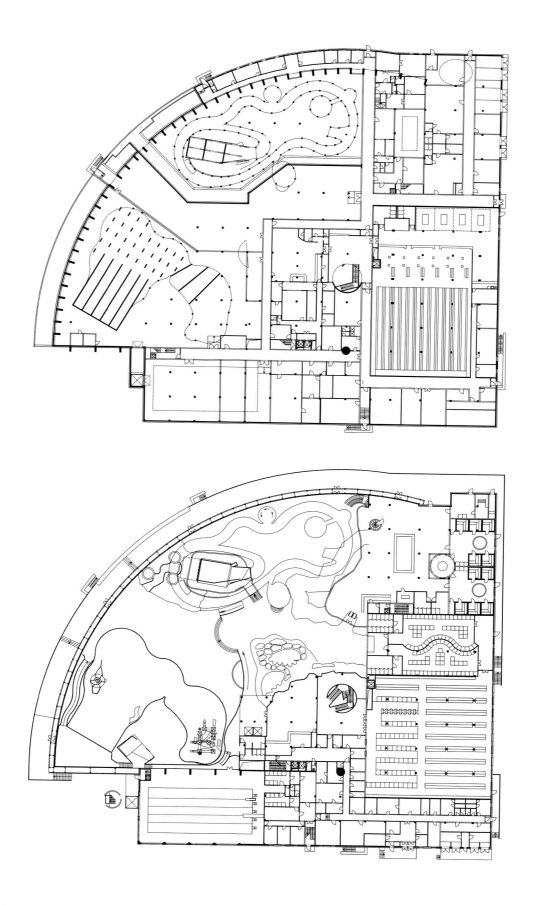

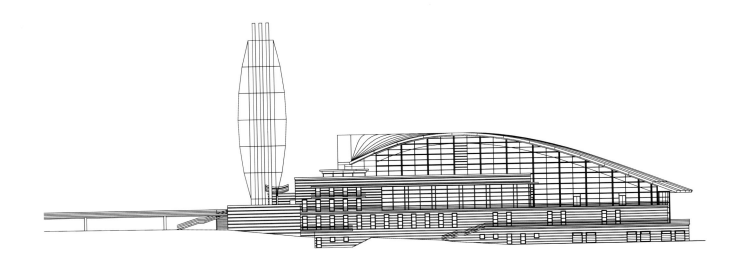

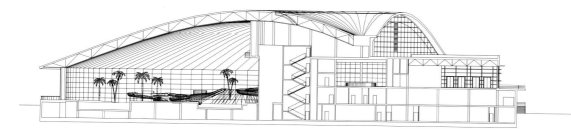

*Form follows function or
form follows fiasco?
The shell collapsed in the
spring of 2004. When will
life return to it?*
Form follows function
oder follows disaster?
Im Frühjahr 2004 stürzte
die Muschel ein. Seitdem
ist sie unbelebt.

Sport and Tennis Centre in Kuntsevo
Sport- und Tenniszentrum in Kunzewo

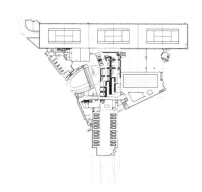

Alexander Asadov
2002

Kuntsevo lies in Moscow's west on Rublyev Avenue on the border between city and countryside, a bit further out from the city than the Olympic sports venues, the new ice stadium and Russia's showpiece Lokomotiv Football Stadium. The tennis centre is also a prime example of the organic building methods, or green architecture, which are favoured in this area. The greater part of the usable area of just under 13,000 square metres is located at the bottom of a gentle slope beyond the fields and the belt of deciduous forest which marks the transition from metropolis to open countryside. The transverse wing with the tennis courts on the roof plays the most important role in setting the supple forms of the surroundings found in the gently rising and open asymmetrical floor plan against the sharp edge of artificiality. The building, with planted roof, turquoise-coloured metal siding and brick masonry, follows the entrance road in a concave sweep, only to return to its natural surroundings. The facilities – a swimming pool, squash courts, a room for aerobics, choreography and bodybuilding, a gym and beauty salon – are largely located inside the hill, as it were, and are accessed through an oval entranceway. From here the visitors can also reach the tennis courts. Only three glass skylights on the planted roof allow daylight into the building. There is parking for approximately one hundred vehicles in the underground car park and partly on the ground level. There are also bowling alleys, a billiard hall with its own bar and a café. In addition to a further parking area, the cashiers, the restaurant, the VIP areas and the squash courts are all arranged on the ground floor. The entrance hall, the fitness relaxation room and the entrance to the VIP tennis courts on the roof are located on the first floor.

Kunzewo liegt im Westen Moskaus an der Rubljow-Chaussee, an der Nahtstelle zwischen Stadt und Landschaft und noch etwas weiter von der Stadt entfernt als die olympischen Sportstätten, die neue Eissporthalle und Russlands Vorzeige-Fußballstadion »Lokomotive«. Aber auch diese Tennisanlage ist ein Musterbeispiel für die in diesem Bereich bevorzugte organische Bauweise oder »grüne« Architektur. Der größte Teil der Nutzfläche von knapp 13.000 Quadratmetern befindet sich unter einem sanften Hügel jenseits von Wiesen und eines Laubwaldgürtels, der den Übergang von der Millionenstadt in die offene Landschaft markiert. Es ist vor allem der Querflügel mit den Tennisplätzen auf dem Dach, der mit dem sanft ansteigenden und begehbaren asymmetrischen Grundriss den geschmeidigen Formen der Umgebung die scharfe Kante des Artifiziellen entgegensetzt, um sich mit begrüntem Dach, türkisfarbenen Metallverkleidungen und Backsteinmauerwerk in einem konkaven Schwung entlang der Zufahrtsstraße dann doch wieder seiner Umgebung zuzuordnen. Das Gros der Einrichtungen – wie Schwimmbad, Squashplätze, eine Halle für Aerobic, Choreographie und Bodybuilding, Fitnessclub und Schönheitssalon – befindet sich gleichsam im Berg, erreichbar durch den ovalen Eingang. Von hier aus gelangen Besucher auch zu den Tennisplätzen. Lediglich drei Glashauben auf dem Rasendach lassen Tageslicht in das Gebäude. Im Tiefgeschoss und im Erdgeschoss befinden sich rund 100 Parkplätze. Dort befinden sich auch Bowlingbahnen, ein Billardraum mit eigener Bar sowie ein Café. Im Erdgeschoss sind neben einer Parkzone die Kassen, das Restaurant, die VIP-Bereiche sowie die Squashplätze angeordnet. Darüber liegen Eingangshalle, Fitnessruheraum und der Zugang zum VIP-Tennisplatz auf dem Dach.

150

Penguin Office Building in Moscow
Bürogebäude »Pinguin« in Moskau

Ostozhenka
2004

This office building occupies a corner lot in the middle of a busy inner-city district of Moscow which, with its extremely dense development on a grid of streets, belongs to the most decidedly urban districts of the Russian capital. Here, between Byelorussian Station and the intersection of Tverskaya and Yamskaya Street, the buildings are taller and the streets narrower. But skyscrapers are not only sprouting up on the main street; the side streets with their humble old buildings are increasingly being drawn into the plans of the real-estate developers. This process of internal urbanisation comes in two forms: either the individual parcels are filled with largely neutral buildings with maximum profitability in mind, or builder and architect develop a formally independent and individual building which not only offers exclusive office space, but also serves as a landmark in the cityscape. The high-rise office building at No. 1 Brestskaya Street is a successful example of the latter. The first task was to create an effective balance to the soaring solitary high-rise buildings within the urban texture of a neighbourhood interspersed with new buildings. The simple form of the building slightly resembles the silhouette of a penguin – hence the name. Actually, the convex glass façade is the minimalist analogy of a Baroque commode. The building's softly rounded flank protrudes into the street and, using only aesthetic means, creates an individual urban posture with high recognition value. Its modern urban vibrancy is achieved by the strictly geometrical perforated façade and cool, smooth materials.

Das Bürogebäude befindet sich mitten in einem geschäftigen Moskauer Innenstadtviertel, das mit einer extrem verdichteten Bebauung in einem schachbrettartigen Straßenraster zu den urbanen Quartieren der russischen Hauptstadt zählen darf. Hier, zwischen dem Weißrussischen Bahnhof und Metrostation Majakowskaja sind die Häuser höher und die Straßen enger. Doch nicht nur in den Hauptstraßen wachsen neue Wolkenkratzer in die Höhe. Zusehends werden auch die Nebenstraßen mit ihrem bescheidenen Altbaubestand in die Pläne der Immobilienentwickler einbezogen. Der Prozess einer inneren Urbanisierung kennt zwei Ausprägungen: Entweder werden die einzelnen Parzellen mit Blick auf maximale Wirtschaftlichkeit einfach mit weitgehend neutraler Bebauung gefüllt, oder Bauherr und Architekten entwickeln ein formal individuelles Gebäude, das nicht nur exklusive Büros bietet, sondern im städtischen Raum als Landmarke funktioniert. Hier galt es zunächst, in der von zahlreichen Neubauten durchsetzten Nachbarschaft einen wirkungsvollen Ausgleich zu den emporschießenden Hochhaussolitären innerhalb der städtischen Textur zu schaffen. Die einfache Form des Gebäudes erinnert zunächst an die Silhouette eines Pinguins – daher leitet sich der Name ab. Doch recht besehen handelt es sich bei der konvexen Glasfassade eher um die minimalistische Entsprechung einer barocken Kommode. Sie ragt mit ihrer sanft gerundeten Flanke in den Straßenraum und schafft allein mit ästhetischen Mitteln eine individuelle städtebauliche Situation mit hohem Wiedererkennungswert.

In the second row behind Tverskaya Street the Penguin shows its dignified and handsome front. If its form and materials focus the surrounding heterogeneity, who will cavil at this office building's slightly exceeding the scale set by its urban context?

In der zweiten Reihe der Twerskaja-Straße präsentiert sich der Pinguin in vornehmer und ästhetischer Weise. Seine Form und seine Materialität geben der heterogenen Nachbarschaft eine neue Ordnung. Da mag es nicht schmerzen, dass das Bürogebäude den Maßstab der Umgebung etwas übersteigt.

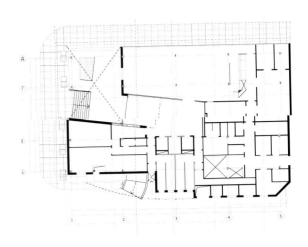

Catamaran Residential Complex in Moscow
Wohnhaus »Katamaran« in Moskau

TPO Reserv
2000

This property is located approximately 250 metres south of Mozhaysky Avenue in a suburb bounded by Zagorsky Drive, Veresayev Street and the deeply incised Setun River. The northern and eastern part of the area is dominated by a cluster of twelve- to fifteen-storey apartment buildings. The suburb is structured around the environmentally protected riverside. The residential complex consists of two parallel units situated opposite one another and connected by four suspended walkways which contain the stairwells in their centres. The rooms on the ground floor of the west wing are occupied by leisure and recreation facilities. The building attempts to scale down the immense vertical dimensions of its surroundings by using its own horizontal ingredient and following the law of functional modernity which transfers ornamental details to the structural cubature. This means that one of the wings has six floors, whereas the opposing wing has four or five storeys, depending on the position on the slope. The surfaces of both buildings are divided into four blocks by the narrow protruding balconies and loggias. Apart from the unanticipated windows, this housing complex is reminiscent of the 1970s. The building seems too cool – it has all the charm of an arrogant office building. Contrary to the original plans, windows with traverse frames were installed in the loggias. This robs the building of much of its original aesthetic statement, a spatial organisational element in the long façade. As a result, the building seems dull, and it can only hope that the passage of time will lend it the same morbid romantic charm it has already bestowed upon the surrounding prefabricated high-rises.

Das Grundstück befindet sich etwa 250 Meter südlich der Moschaiki-Chaussee in einem Viertel, das von der Sagorski-Straße, der Weresaew-Straße und der Schlucht des Setuni-Flusses begrenzt wird. Den nördlichen und östlichen Teil dieses Areals dominiert ein zwölf- bis fünfzehngeschossiger Massenwohnungsbau. Das Quartier gruppiert sich um die naturgeschützte Schlucht. Der Wohnkomplex besteht aus zwei parallelen, einander gegenüber liegenden Gebäudekörpern, die durch vier Bügelbauten miteinander verknüpft sind, in deren Mitte sich jeweils die Treppenhäuser befinden. Die Räume im Erdgeschoss des westlichen Flügels werden für Freizeit- und Erholungseinrichtungen genutzt. Der Bau versucht in sich die unmaßstäbliche Vertikale seiner Umgebung in der Horizontalen überschaubar zu machen und – dem Gesetz der funktionalen Moderne folgend – setzt das Ornament in der baulichen Kubatur um. Das heißt, dass ein Gebäuderiegel einmal sechsgeschossig ist, während der gegenüber liegende Baukörper je nach Standort an der Hanglage vier- und fünf Etagen hat. In der Fläche sind beide Riegel durch vier Vorbauten geordnet, die bänderartigen Loggien und Balkone. Abgesehen von den einsprossigen Fenstern erinnert die Wohnanlage an die Siebzigerjahre. Sie wirkt unterkühlt, entfaltet den Charme eines schnöden Bürobaus. Entgegen den ursprünglichen Plänen wurden in die Loggien Fenster eingebaut und der Rahmen durchgezogen. Das nimmt diesen Baukörpern das ästhetische Moment als räumlich gliederndes Element in der langen Fassade. Das Haus darf auf das Altern hoffen, das auch den Plattenbauten ringsum den Charme einer morbiden Romantik verliehen hat.

158

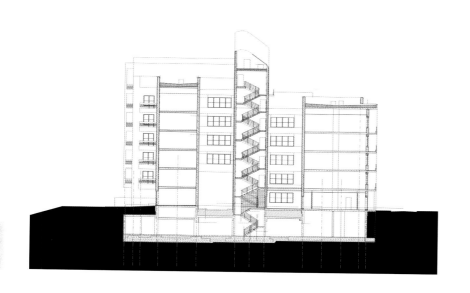

The architects of this residential building tipped over the vertical lines that dominate the surroundings and introduced a strong horizontal element. The distinctive loggias running along the façades of the neighbouring highrises were taken up in the new building to establish a link to the architectural context.

Mit diesem Wohnhaus haben die Architekten die Vertikale der Umgebung in die Horizontale befördert. Die Loggienbänder als stilprägende Elemente der Hochhäuser sind der optische Bezugspunkt des Neubaus zu seinem architektonischen Umfeld.

Tatarovskaya Poyma Residential Complex in Moscow
Wohnsiedlung »Tatarowskaja Pojma« in Moskau

TPO Rezerv
2003

This 25.5-hectare area, a part of the Moskvoretsky Nature Park in west Moscow, is situated between the Olympic rowing canal and the golf club. The environs are characterised by the delightful countryside in the catchment basin of the Moskva River, by sports venues and the backdrop formed by the district of Krylatskoye with its huge residential buildings. The Soviets planned to develop half of the scant thirty-hectare area and set aside the other half as a park. Today, developers have created a garden city with conspicuously many stylistic and formal references to the 1920s. The social centre of the project is a semicircular public square at the end of a main street lined with blocks of houses. There are a total of twelve four-storey multiple dwellings with commercial units, nineteen separate cottages, a sports and medical facility as well as shops and public buildings. Additional earthen mounds and a canal lend this area its own unique character. The references to early modernism include the letter-shaped arrangements of the blocks, which form greened courtyards open to the street and thus blur the traditional urban division between social and private space, between interior and exterior. Detailed architectural references are evident in the form of the white façades with horizontal, encompassing bands of windows on the front side and in the overall coherent composition of the estate. Nothing is superfluous or overstated; the composition is reduced to a pleasant, comfortable minimum. In this manner even the pergolas, which connect the houses on the main square with one another while closing off the semicircle to the street, support the notion of community space in the estate.

Das 25,5 Hektar große, zum Naturpark Moskworetski gehörige Areal im Moskauer Westen befindet sich zwischen dem olympischen Ruderkanal und dem Golfklub. Die Umgebung wird von einer reizvollen Landschaft im Einzugsgebiet der Moskwa, von Sportstätten und der Kulisse des von Massenwohnbauten dominierten Stadtteils Krylatskoje bestimmt. Bereits zu Sowjetzeiten gab es einen Bebauungsplan, der vorsah, das knapp 30 Hektar große Gelände in eine Bauzone und eine Parkzone zu unterteilen. Verwirklicht wurde nun eine Gartenstadt mit auffällig vielen Stil- und Gestaltungszitaten der Zwanzigerjahre, deren gesellschaftlicher Mittelpunkt ein halbkreisfömiger Ortsplatz am Ende einer von Häuserblöcken gesäumten Hauptstraße ist. Insgesamt umfasst es zwölf viergeschossige Mehrfamilienhäuser mit Gewerbeeinheiten, 19 separate Cottages, ein Sport- und Ärztehaus sowie Geschäfte und öffentliche Bauten. Zusätzliche Erdaufschüttungen und ein Kanal geben dieser neuen Gartenstadt einen ganz eigenen Charakter. Anleihen an die Frühmoderne sind beispielsweise die im Grundriss buchstabenförmig angelegten Blöcke, die zur Straße hin offene, begrünte Innenhöfe bilden und damit die für die traditionelle Stadt klare Trennung zwischen gesellschaftlichem und privatem Raum verwischen. Im Architekturdetail sind es die weißen Fassaden und deren Gestaltung mit horizontalen Fensterbändern, umlaufenden Fensterbändern an den Stirnseiten und die insgesamt klare Komposition der Siedlung. Nichts ist überflüssig, nichts erscheint zu viel und wird so auf ein wohltuend Angenehmes reduziert – selbst die Pergolen, die die Häuser am Ortsplatz miteinander verbinden.

161

Everyone knows Berlin's "Weisse Siedlung". Now Moscow has one too. Seventy years after its predecessor was built in Berlin, this new garden city features all the time-honoured stylistic elements of the avantgarde.

Eine »Weiße Siedlung«, diesmal nicht in Berlin sondern in Moskau. Siebzig Jahre nach dem Bau des Berliner Vorbildes entstand diese Vorstadtsiedlung mit den bewährten Stilzitaten der Avantgarde.

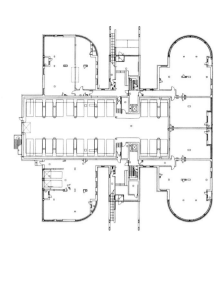

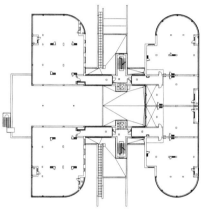

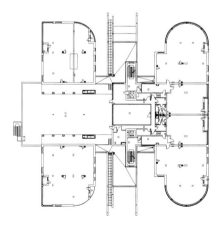

Multi-storey dwellings, small front gardens, a clear orientation towards the street and a centre of its own – almost a small town in itself.

Mehrstöckige Häuser, kleine Vorgärten, aber eine klare Lage zur Straße und eine eigene Ortsmitte als Bezugsgröße – fast eine Kleinstadt für sich.

Central Railway Station in Samara
Hauptbahnhof in Samara

Yury V. Khramov
2002

When confronted with the tall tower with its reflecting, brightly illuminated façade, trapezoidal extensions, soaring lift tower and tube-shaped concourse the traveller is more likely to believe he has arrived at a futuristic space station rather than a train station. Maybe he should check to see if his feet are still planted firmly on the ground and gravity still exerts its pull. No, the traveller is in the Here and Now. This project realised in 2002 is not only a new train station but also a redevelopment of the central Komsomolsky Square within an urban-planning context. The station is striking in its functional construction. A tube-like steel and glass construction optimally channels passengers to the six platforms. Arriving passengers have separate entrances from departing passengers or passengers on interregional transit trains. Its area of 47,800 square metres makes the Samara station one of the largest new stations in Europe, and its organisation was completely overhauled to integrate aspects of airport management systems for regulating passenger flow. In the context of urban planning, the station is a multifunctional venue, whose planners were thinking far into the future. In addition to a hotel with offices and conference rooms, the station is a centre of business and mobility serving as a business port with direct railway access. It could not be more efficient. As an urban location, the station includes a cultural facility, shops, cafés and restaurants.

Der hohe Turm mit der spiegelnden und hell erleuchteten Fassade, den trapezförmigen Anbauten, dem schornsteinähnlichen Aufzugsturm, mit der röhrenförmigen Bahnsteighalle: Bei alledem glaubt der Reisende nicht, in einem Bahnhof, sondern in einer futuristischen Weltraumstation angekommen zu sein. Dann doch noch einmal vorsichtshalber prüfen, ob die Füße die Erde berühren und auch drumherum die Erdanziehungskraft die Materie nicht verlassen hat. Nein, der Besucher befindet sich im Hier und Jetzt. Mit dem neuen Bahnhof wurde nicht nur einen Bahnstation gebaut, sondern 2002 gleich der Komsomolski-Platz inmitten der Stadt städtebaulich neu geordnet. Verblüffend ist der Bahnhof in seiner funktionalen Konstruktion. Eine röhrenartige Stahl-Glas-Konstruktion lenkt die Fahrgäste zu den sechs Bahnsteigen und zwar gezielt nach den Bewegungsflüssen: nach ankommenden und abreisenden Fahrgästen. Mit 47.800 Quadratmetern einer der größten Bahnhofsneubauten Europas, wurde in Samara auch die Organisation neu gedacht und in Teilen das Leitsystem eines Flughafens übernommen. Städtebaulich ist der Bahnhof eine multifunktionale Adresse – und auch in dieser Hinsicht weit über das Hier und Heute geplant, wenn er gleichzeitig neben Hotel mit Büros und Konferenzräumen, ein Standort für das Geschäftsleben, aber auch für dessen Mobilität ist und in diesem Sinne auch als *Business Port* mit Gleisanschluss fungiert. Ökonomischer geht es nicht.

167

It's a nuclear power station, it's a space station, no, it's a train station! Futuristic aesthetics may be a question of taste, but everyone welcomes functionality.

Ein Bahnhof wie ein Atommeiler, wie eine Raumstation, wie ein... An der futuristischen Ästhetik scheiden sich die Geister. Nicht aber an der Funktionalität.

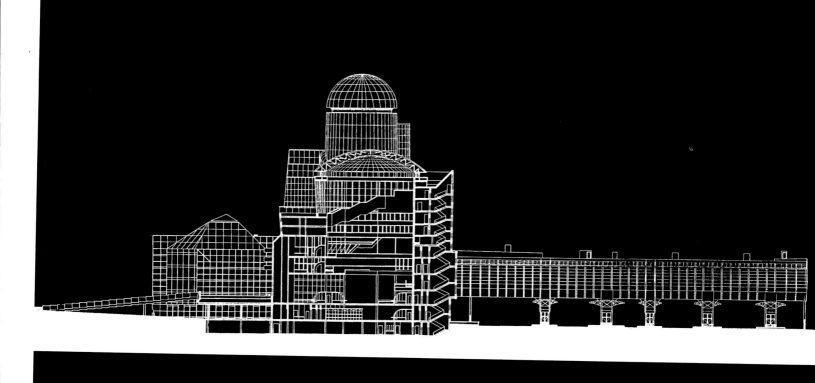

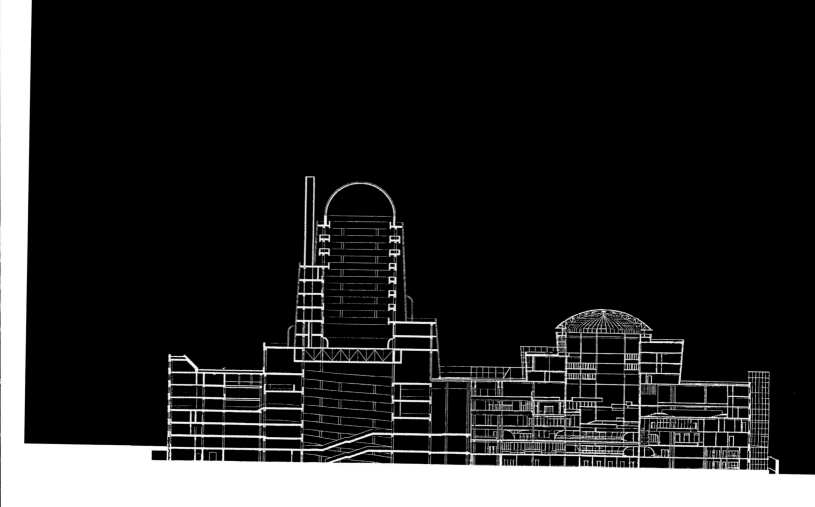

National Centre for Contemporary Arts in Moscow
Nationales Zentrum für zeitgenössische Kunst in Moskau

Mikhail Khasanov
2004

For the National Centre for Contemporary Arts (NCCA) in Moscow, a former workshop for theatre and stage sets located in the middle of the city was converted into a modern museum complete with exhibition spaces, research spaces and offices for curators and museum staff. An open exhibition hall was to be installed on the second floor of the old factory building. The biggest challenge for the structural engineers and architects was to construct this without supporting structures. The removal of all existing columns jeopardised the plan of suspending a conference hall as a room within a room. The solution was an external support structure. A metal frame was fixed to the façade. It has a static as well as an aesthetic function and lends the old brick wall a modern feel without fundamentally changing it. This brings out the contrast between old and new, but also the continuity and classicism of old industrial architecture. There is no trace here of purely decorative ornament or disguised functionality. The design of this building heralds the advent of a new era. The supporting structures as well as the metal banisters and steps remain bound to the classical canon of factory aesthetics, but the bold red of the wall and the plinth speaks of a post-industrial function. The light, floating impression is created by the filigree mountings connected by delicate struts on the slightly curved roof, which glides with a gentle sweep over the stone weight of the old factory walls.

Für das National Centre for Contemporary Art (NCCA) in Moskau wurde eine ehemalige Fabrikationsstätte für Theater- und Bühnenbedarf mitten in der Stadt zu einem modernen Museumskomplex mit Ausstellungsräumen, Bereichen für Forschungszwecke sowie Büros für Museumsangehörige und Kuratoren umgebaut. Die große Herausforderung für Statiker und Planer bestand darin, im zweiten Geschoss des alten Fabrikgebäudes eine weitläufige Ausstellungshalle zu platzieren, die ohne tragende Strukturen auskommt. Deshalb wurden sämtliche vorhandenen Säulen entfernt. Allerdings erwies sich nun der vorgesehene Konferenzsaal als Problem, der als Raum im Raum aufgehängt werden sollte. Es fehlte an einer statischen Grundlage. Die Lösung lag in einer externen Stützkonstruktion. An der Fassade wurde ein Metallrahmen arretiert, der sowohl statische als auch ästhetische Funktion hat: Er verleiht dem alten Ziegelgemäuer einen modernen Charakter, ohne es grundsätzlich zu verändern. Rein dekorativen Zierrat sucht man hier ebenso vergeblich wie verkleidete Funktionalität. Zwar bleiben die statischen Konstruktionen ebenso wie Treppengeländer und Stufen aus Metall der klassischen Fabrikästhetik verhaftet, doch spätestens die Wand- und Sockelflächen in kräftigem Rot künden von einer post-industriellen Nutzung. Die Leichtigkeit ist den filigranen Details zu verdanken. Sensibel nehmen sie den alten Fabrikmauern ihre steinerne Schwere.

New and Old formulate a clear relation in this converted building. Its structure rests on supports that now characterise the façade and the exterior as a whole. Located near the zoo and hidden away among urban greenery, the art centre is not all that easy to find.

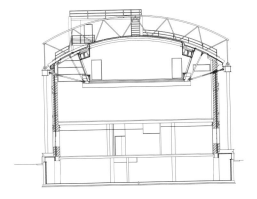

Klar ablesbar ist bei diesem Umbau das Verhältnis zwischen Alt und Neu. Die Konstruktion des Umbaus lastet auf den Stützen, die nun die Fassade und das gesamte Äußere prägen. In unmittelbarer Nachbarschaft zum Zoo ist das Kunstzentrum – versteckt zwischen Stadtgrün – nur schwer zu finden.

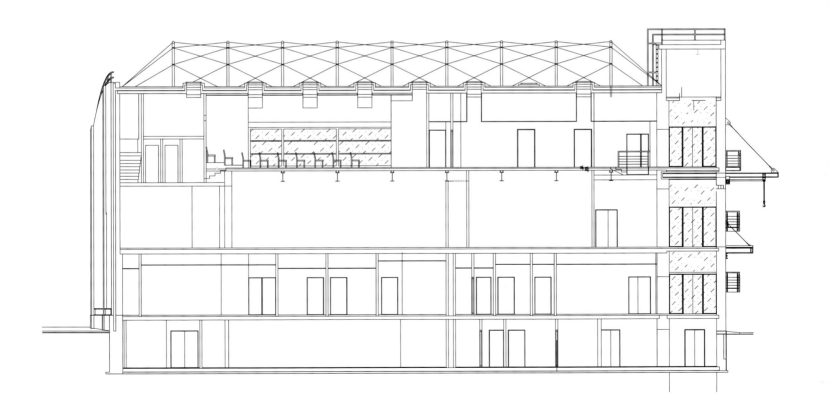

Panorama Residential Building in Moscow
Wohngebäude »Panorama« in Moskau

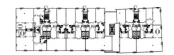

Ostozhenka
2003

This colossal residential complex was built on a former industrial site in the centre of Moscow. Its crystalline corpus reaches up over the roofs of its polymorphous urban surroundings. The outstretched, glistening façade reflects the light like the smooth surface of a lake and brings the whole area alive with light. Without a doubt, a residential building of this type has never been seen before in Moscow. The projecting glass façade, comprised of a number of variously-sized glass panels, rises above a massive two-storey plinth. The precision working of the glass and the kaleidoscope of effects, which result from various views into, from and through the building as well as the reflections, convey an impression of lightness and transparency. The façade's irregular grid provides no indication of the internal structure of the building; only the even, narrow vertical bands mark the course of the individual floors. To prevent the massive body of the building from seeming like a monolithic mass, a deep incision divides the façade in two. This created two structural elements: a small, simple rectangular solid and a larger trapezoidal cube. The individual, largely open-plan floors within the building contain modern apartments which are largely free of supporting structures and can therefore be furnished according to the occupants' individual desires.

Der mächtige Wohnkomplex entstand auf einem ehemaligen Industrieareal mitten in Moskau. Er wächst als kristalliner Korpus über die Dächer seiner vielgestaltigen städtischen Umgebung. Seine weit aufgespannte, gleißende Fassade reflektiert das Licht wie die ruhige Oberfläche eines stehenden Gewässers und lässt das ganze Viertel glitzern. Keine Frage, ein Wohnhaus dieser Art ist in Moskau ein Novum. Über einem zweigeschossigen, massiven Sockel erhebt sich die auskragende, gläserne Fassadenfront, die aus einer Vielzahl von unterschiedlich großen Glaspaneelen zusammengesetzt wurde. Der Eindruck von Leichtigkeit und Transparenz verdankt sich vor allem der exakten Verarbeitung des Glases und den vielfältigen Sichtbeziehungen, die sich durch Ein-, Aus- und Durchblicke sowie Spiegelungen ergeben. Das unregelmäßige Fassadenraster gibt keinen Hinweis auf die interne Struktur des Hauses. Lediglich die gleichmäßigen schmalen Vertikalbänder markieren den Verlauf der einzelnen Geschosse. Um das mächtige Volumen nicht wie eine monolithische Masse wirken zu lassen, wurde die Fassade mit einem tiefen Einschnitt zweigeteilt. So entstanden zwei Baukörper: ein kleiner, einfacher Quader und ein großer, trapezoider Kubus. Im Inneren des Gebäudes wurden weitgehend offene Grundrisse wie beim Bürobau möglich.

Bathed in the rays of a winter sun low on the horizon, the glass building resembles a blue crystal, but the glare of summer turns it into a fiery rock. The new building sets an important accent in the quarter's panorama and offers an attractive view of the church situated to its south.

In der tiefen Wintersonne wirkt der Glasbau wie ein blauer Kristall. Im gleißenden Licht des Sommers entpuppt er sich als feuriger Stein. Die neue Architektur setzt durchaus einen neuen Akzent im Panorama der Nachbarschaft. Auch der Ausblick hat seine Reize: wenn der Blick Richtung Kirche im Süden gerichtet ist.

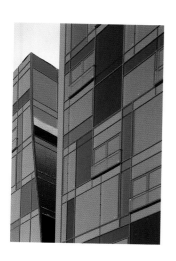

Ladozhsky Railway Station in St Peterburg
Ladoschski-Bahnhof in Sankt Petersburg

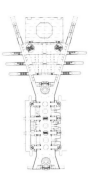

Studio 44
2003

With its steel cross-ribbed arches, the station is reminiscent of the great epoch of railway stations, when stone-hewn neo-Romanesque and neo-Gothic cathedrals of mobility attested to the unshakable faith in the technological power of the steam age. This faith may have long since faded, but the builders of the Ladozhsky Railway Station have made a grand gesture to the spirit of the era, which manifests itself in two distinct ways. Ladozhsky Station is really very big; and it is a result of the ever-present freedom to borrow from the catalogue of period styles. The steel crossbeams have a purely aesthetic function and belong to the postmodern repertoire, which the architects have exploited to the fullest. Looking upon the station, project manager Nikita Yaveyn speaks of Roman baths. The architects oriented their design on Ivan Fomin's (unrealised) entry to the 1912 competition for the Nikolaevsky Railway Station. Though the Studio 44 architects borrowed from his three-part spatial composition flanked by two round towers, they replaced the plan's "red Doric" classical details with industrial aesthetics. Nonetheless, the passageways, for example the escalator shafts, are as imposing as Piranesi's. With its multilevel construction, unique expressiveness and role as junction on the Moscow-Helsinki line, the station refers back to itself and its Russian surroundings regardless of the demands of functionality. In design terms it is thus somewhat disconnected from the course of time.

Der Bahnhof erinnert mit seinen Kreuzrippegewölben ähnelnden Stahlverstrebungen an die große Epoche der Bahnhöfe, als in Stein gehauene neoromanische oder neo-gotische Kathedralen der Mobilität Zeugnis von einem unerschütterlichen Glauben an die Macht der Technik des Dampfmaschinenzeitalters ablegten. Dieser Glaube hat sich längst relativiert, dennoch üben sich die Erbauer des Ladoschski-Bahnhofes in eben jener erhabenen Gestik. Zu erklären ist dies mit zweierlei: Zum einen ist der neue Bahnhof wirklich groß. Zum anderen liegt es aber auch an der allgegenwärtigen Freiheit, sich im Katalog der Epochenstile zu bedienen. Denn die stählernen Verstrebungen erfüllen eben nur jene ästhetische Funktion und gehören zum postmodernen Repertoire, das die Architekten hier ausschöpfen. Der Projektleiter Nikita Jawejn spricht beim Blick auf den Bahnhof von römischen Thermen. Denn orientiert haben sich die Architekten am 1912 durchgeführten, aber nie verwirklichten Wettbewerb für den Nikolaewski-Bahnhof von Iwan Fomin. Von ihm entlehnte das *Studio 44* die aus drei Teilen bestehende Komposition des Raums, der von zwei runden Türmen flankiert wird. Das Gebäude mit seinem mehrstufigen Aufbau, seiner ihm eigenen Ausdruckskraft und Rolle als Schnittstelle auf der Bahnlinie Moskau-Helsinki ist trotz seiner Bedeutung über alle Funktionalität hinweg doch wieder auf sich und sein russisches Umfeld bezogen.

181

Industrial architecture
from the nineteenth
century and round towers
in a postmodern style –
this is how the architects
realised a design ninety
years after it won a com-
petition in 1912.

Industriearchitektur des
19. Jahrhunderts und
Rundtürme in post-
moderner Manier. In
dieser Ästhetik haben die
Architekten einem 1912
prämierten Wettbewerb
neunzig Jahre später
ins Dasein verholfen.

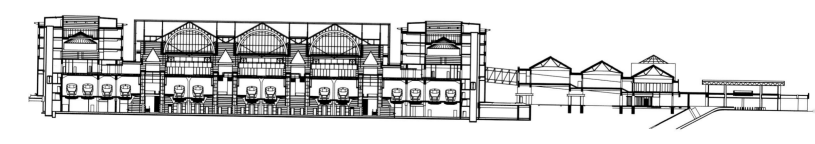

Triumf Palace Residential High-rise Building in Moscow
Wohnhochhaus »Triumf Palas« in Moskau

Don Stroy
2006

A 270-metre-tall skyscraper has been built in Moscow to accommodate an increase in moneyed residents in an area close to Aeroport Shopping Centre. Some speak of neo-Stalinism when they see the thousand-unit apartment complex, a posthumously completed addition to the seven Stalinist high-rise buildings which mark the inner-city ring. The developers, however, refer to its modern comforts. Only in its shape this backdrop does the new high-rise building appear as the eighth of the Stalinist symbols of power which celebrate the Tsarist stylistic elements representing the potency of the state in general and Stalin in particular as the great architect of communism. In the Triumf Palace, the creative trilogy of fillet, string-course and capitals typical of these buildings is nowhere to be seen. Nevertheless, pathos is at work in this building. The demand for prestigious architecture has already engendered a building programme, initiated by Moscow's mayor Yury Luzhkov, which calls for a further sixty buildings in this style. This is Europe's largest residential building and it expresses the desire to maintain a unique style and, simultaneously, be taken seriously. With its flush white balconies and ornamentation, the style is reminiscent of the American high-rise buildings of the last century, such as the Singer Building in New York City. The building is furnished with a spire in the shape of a spiked helmet reminiscent of Baptist churches in small American towns. From the plinth to the spire the gargantuan building looks as if it were built from a child's building blocks. It is as kitschy as a commonplace prefabricated high-rise dressed up in white plaster and is therefore nothing more than a caricature of Stalin's venerable people's palaces.

Unweit des Einkaufszentrums Aeroport hat Moskau kaufkräftigen Bevölkerungszuwachs bekommen. Neo-Stalinismus sagen die einen, die in der hufeisenförmigen Anlage mit über 1.000 Apartments das posthum gelieferte achte der sieben stalinistischen Hochhäuser sehen, die den inneren Stadtring markieren. Der Entwickler hingegen verweist auf den zeitgemäßen Komfort. Nur in seiner Kulisse mutet dieses neue Hochhaus wie das Achte der stalinistischen Machtsymbole an, bei denen die zaristischen Stilelemente die Potenz der siegreichen Staatsmacht im Allgemeinen und die Stalins als großen kommunistischen Architekten im Besonderen feierten. Der *Triumf Palas*, mit 265 Metern das höchste Wohngebäude Europas, lässt nicht einmal die für diese Bauten gestaltgebende Trias aus Leisten, Borden und Kapitellen erkennen. Nichtsdestoweniger ist auch an diesem Gebäude Pathos im Spiel. Die Nachfrage nach repräsentativer Architektur hat bereits ein von Moskaus Oberbürgermeister initiiertes Bauprogramm hervorgebracht, das weitere 60 Hochhäuser in dieser Art vorsieht. Der Stil erinnert mit den abschließenden weißen Balkonen und dem Zierrat an die amerikanischen Hochhäuser der vorherigen Jahrhundertwende wie etwa an das Singer-Building in Soho in New York – versehen mit der Dachkrone in Gestalt einer Haube, die an den Turm einer Baptistenkirche einer amerikanischen Kleinstadt erinnert. Vom Sockel bis zur Spitze wie ein riesengroßes Gebäude aus dem Spielzeugbausatz, sieht es fast kitschig aus – bei genauer Betrachtung wie ein banaler Plattenbau, der mit weißem Stuck verhübscht wurde und somit einer Karikatur der ehrwürdigen stalinistischen Volkspaläste gleichkommt.

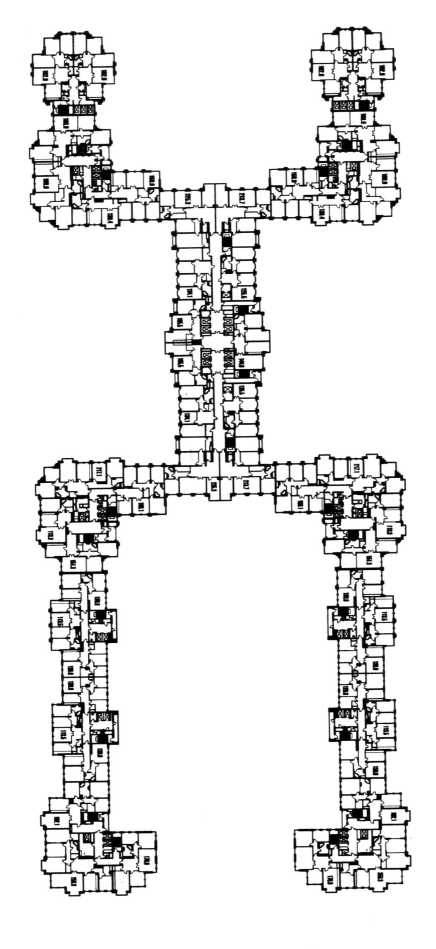

The Triumf Palace harks back to Stalin's idea to build "people's palaces" and house the masses in elegant interiors. The political situation has changed, the laws of housing less so. Luxury apartments are still firmly in the hands of the nomenklatura, though the new upper crust is defined by money rather than party membership.

»Triumf Palas« erinnert an Stalins Philosophie der Arbeiterpaläste: Massenwohnungsbau in feudalen Räumen. Die politischen Umstände haben sich geändert, die Gesetze der Wohnungsverteilung dagegen weniger. Auch heute kommt nur die Nomenklatura an Luxus-Wohnungen. Die neue Oberschicht zeichnet sich heute aber nicht mehr durch Parteibücher, sondern durch dicke Geldbeutel aus.

The tallest residential building in Europe may not be Stalin's "eighth sister", but it is a symbol of the new will to high-flying pomp.

Stalins »achte Schwester« ist das höchste Wohnhaus Europas nicht. Aber ein Sinnbild des neuen Willens zum Pomp im Höhenrausch schon.

Patriarch Residential Building in Moscow
Wohngebäude »Patriarch« in Moskau

SPAT/Sergey Tkachenko
2002

The Patriarch Building is located near the Kremlin next to Tverskaya Street, one of Moscow's main shopping streets. The building is influenced by architecture from the turn of the last century as well as Stalinist classicism. The architectural character of the environs has rubbed off on the architecture of this new building. A corner building, it has incorporated the dominant style of the immediate surroundings and closed a gaping wound in the urban fabric. The building takes on a quality embodied in its high ceilings and latticed windows and, using breathtaking stylistic devices, unites classical elements with those of early modernism in a contemporary structure. The generous loggias in the façade, which is structured with columns, pilasters and ornate shoulder pieces, are particularly striking. The street corner is marked by a tapered, rounded building with a cornice that is crowned with three structures of various styles: a classical rotunda with half-columns is followed by a baroque, octagonal superstructure and finally a twin of the spiral-shaped monument designed by Vladimir Tatlin for the Third International in 1919. The main building is crowned by a giant neo-classical cupola with an undulating domed roof. This building makes no secret of the luxury to be found within. The leading figures in Moscow's real-estate business, including Moscow's chief architect Alexander Kuzmin, are depicted in larger-than-life statues on the building's balustrade. The ground floor is clad in stone and the apartments are also fitted in stone, ceramics and parquet flooring. The facilities located on the ground floor include a concierge, a swimming pool, steam baths, a freight lift and three passenger lifts in addition to two underground car parks.

Der architektonische Charakter der benachbarten Twerskaja-Straße hat auf die Architektur des »Patriarch« abgefärbt. Mit dem Eckbau wurde eine offene Wunde, die im Stadtkörper klaffte, durch eine das nähere Umfeld Stadtbild prägende Dominante geschlossen. Das Gebäude greift die Qualität hoher Räume mit hohen Sprossenfenstern auf und vereint in einem geradezu atemberaubenden stilistischen Kunstgriff klassizistische Elemente mit solchen der Frühmoderne in einer zeitgemäßen Konstruktion. Markant sind die großzügigen Loggien der von Pfeilern und Pilastern strukturierten Fassade mit verzierten Verkröpfungen. Die Straßenquerung wird von einer stufenförmig verjüngten Gebäuderundung mit Kranzgesimsen geprägt, die von drei Aufbauten unterschiedlicher Stile gekrönt ist: einem klassizistischen Rundbau mit Blendsäulen folgt ein achteckiger Aufbau in barocker Manier und diesem eine Ausformung des spiralförmigen Monuments für die III. Internationale, das Tatlin 1919 entwarf. Das Haupthaus wird von einem riesigen neoklassizistischen Kuppelrundbau mit gewellter Dachhaube gekrönt. Die Stadtvilla macht aus ihrem Luxus von außen nach innen keinen Hehl. Auf der Balustrade sind die führenden Akteure im Moskauer Immobiliengeschäft in überlebensgroßen Statuen abgebildet, darunter etwa Moskaus Chefarchitekt Alexander Kusmin. Das Erdgeschoss ist mit Naturstein verkleidet, und auch die Wohnungen sind mit Naturstein, Keramik und Parkett ausgestattet. Im Erdgeschoss befinden sich die für die Hausbewohner gemeinschaftlichen Einrichtungen: ein inzwischen obligatorischer Concierge-Dienst, eine Schwimmhalle mit Dampfbädern, ein Lastenaufzug, drei Aufzüge sowie zwei Tiefgaragen.

An architectural best-of collection makes quite an impressive building, which celebrates itself and the leading figures in Moscow's real-estate business, all depicted in statues on the building's balustrade.

Gestapelte architektonische Stilblüten ergeben in der Summe ein imposantes Gebäude, das sich selbst und in Statuen auf der Balustrade die Größen des Moskauer Immobiliengeschäfts gleich mitfeiert.

Monolith Residential Building in Moscow
Wohnanlage »Monolith« in Moskau

Mikhail Belov
2004

If one walks eastwards through the park of Lomonossov University at the Pioneer Palace, one inadvertently arrives at a generous five-storey building in neoclassical style. This exclusive residential complex for well-to-do families is located near the meandering Moskva River and the sport venues from the 1980 Olympics situated on the other side of the river in an attractive and quiet location. The area, however, is within easy reach of the main traffic arteries of the pulsing metropolis. There are buildings in the new Russia whose name stands written above the main doorway, saying everything about the building if there is any room for doubt about its purpose and aesthetics. This is true of this three-winged complex with the stately park at the back and the unforthcoming wrought-iron fence at the front. When approaching the building from the north, one is immediately struck by a portal consisting of four smooth marble columns with Corinthian capitals supporting a quite common portico with lattice windows and the monogram of the complex. Behind the columns is not the grand entrance one might expect, but simply the façade with an entrance which seems more like a mouse hole in relation to the declamatory gesture of the portico and the dimensions of the entire building. It is a mistake which really should not have been made and cannot be excused in the light of the otherwise regular front of the building with its partially roofed windows, cornices, Ionic pilasters and bas-reliefs depicting classical family scenes. The building illustrates the danger inherent in borrowing from proven motifs, as such eclecticism can soon grow wearying. Nothing fits together in this skewed building, yet it fulfils the long-repressed desire for a prestigious lifestyle.

Wenn man durch den Park der Lomonossow-Universität am Pionierpalast nach Osten geht, gelangt man unversehens zu einem großzügigen fünfstöckigen Bau in neoklassizistischer Manier. Nahe der mäandernden Moskwa und den auf der anderen Flußseite gelegenen Sportstätten der Olympischen Spiele von 1980 befindet sich diese exklusive Wohnanlage für wohlhabende Familien in exzellenter und ruhiger Lage, zugleich aber unweit der Hauptverkehrsadern des pulsierenden Stadtbetriebs. Fraglos gibt es im neuen Russland Bauten, deren Name, im Zweifelsfalle sogar über dem Hauptportal stehend, alles über die Bestimmung des Hauses und dessen Ästhetik sagen. Dazu zählt auch diese dreiflügelige Anlage, die rückwärtig einen herrschaftlichen Park umschließt und zur Straße hin standesgemäß mit einem feinen schmiedeeisernen Zaun umfriedet ist. Wer von Norden her auf das Gebäude zusteuert, dem fällt sofort das von vier glatten Marmorsäulen mit einem korinthischen Blattkapitel geprägte Portal auf, das aber nur einen gewöhnlichen Vorbau mit Sprossenfenstern mit dem Monogramm der Wohnanlage trägt. Hinter den Säulen ist aber nicht wie zu erwarten ein adäquates Entree, sondern die gewöhnliche Fassade mit einem Eingang, der sich im Verhältnis zu der pathetischen Geste im Portikus und zu den Dimensionen des gesamten Bauwerks wie ein Mauseloch ausnimmt. Ein Missgriff, der angesichts der sonst gleichmäßigen Hausfront mit teilweise verdachten Fenstern, Gesimsen, ionischen Pilastern und Reliefs mit antiken Familienszenen ohne Not geschehen und so recht nicht zu entschuldigen ist. Aber das Haus erfüllt den Zweck eines lang unterdrückten Bedürfnisses nach repräsentativem Lebensstil.

Tsar for a day? The desire for a prestigious lifestyle persists in post-Soviet Russia, as does the habit to borrow stylistic elements from all periods. This building is a case in point – a kind of Winter Palace for the really rich.

Die Lust, zaritisches Lebensgefühl zur Schau zu stellen, ist im postsowjetischen Russland ebenso ungebrochen, wie sich dafür aus dem Stilkatalog der Epochen zu bedienen. Dieses Haus ist ein Beispiel dafür: eine Art Winterpalais steinreicher Familien.

Pompey Residential Building in Moscow
Wohnhaus »Pompeji« in Moskau

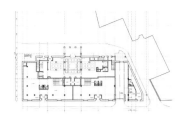

Michail Belov
2005

Filippovsky Lane is a narrow alley in the old Arbat Quarter. It lies between the Cathedral of Christ the Savior in the east and the foreign ministry in the west. The streets in this part of the city are so narrow that the building can hardly be taken in as a whole. Therefore it is not surprising that the Moscow architect Mikhail Belov chose to concentrate solely on the upper two floors when designing the façade of his seven-storey residential building. The upper levels rise above the neighbouring buildings and form a virtual calling card for the occupants. The building shines over grey Arbat with the elegance of an Italian renaissance palace in colourful shades of bright orange, vermilion and royal blue. A heavy cornice, supported by two-storey forward columns, unleashes a fiery architectural display with its floral ornamentation and classical forms. The capital was designed by Belov himself and cast in a new type of synthetic material which gives the impression of bronze. The Pompey Building is an architectural statement which can be seen as the antithesis of the anti-ornamental dogma of the modern era. According to Belov, who made a name for himself in the international scene at the end of the 1980s as one of Russia's best Paper Architects, the building also overcomes the present weariness of the deconstructivists and even the "bionic architects", as he calls them. Consequently, this building, commissioned by a private individual, could only be orchestrated on Moscow's architectural stage – one which is free of political ideology, free of theoretical dictates and ultimately free of the tradition of the *genius loci*. It is Italy in Russia. Belov sees his architecture quite pragmatically: "To me, the Pompey Building is not retro-style. To me it is neither historical nor postmodern."

Die Filippowski Pereulok ist eine schmale Gasse im alten Arbat-Viertel. Sie liegt zwischen der Christus-Erlöser-Kathedrale im Osten und dem Außenministerium im Westen. Die Straßen sind hier so schmal, dass die Gebäude kaum als Ganzes wahrnehmbar sind. Es verwundert daher nicht, wenn sich der Moskauer Architekt Michail Below bei der Fassadengestaltung seines siebengeschossigen Wohnhauses ganz auf die beiden oberen Etagen konzentriert hat. Sie ragen über die Nachbarbebauung hinaus und stellen so etwas wie eine Visitenkarte für die Bewohner dar. Farbenfroh in Signalorange, Zinnoberrot und Königsblau thront auf dem grauen Arbat die Eleganz eines italienischen Renaissance-Palais'. Vorgelagerte Säulen tragen über zwei Geschosse ein schweres Gesims, das mit floralem Ornament und klassischem Formenvokabular ein regelrechtes Feuerwerk der Architektur entfacht. Die Kapitelle hat Below selbst entworfen und in einem neuartigen Kunststoff, der wie Bronze wirkt, gießen lassen. Das Pompeji-Gebäude ist ein architektonisches Statement, das als Antithese gegen das ornamentfeindliche Dogma der Moderne gelesen werden kann. Folgt man Michail Below, der sich Ende der Achtzigerjahre international einen Namen als einer der russischen Papierarchitekten schlechthin gemacht hat, überwindet das Gebäude auch die gegenwärtige Müdigkeit der Dekonstruktivisten und selbst der »bionic architects«, wie er es beschreibt. Folglich konnte dieses Haus, das ein Privatmann in Auftrag gegeben hat, nur auf der architektonischen Bühne in Moskau inszeniert werden: frei von politischen Ideologien, frei von theoretischen Zwängen und letztlich frei von der Tradition des Genius loci. Italien in Russland.

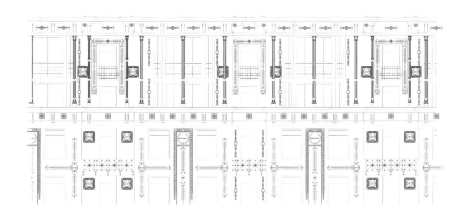

Warum dieses Gebäude »Pompeji« heißt, ist so recht nicht klar. Aber das Haus zählt zu den imposanten Beiträgen der Stadtreparatur. Ihm ist zu wünschen, dass ihm das Schicksal der gleichnamigen antiken Stadt erspart bleibt.

How this house got its name – Pompey – is something of a mystery. Yet it is one of the more impressive examples in the urban repair programme, and it is to be hoped that it will be spared the fate of the eponymous ancient city.

The details reveal Mikhail Belov's love for finery. The capitals were cast in a new type of synthetic material, and the other ornaments are also custom-made. Rarely does an architect enjoy such licence, but getting it evidently puts him on his mettle.

Im Detail offenbart sich Michail Belows Liebe zum Ornament. Die Kapitelle ließ der Architekt aus einem neuartigen Kunststoff fertigen. Die sonstigen Schmuckelemente sind ebenfalls individuelle Sonderanfertigungen. Selten darf sich ein Architekt so austoben. Wenn er es dennoch darf, muss er wohl sein ganzes Können zeigen.

Residential Building in Moscow
Wohnhaus in Moskau

Ilya Utkin
2004

This residential building is also located in Moscow's city centre. It is an area in which the nomenklatura indulged themselves in fine brick buildings while the rest of the country was plastered with the unimaginative architecture of the Leonid Brezhnev era of the 1970s. Matter-of-fact design would strike an incongruous note in this context, and might be seen to bring into discredit the predominant form of building, which hails from the second half of the nineteenth century to the beginning of the twentieth century, when the old Moscow tenements and town houses were built in this area. The resulting building is a five-storey corner development with the rounded edge typical of this quarter. It features an unusual mixture of basic classical elements and the Art-Deco forms found in this area, and uniquely incorporates them into the large corner building. The building is worthy of its role as visual focal point on a corner of Prechistensky Lane. The façade's basic architectural pattern is unpretentious. The ground level, clad in stone and with semi-basement and plinth cornice, is followed by a one-storey piano nobile with cross windows and light and dark brickwork. An attic level rises above the building with a blind wall which is quite striking when seen from street level. A glazed rotunda with pergolas serves as a crowning finish. The wall, which serves as an interface between exterior and interior, between shared and private space, is more than a mere functional element. It is the stone skin of the building and also a work of art.

Auch dieses Wohnhaus befindet sich in der Moskauer Innenstadt. Eine Gegend, in der sich in den Siebzigerjahren zu Leonid Breschnews Zeiten, als das übrige Land mit einfallsloser Lagerarchitektur überzogen wurde, die Nomenklatura Ziegelsteinbauten gönnte. Ein Entwurf im sachlichen Stil hätte darum die Auguren für diese Umgebung auch gar nicht überzeugt. Und das allein schon deshalb, weil er die vorherrschende Bebauung aus der zweiten Hälfte des 19. Jahrhunderts bis zu Beginn des 20. Jahrhunderts, als in dieser Gegend die so genannten Alt-Moskauer Miets- und Herrenhäuser entstanden, diskreditiert hätte. Das gebaute Resultat ist darum ein fünfgeschossiges Eckhaus mit der für dieses Viertel auch typischen abgerundeten Kante, das die eigenartige Mischung klassizistischer Grundzüge und Formen des Art Deco dieser Umgebung aufgreift. Entstanden ist ein Gebäude, das zugleich seiner Rolle als ästhetischer Blickfang an der Straßenkreuzung zur Pretschistenski-Gasse gerecht wird. Das architektonische Grundmuster der Fassade ist unprätentiös. Einem mit Natursteinen verkleideten Sockelgeschoss mit Souterrain und Sockelgesims folgt die mit hellen und dunklen Ziegelsteinen verkleidete Beletage mit Kreuzfenstern. Darüber und abschließend erhebt sich ein Dachgeschoss, das in Höhe der Straßenquerung mit einer Blendfassade auffällt. Hinter dieser verbirgt sich eine verglaste Rotunde mit Pergolen als Kopf eines Penthouses und als krönender Abschluss des Gebäudes.

204

Elegant proportions and elements from different historical periods are combined harmoniously in this façade. The rooftop rotunda gives a view of a model example of reconstruction – the Cathedral of Christ the Saviour.

Alles an der Fassade ist wohlproportioniert und aus dem Stilkanon der Epochen aufeinander abgestimmt. Von der Dachrotunde fällt der Blick auf ein Musterbeispiel der Rekonstruktion: die Christus-Erlöser-Kathedrale.

The building fits into the neighbourhood of old tenements and town houses as if it had always been here.
Mitten in diese Gegend Alt-Moskauer Miets- und Herrenhäuser fügt sich dieser Bau ein, als hätte er schon immer hier gestanden.

Administrative Buildings at Paveletskaya Square in Moscow
Verwaltungsgebäude am Pawelezker Bahnhof in Moskau

SPAT/Sergey Tkachenko
2003

In 1988, the Moscow City Council held a competition for the design of three high-rise buildings which were to "complete the visual succession of the Garden Ring" in the south-east of the inner-city circle, which follows the course of the city's main fortifications. Even today the monasteries, such as the Andronikov Monastery (1360), Saviour Monastery (1420), Semyonovsky Monastery (1379) or Donskoy Monastery (1591) hark back to the ring of fortified cloisters built beyond Moscow's city walls between the fourteenth and sixteenth centuries. The Soviet state's secular cue followed the same principle – this time directly on the circuit of the former city wall where the gates had once been. This ring of imaginary city gates was continued after 1990. New high-rise buildings were erected, e.g. the Riverside Towers in Oruzheyny Lane in the Krasniye Kholmy district. These have now been followed by the project on Paveletskaya Square, one of the largest squares in the southern city centre. The twenty-six-storey office tower with its two side wings is the only project from the competition to be realised. The ensemble is the focal point of this lively square located at a railway and metro station of the same name. Originally designed in an eclectic mixture of styles, including neo-Gothic garb as a copy of Big Ben in London, the tower now presents itself as a variation on Moscow baroque and Stalinist classicism in the spirit of American New Urbanism with its dash of postmodernism. When illuminated, the building radiates a certain longing for urban entertainment. A little bit of Las Vegas is never out of place when it helps liven up the urban apartment.

Bereits 1988 wurde vom Moskauer Stadtkommitee der Wettbewerb für drei Hochhäuser ausgelobt, die »die visuelle Reihe des Gartenringes vollenden sollten« im Südosten des inneren Stadtrings, welcher der großen Stadtbefestigung folgt. Noch heute künden die Monasterien, wie das Andronikowkloster (1360), das Erlöserkloster (1420), Semjonowski (1379) oder das Donskojkloster (1591), von einem zusätzlichen Ring befestigter Klöster, die zwischen dem 14. und 16. Jahrhundert rund um Moskau außerhalb der Stadtmauer angelegt wurden. Die säkularen Fingerzeige des sowjetischen Staates folgten demselben Prinzip. Nur eben unmittelbar am Verlauf der ehemaligen Stadtmauer, dort, wo sich früher die Stadttore befanden. Nach 1990 wurde dieser Ring von imaginären Stadttoren weiter komplettiert. Neue Hochhäuser wurden in der Oruschejni-Gasse im Viertel der Krasnije Cholmy in Gestalt der Riverside Towers gebaut. Und später am Pawelezker Platz, einem der größten Plätze im Süden der Innenstadt. Der 26 Stockwerke hohe Büroturm mit seinen beiden Seitenflügeln ist das einzige Resultat, das aus dem fast zwei Jahrzehnte zurückliegenden Wettbewerb verblieben ist. Der eigentlich in anderen Stileklektizismen gedachte Turm unter anderem im neogotischen Gewand als Nachbildung des Big Ben in London präsentiert sich nun als eine Adaptation Moskowiter Barocks und stalinistischen Klassizismus im Sinne des postmodern angehauchten amerikanischen New Urbanism. In der Illumination scheint auch ein wenig Sehnsucht nach Urban Entertainment durch, nach dem Motto: Ein wenig Las Vegas ist nie verkehrt.

I'd like to be in America…
When staging glamour,
anything goes, as long as
it enhances the overall
effect. At night the cunnin-
gly lit ensemble on the
vast square shows the
way to the train station.
Etwas Amerika darf es
sein: Geht es um die
Inszenierung von Glanz,
ist alles recht, um das
Gesamtbild zu bereichern.
Nachts ist das illuminierte
Ensemble ein Wegweiser
zum Bahnhof.

Residential Building in Mashkova Street in Moscow
Wohnhaus in der Maschkowa-Straße in Moskau

SPAT/Sergey Tkachenko
2002

The imagination of the architects who created their own designs despite the state-decreed monotony in the arts knew no bounds. These Paper Architects were prevented from proving the feasibility of their designs in the Soviet Union. After the political restructuring of the former Soviet Union the situation changed, at least in Russia. Utopias which follow a renewed taste for architecture are suddenly in demand, and perhaps this is also the case when architecture takes on the role of an artistic happening. One of these former Paper Architects is Oleg Dubrovsky. After contemplating several possible sites, his egg-shaped building rolled to its home in Mashkova Street – wilfully defying the time-honoured quadrature of space and the relationship between block and street. As if that were not impertinent enough, this four-storey building clad in an Art-Nouveau outer skin has attached itself to a conventional building. Its design rebels against merely restorative art design similar to the way the young avant-garde at the turn of the previous century did, whose proponents also presented unique forms of expression. The Egg is just that – the detail of stylistic idiosyncrasy is transferred to the structure. Two Eggs should have been built, in fact, including a large one in a kind of eggcup with Palladian arches and a ring supported by Corinthian columns. But to date only the smaller Egg described here has been completed.

Die Fantasie der Architekten, die gegen die staatlich verordnete Monotonie in der Kunst anzeichneten, kannte bekanntlich keine Grenzen. Diese »Papierarchitekten« waren in der Sowjetunion zwangsweise vom Beweis des Machbaren ihrer Entwürfe entbunden. Seit der politischen Neuordnung der Sowjetunion ist das zumindest in Russland anders. Plötzlich sind die Utopien gefragt, so sie einem restaurativen Architekturgeschmack folgen, vielleicht auch dann, wenn Architektur die Funktion einer Kunstaktion übernimmt. Einer von diesen ehemaligen »Papierarchitekten« ist Oleg Dubrowski, Mitarbeiter im Atelier von Sergei Tkachenko. Sein Objekt ist ein eiförmiges Gebäude, das als Idee von mehreren möglichen Standorten buchstäblich in die Maschkowa-Straße kullerte, um sich hier höchst eigenwillig der jahrhundertelang erprobten Quadratur des Raumes und der Beziehung von Block und Straßenkante zu widersetzen. Frech um so mehr, als sich das vierstöckige Gebäude in einer jugendstilartigen Außenhaut an ein konventionellen Haus angliedert. Zugleich war die Aufsässigkeit gegen restaurative Formen in der Kunst die Methode der jungen Moderne. Nichts anderes verkörpert auch das Ei, in dem die stilistische Eigenart im Detail auf den Baukörper übertragen wird. Ursprünglich sollten zwei Eier gebaut werden: ein kleines, das auch realisiert wurde, sowie ein zweites, in einer Art Eierbecher mit Palladiobögen und einem von korinthischen Säulen getragenen Ring.

FOR SALE 980 7733

PAUL'S YARD

An unusual interpretation
of traditional style.
Originally two Eggs were
planned, but in the end
only the smaller one was
realised.
*Heimatstil in seiner
eigensinnigsten Spielart.
Eigentlich waren zwei Eier
geplant. Gebaut wurde
aber eben nur dieses –
das kleine.*

50.000
48.700
47.800
44.500
41.200
37.900
34.600
31.300
28.000
24.700
21.400
19.100
14.800
11.500

0.315
0.000

215

Office Building in Dolgorukovskaya Street in Moscow
Bürogebäude in der Dolgorukowskaja-Straße in Moskau

MNIIP Mosproyekt-2,
Studio 14
2001

Located in Moscow's city centre, the office building's outer form submits to the area's older buildings while at the same time setting its own unique stylistic note. This can be seen in the way the fourteen-storey building rises far above the surrounding structures. In order for the fifty-metre tall building to blend into the streetscape, it was designed as a series of progressive levels which gradually rise to the maximum height. The building appears to consist of several separate interlocking buildings with a common façade finished with glazed lofts and an overhanging roof. The central structure dominates with a vertical glass band which ends at the ground floor with a colonnade. The building thereby refers to the aesthetics of the adjoining building, which was designed by the constructivist Ilya Golosovoy. The neighbouring building not only influenced the architectural elements of the new building. The structure of its façade is uniquely echoed in the height of the floors, the façade bands and the design of the cornice.

Das Bürogebäude liegt in der Moskauer Innenstadt in einem Viertel mit überwiegend alter Bebauung, in das sich das neue Bürohaus in seinem Äußeren fügt und zugleich einen eigenen Akzent setzt. Zum einen dadurch, dass das insgesamt 14 Stockwerke hohe Haus die Häuser der Umgebung bei weitem überragt. Damit sich der über 50 Meter hohe Neubau auch ins Straßenbild des Viertels einfügt, wurde das Haus stufenförmig angelegt, so dass es stufenförmig die maximale Höhe erreicht und wirkt, als ob es aus mehreren ineinander greifenden Einzelhäusern bestünde. Der mittlere Baukörper dominiert durch ein gläsernes Vertikalband, das auf dem Sockelgeschoss mit Säulengang abschließt. Ästhetisch orientiert sich das Haus unmittelbar am angrenzenden Gebäude, dessen Entwurf von dem Konstruktivisten Ilia Golosovoj stammt. Dieses Nachbarhaus hat nicht nur den Architekturkörper des Neubaus beeinflusst, sondern dessen Fassadengliederung findet sich indirekt in der Geschosshöhe, den Fassadenbändern und im Gesims wieder.

Multi-storey Car Park in Moscow
Parkhaus am Jakimanka-Kanal in Moskau

MNIIP Mosproyekt-2,
Studio 11/Veiko
2001

Located at Nos. 1–4 Golutvinsky Lane in the middle of Moscow's city centre, this multi-level car park with space for 445 vehicles may be the best building to corroborate the theory that architecture is an artistic happening – it certainly is in this instance. This building is a proper imitation of all which is old in a quarter where white villas and romantic front gardens contrast both with old and grey yet venerable industrial administration buildings and with the sleek façades of the most recent architectural styles, which from any perspective are lacklustre backdrops. Everything that lends stylistic character to the façade – cornices, embrasures and the plinth – is presented in the gleaming white of the old buildings. The façade, however, is done in the red brickwork found in factory architecture. In addition, there are the round arch windows in various sizes, even in the form of twin church windows. Yet the building houses neither a school, nor a church, nor an industrial firm. It is just a car park, and a first-class architectural illusion at that, whose rich façade makes it much more honest than the surrounding postmodern architecture. The five-storey car park is particularly impressive when seen from Bolshaya Yakimanka. From here the building enters into a dialogue with the little white houses with their saddle and hipped roofs, and the buildings become actors on the urban architectural stage.

Das mehrstöckige Parkhaus für 445 Parkplätze an der Schnittstelle der 1. und 4. Golutwinski-Gasse inmitten der Moskauer Innenstadt mag noch am ehesten die These von der Architektur als Kunstaktion bestätigen. In diesem Viertel am Jakimanka-Kanal mit den weißen Stadthäusern und ihren romantischen Vorgärten einerseits, den alten grauen, aber nichtsdestoweniger ehrwürdigen Verwaltungsbauten und den aalglatten Fassaden jüngster architektonischer Stilübungen andererseits, stellt dieses Gebäude eine stilechte Imitation dar. Alles, was an der Fassade formprägenden Charakter hat – Gesimse, Laibungen, Sockelprofile – ist in jenem strahlenden Weiß der alten Häuser gehalten. Die Fassadenoberfläche ist dagegen im roten Backstein der Fabrikarchitektur ausgeführt. Dazu passen die großen Rundbogenfenster, selbst in der Façon schmaler Zwillingskirchenfenster. Aber das Haus beherbergt weder eine Lehranstalt, noch eine Kirche oder einen Industriebetrieb. Es ist schlicht ein Parkhaus und dafür eine architektonische Täuschung erster Güte. Und doch ist es in seiner Fassadenplastik ehrlicher als die postmodernen Kulissen im Umfeld. Besonders eindrucksvoll ist das fünfstöckige Parkhaus von der Bolschaja Jakimanka, wo es als Kulisse inmitten der kleinen weißen Häuser und ihren Sattel- und Walmdächern als neuer Akteur auf der städtischen Architekturbühne wirkungsvoll in Dialog tritt.

The Fifth Element Residential Complex in St Peterburg
Wohnanlage »Das fünfte Element« in Sankt Petersburg

Yevgeny Gerasimov
2004

As the Venice of the north, St Petersburg offers excellent and charming domiciles for city residents with discriminating tastes on the offshore islands near the Old City in the Gulf of Finland. Krestovsky Island, for example, has such niches on offer. This new apartment hotel is located at No. 2 Yuzhnaya Avenue, directly at the front of Yuzhny Weir in the middle of the heritage-listed ensemble of historical buildings in Primorsky Park. The new four-storey building shows deference to the Arcadian surroundings while opening its horseshoe-shaped layout to the water – the immediate visual point of reference. Everything about the building yearns to be a part of the landscape, as articulated in the green steel strutting on the protruding roof, the columns on the front of the side wings, the oriels and the window frames. This lends the stone and brick façade the desired lightness. The filigree steel construction seems to rest lightly on the building like a delicate meshwork. The glass and green steel strutting, but also the metal window borders on the front side of the wings and the corresponding oriels on the side walls emphasise the fact that this large building (almost 12,400 square metres) seeks to belong to the landscape while eschewing organic conformity. The building is confident yet harmonious. Its sweeping, finely-woven glass roof joins the two wings together and creates a comfortable courtyard, which transforms the house into a stage when the residents emerge from their suites to see and be seen. The suites offer princely living with their three to four rooms, the ceilings almost four metres high, on a floor area of at least 180 square metres.

Sankt Petersburg bietet als Venedig des Nordens auf den zahlreichen der Altstadt vorgelagerten Inseln im Finnischen Meerbusen exzellente und reizvolle Wohnidyllen. Auch die Krestowsk-Insel hält solche urbane Nischen parat. In der Juschnaja-Allee 2, inmitten des denkmalgeschützten Ensembles mit dem Primorski-Park, befindet sich der Neubau dieses Apartmenthotels unmittelbar an der Stirnseite des Juschni-Weihers. Dieser arkadischen Umgebung fügt sich der vierstöckige Neubau ein und öffnet sich zugleich mit seinem hufeisenförmigen Grundriss dem Gewässer als seinem unmittelbaren optischen Bezugspunkt. Alles an dem Gebäude will zu seiner Landschaft, was sich von den grünen Stahlverstrebungen des überkragenden Daches, den Säulen an den Stirnseiten der Flügelbauten, den Erkern bis hin zu den Fensterrahmen im Detail artikuliert. Die filigrane Stahlkonstruktion scheint sich wie ein zartes Geflecht um das Gebäude zu legen. Glas und grüne Stahlverstrebungen unterstreichen, dass das Gebäude mit fast 12.400 Quadratmetern zu seiner Landschaft gehören will, ohne sich in organischer Fügsamkeit dieser anzubiedern. Souverän steht das Haus da, mit seinem geschwungenen, fein gewobenen Glasdach eingefasst, das die beiden Seitenflügel miteinander verbindet und damit einen komfortablen Innenhof schafft. Das Dach verwandelt das Haus zugleich zur Seebühne, auf der die vornehmen Kreise ihr Gesellschaftsspiel aufführen, wenn sie sich aus ihren Suiten bewegen. Diese bieten über drei bis vier Räume auf reichlich 180 Quadratmetern in fast vier Meter hohen Wänden fürstliche Möglichkeiten zum Logieren.

Four substances compose the physical universe: fire, earth, air and water, represented by four geometric bodies. The fifth element in this case is architecture, artistic creativity. And that is what relates this residential development to its surroundings.

Vier Elemente kennt die Urmaterie: Feuer, Erde, Luft und Wasser – symbolisiert in vier geometrischen Körpern. Als fünftes Element gilt in diesem Fall die Architektur: als künstlerische Neuschöpfung. Und gerade so verhält sich diese Wohnanlage zu und in ihrer Umgebung.

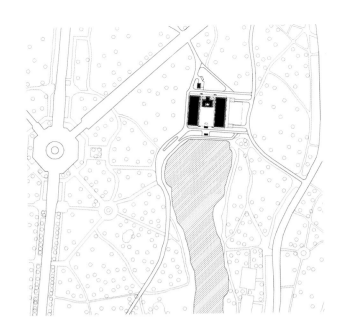

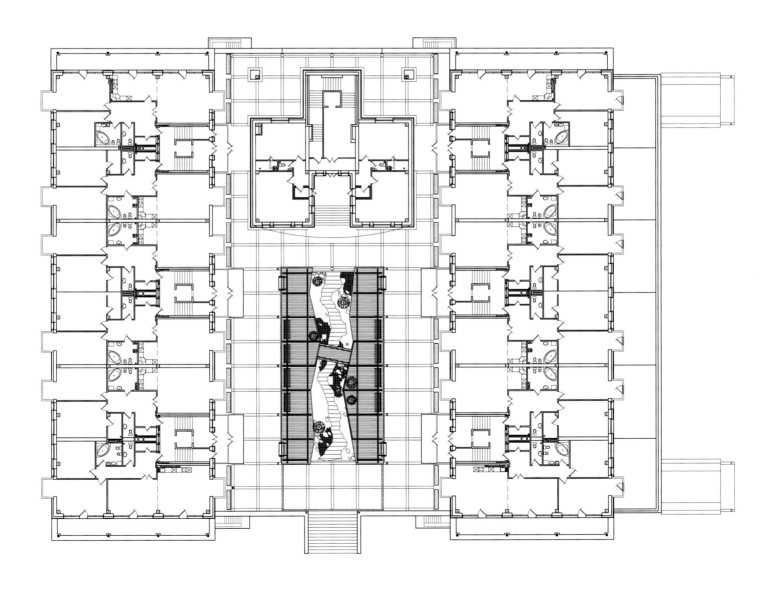

223

Kul Sharif Mosque in Kazan
Moschee »Kul Scharif« in Kasan

Tadinvestgrazhdanproyekt
2001

The list of ecclesiastical buildings built since the break-up of the Soviet Union includes not only Christian, but also Islamic houses of worship. Among these, the Kul Sharif Mosque is an unusual example because it is located in Kazan's fortified city centre, the kremlin. The mosque forms the geographical centre of the kremlin, and the minarets, nearly sixty metres high, define the skyline of the old city centre. Until recently the city skyline was characterised by the pointed spires of Annunciation Cathedral, built in 1562, the churches of the Transfiguration Monastery and the St Peter and Paul Cathedral. The dominant Christian symbolism has now been called into question by this mosque – a step which is both understandable as well as long overdue, as Kazan was the seat of the Sunni mufti in the European part of the Soviet Union. The construction of the mosque is the ultimate manifestation of this important role. The mosque's dominant urban and functional position is underscored down to the last detail by the structure's dimensions and formal expression. The mosque is quite unusual with the all-supporting central cupola with its window wreath executed in the old Russian style and the nave's untypical Gothic cross-rib arches of reinforced concrete. The disconcerting yet sublime architectural face of the mosque is completed by the lancet windows with colourful glass patterns typical of the early Gothic combined with oriental imagery. In addition to the obligatory crescent moons on the minarets and cupola, unmistakably oriental ornamentation adorns the lower part of the mosque, and verses from the Koran are carved on the frieze of the pointed arch portals. The structure thus unites various stylistic elements in an original manner which has finally emerged after decades of aesthetic unimaginativeness decreed by Moscow.

Zu den zahlreichen Sakralbauten, die in Russland nach der Auflösung der Sowjetunion entstanden sind, gehören neben christlichen auch islamische Gotteshäuser. Die Moschee Kul-Scharif ist unter diesen ein ausgefallenes Beispiel – und zwar allein schon wegen ihrer Lage im befestigten mittelalterlichen Stadtkern. Die Moschee bildet den geographischen Mittelpunkt des Kreml und bestimmt heute mit den fast 60 Meter hohen Minaretten die Silhouette. Bislang war diese vom spitz aufragenden Türmen der 1562 erbauten Verkündigungs-Kathedrale sowie der Kirchen des Verklärungsklosters und der Sankt Peter- und Pauls-Kathedrale bestimmt. Diese dominante christliche Zeichensprache ist nun relativiert. Ein Schritt, der historisch begreiflich und längst überfällig war, war doch Kasan schon zu kommunistischen Zeiten Sitz des Muftis der sunnitischen Muslime der europäischen Sowjetunion. Der Bau dieser Moschee unterstreicht und manifestiert diese Bedeutung endgültig. Diese städtebaulich und funktional beherrschende Stellung der Moschee unterstreicht die Architektur von den Ausmaßen und der Formensprache des Baukörpers bis ins Detail. Ungewöhnlich ist die Kirche mit dem alles in der Mitte zusammenhaltenden Kuppelhelm, mit einem Fensterkranz altrussischer Manier und einem für Moscheen völlig untypischen gotischen Kreuzrippengewölbe. In der Frühgotik übliche Lanzettfenster mit blumigen Buntglasmustern komplettieren das gleichermaßen befremdliche wie erhabene Architekturgesicht der Moschee und vereinen sich mit orientalischen Sprachbildern. Zugleich findet sich neben den obligatorischen Mondsicheln auf Minaretten und Kuppel vor allem am Unterbau des Gotteshauses unverkennbar orientalische Ornamentik. In die Friese der Spitzbogenportale sind Verse aus dem Koran eingemeißelt.

The return of religion changes the silhouettes of cities. Situated right in the centre of the kremlin, the mosque now overshadows the Christian churches. With reason, for even in Soviet times Kazan was the seat of the Sunni mufti in the European part of Russia. The only thing that was lacking was a splendid place of worship. Not anymore.

Die Rückkehr der Religionen markiert die Silhouette der Städte. Mitten im Kreml drängt die Moschee nun die christlichen Kirchen in den Schatten. Folgerichtig: Denn Kasan war schon zu Sowjetzeiten Sitz des Muftis der sunnitischen Muslime im europäischen Russland. Jedoch ohne repräsentatives Gotteshaus. Bislang.

The Cathedral of St George the Vanquisher in Samara
Kathedrale des »Heiligen Georg des Siegers« in Samara

Yury I. Kharitonov
2000

This cathedral was completed on the fifty-fifth anniversary of the end of the Second World War. The important state character of this cross-cupola church with its four side towers and a single main dome as a historical memorial is emphasised by its location on Slava Square, which is also the site of the White House, the seat of the regional government, and the war memorial with the eternal flame. In this location the obelisk-like form of the church hallows remembrance and is at the same time a visual cue. Below, life goes on in the rambling city and the marina by the Volga terraces. The five cupolas of the church, crowned with crosses held by chains of pearls, are coated with titanium nitrate – a gold-coloured alloy – and can be seen glistening in the sun from a distance. At night the whitewashed walls of the cathedral are bathed in light, giving it the appearance of a heavenly apparition. The visual effect overlaps with the cathedral's function on Slava Square and beyond. The church occupies only two hundred square metres of floor space and is a mere thirty-five metres tall, this making it rather more like a chapel, yet its radiance outshines its material size. At the same time, the church is a sacral pendant to the obelisks of the monument to the women who worked in the munitions industry on the home front, from which it is separated only by a park with a stand of old trees.

Die Kathedrale wurde genau 55 Jahre nach dem Ende des Zweiten Weltkrieges eingeweiht. Der staatstragende Charakter dieser Kreuzkuppelkirche mit vier Seitentürmen und einer Hauptkuppel als geschichtlicher Gedenkort wird zusätzlich durch die Lage am Slawa-Platz unterstrichen. Also dort, wo sich das Weiße Haus, der Sitz der Regionalregierung, und das Kriegsmonument mit dem ewigen Feuer befinden. So verleiht die Kirche dem Gedenken in Gestalt des Obelisken so etwas wie höhere Weihen. Zugleich ist sie ein städtebaulicher Fingerzeig oberhalb der Wolga. Schon von weitem sind die fünf mit einer Nitrotitan – einer goldfarbenen Legierung – überzogenen und in der Sonne glänzenden Kuppeln zu sehen. Gekrönt sind sie mit von Perlenketten gehaltenen Kreuzen. Nachts ist die Kirche mit ihrer weiß getünchten Fassade in Licht getaucht und entfaltet ihre Wirkung als himmlische Erscheinung. Die optische Wirkung deckt sich mit der Funktion des Sakralbaus an diesem Platz: eine Kirche, die mit 200 Quadratmetern Grundfläche und 35 Metern Höhe als Baukörper eher eine Kapelle ist und eine Strahlkraft entfaltet, die über ihre materielle Größe hinausweist. Die Kirche bildet das sakrale Pendant zum Obelisken des Ehrenmals für die Frauen, die an der Heimatfront in der Rüstungsindustrie arbeiteten. Beide trennt nur ein mit alten Bäumen bestandener Park voneinander.

In New and Old Russia alike, the Church has always commissioned a large number of buildings, and buildings of high symbolic value, too. The aura of this small church is such that it easily outshines the Stalin-era war memorial.

Die Kirche ist im neuen wie im alten Russland einer der größten Auftraggeber – und zudem der symbolträchtigste. Die kleine Kirche konkurriert mit ihrer Strahlkraft mühelos mit dem Fingerzeig des Vaterländischen Kriegsdenkmals aus der Stalin-Ära.

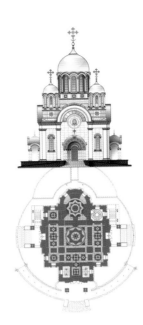

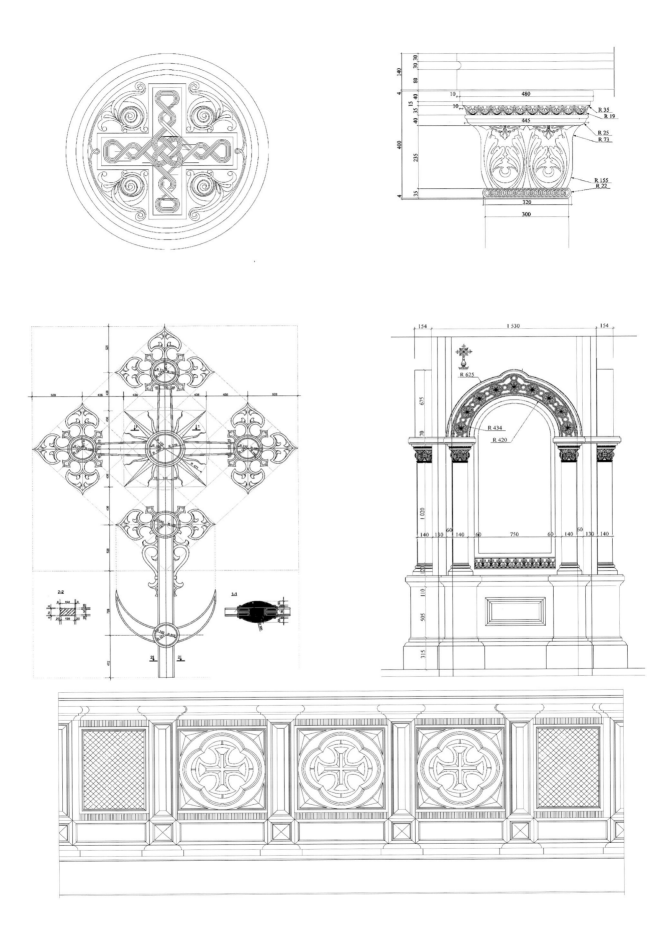

Cathedral of Christ the Savior in Moscow
Christus-Erlöser-Kathedrale in Moskau

MNIIP Mosproyekt-2,
Studio 12
2000

Let there be no mistake: this basilica is new. It was completed in 2000 and its architectural guise leaves no doubt as to its historical import. Everything seems just right – and it truly is when the visitor raises his head to marvel at the cupola's richly adorned rotunda. The original cathedral fell victim to the demolition squads of Stalin's cultural revolution, as did over eight thousand other churches. A Palace of the Soviets was planned for the former site of the building so rich in symbolism. With its 103-metre central cupola, it was the tallest building in Moscow when it was completed in 1883. Not only was the church's demolition an affront from an aesthetic point of view, but the church, whose construction began in 1839 according to plans by the architect Konstantin Ton for a cathedral commemorating the defeat of Napoleon in 1812, was a patriotic building of the highest order. Today, 177 tablets commemorating the names of battles and heroes in the Napoleonic War are set in niches along the walls. On the site of the Saviour Cathedral the Soviets had planned a 315-metre tiered building crowned by a 100-metre statue of Lenin. The Palace of the Soviets was intended as an architectural apogee of a restructured Moscow while at the same time providing something of a secular celebratory venue for the regime near the Kremlin in the south-west of Moscow's city centre. The project, however, never got off the ground. Instead, Stalin's successor, Nikita Khrushchev, had a heated, and therefore quite popular, open-air swimming pool built for the health of the city's workers. The steam which rose from the pool, however, damaged the art collection in the neighbouring Pushkin Museum, causing Mayor Yury Luzhkov to begin construction of the cathedral without further ado.

Damit keine Missverständnisse auftreten: Diese Basilika ist neu. Fertig gestellt im Jahr 2000, zeigt sie sich in einem architektonischen Gewand, das keinen Zweifel an ihrer Geschichtlichkeit aufkommen lässt. In den Dreißigerjahren fiel diese Kirche – wie über 8.000 weitere – den kulturrevolutionären Sprengkommandos Stalins zum Opfer. An die Stelle des symbolträchtigen Baus, der mit seiner 103 Meter hohen mittleren Hauptkuppel nach seiner Fertigstellung 1883 das damals höchste Gebäude Moskaus war, sollte der »Palast der Sowjets« entstehen. Allein der Abriss der Kirche war selbst aus atheistischer Sicht ein Affront, wurde doch die Kirche 1839 nach Plänen des Architekten Konstantin Ton als Kathedrale für die Befreiung von Napoleon 1812 erbaut und war somit ein patriotisches Bauwerk erster Güte. Über die Wände verteilt sind heute wieder in 177 Nischen Tafeln, auf denen Schlachten- und Heldennamen des Krieges von 1812 gegen Napoleon erinnern. An Stelle der Erlöser-Kathedrale war ein 315 Meter hohes stufenförmiges Gebäude gedacht, mit einer 100 Meter hohen Lenin-Statue als krönenden Abschluss. Über die Fundamente kam der Bau jedoch nicht hinaus. Stattdessen ließ Stalins Nachfolger Nikita Chruschtschow für die Gesundheit der Werktätigen ein beheiztes und darum bei den Moskauern beliebtes Freiluftschwimmbad bauen. Aber die Dämpfe des Bades schädigten die Kunstsammlungen des benachbarten Puschkin-Museums und so entschloss sich Oberbürgermeister Juri Luschkow, kurzerhand den Aufbau der Kathedrale zu betreiben. Der historisierende Neubau war höchste Staatsangelegenheit – nicht nur wegen der überwiegend vom Staat getragenen Kosten von umgerechnet 150 Millionen Euro. Unter den heiligen Hallen wurde zudem eine Tiefgarage errichtet.

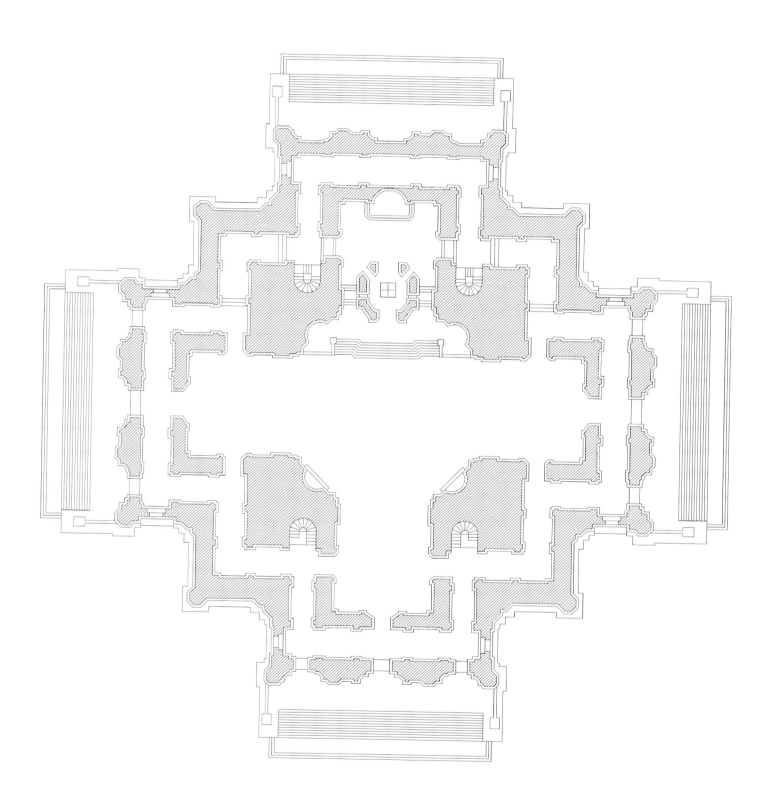

233

The central dome of St Peter's in Rome reaches 132 metres. The central dome of this cathedral near the Kremlin reaches 103 metres, symbolising Moscow's religious importance. Impressive views of the new cathedral are to be had from all side streets.

132 Meter misst die Hauptkuppel von St. Peter in Rom. 103 Meter misst die Hauptkuppel dieser Kathedrale – Sinnbild für Moskau als östliches Rom unweit des Kreml. In allen Seitenstraßen eröffnen sich imposante Blicke auf den Neubau.

The reconstructed cathedral shines in seemingly old splendour, belying the historical rupture. Yet hidden underneath all this ecclesiastical ornament is an underground car park.

Außen so wie innen erstrahlt die Kirche seit ihrem Wiederaufbau in einem täuschend alten Glanz, der über den Geschichtsbruch hinwegtäuscht. Unter so viel Kirchenschmuck verbirgt sich im Keller heute eine Tiefgarage.

Architektur nach dem Kommunismus

Architektur nach dem Kommunismus

Bart Goldhoorn

Revolutionär! Alles neu! Alles ganz anders! Große Auswahl! Freiheit! Nicht umsonst werden diese Vokabeln gern für Reklamezwecke benutzt – ihr Reiz ist so universell wie bezwingend. Wandel und Revolution sind Worte mit einer positiven Strahlkraft. So ähnlich war es auch mit Russland zu Beginn der Neunzigerjahre. Die ganze Welt blickte in Erwartung einer wundersam blühenden Kultur und einer prosperierenden Wirtschaft auf das riesige Land, das sich vom Joch des Kommunismus befreit hatte. Seither sind mehr als 15 Jahre vergangen. Und man muss nur die Nachrichten einschalten, um einzusehen, dass Russland mit Problemen kämpft, die weitaus gravierender sind als ursprünglich angenommen. Das gilt nicht nur für Wirtschaft und Gesellschaft, sondern auch für Architektur und Städtebau. Die russischen Städte werden noch über lange Jahrzehnte die deutlichen Spuren von siebzig Jahren Kommunismus tragen. Darin unterscheiden sie sich grundlegend von ehemals kommunistischen Städten in den anderen Ländern Mitteleuropas, die dieses historische Erbe leichter überwunden haben. Dafür gibt es eine Vielzahl von Gründen. In Russland begann die Industrialisierung viel später als in Mitteleuropa, der Kommunismus jedoch um einiges früher. Die vorrevolutionäre russische Stadt, mit Ausnahme von Sankt Petersburg und Moskau, bestand zu einem großen Teil aus Holzbauten. Davon hat kaum etwas die Zeiten überdauert. In den Städten sind heute deshalb fast gar keine Spuren ihrer langen, mitunter mehr als 1000 Jahre alten Geschichte zu finden. Die physischen Strukturen der russischen Stadt, wie wir sie heute vorfinden, wurden in den Jahrzehnten des Kommunismus manifestiert. Der Kommunismus ist also nicht bloß eine Schicht, die sich einfach abkratzen ließe, damit die »echte« Stadt darunter zum Vorschein kommt, und er ist

auch kein »historischer Irrtum«, den man am besten so schnell wie möglich vergisst. Nicht die Vielzahl von Monumenten, Parolen und politischen Symbolen im öffentlichen Raum begründen den kommunistischen Charakter der russischen Stadt, sondern die Tatsache, dass die Stadt unter Bedingungen einer Gesellschaft geschaffen wurde, die nach kommunistischen Prinzipien funktionierte: Kein Privateigentum, geringe Einkommensunterschiede, zentrale Wohnungsvergabe, serielle Industriebauweise. Und selbst hier war nicht der ideologische Überbau entscheidend, sondern seine praktischen Auswirkungen im Alltag. Gesetze, die wie wasserdichte Umsetzungen der kommunistischen Ideologie aussahen, zeitigten unbeabsichtigte Folgen und nicht selten das Gegenteil des eigentlich erwünschten Effekts. Ich habe diesen Mechanismus als »sowjetisches Paradox« bezeichnet. Denn in Architektur und Städtebau der einstigen Sowjetunion ging es weder rigide noch rational zu, sondern chaotisch und amorph.

Die Vierte Revolution

Die unvorhersehbaren Auswirkungen ideologischer Prinzipien finden sich überall. Rem Koolhaas, der zum ersten Mal seit den Siebzigerjahren wieder nach Moskau kam, hat den Grund für die Begeisterung vieler westlicher Architekten für die russische Stadt vielleicht am treffendsten formuliert: Das Faszinierende an der vom sowjetischen Kommunismus geprägten russischen Stadt ist ihr radikales Konzept. Keine Grundstücksspekulation, kein unkontrollierbarer Markt – nur Architektur, die auf einer strengen Ideologie basiert. Eine totalitäre Planung; eigentlich der Traum jedes Architekten. Der ideologische Gehalt der Architektur zeigt sich

immer dann, wenn die jeweilige politische Macht einen Paradigmenwechsel anstrengt. Innerhalb der Sowjet-Ära gab es insgesamt drei Revolutionen dieser Art. Die konstruktivistische Revolution der Zwanziger- und Dreißigerjahre wollte mit ihren modernen Experimenten alle Spuren des bürgerlichen Eklektizismus der vorrevolutionären Zeit tilgen. Die Stalinistische Revolution hingegen ersetzte die Bauten des modernen Konstruktivismus durch einen fast barock anmutenden Neo-Klassizismus und propagierte eine Rückkehr zum traditionellen Städtebau. Die Chruschtschow-Revolution verdammte das Ornament und setzte eine fast absolute Form der Moderne durch: riesige, serielle Bauten aus industriell vorgefertigten Elementen.[1] Und es gab eine vierte Revolution. Sie fand in den Jahren nach 1990 statt und steht ihren Vorgängern an Radikalität in nichts nach. Sie erfolgte nicht per Dekret, sondern war in erster Linie eine Reaktion der Architektur auf den Kollaps des Sozialismus, der sich in der Sowjetunion sicher am stärksten auswirkte, mit seinen Ausläufern jedoch auch in Westeuropa spürbar war. Denn auch dort wurden sozialdemokratische Planungsgrundsätze, die nach dem Zweiten Weltkrieg den Städtebau beherrschten, zugunsten kapitalistischer Ansätze aufgegeben.

Papierarchitektur

Die vier Revolutionen sind sich in ihrer Ablehnung des jeweils Vorangegangen gleich. So geht es der vierten Revolution um eine Überwindung der sowjetischen Moderne, die von Chruschtschow in den Sechzigerjahren initiiert wurde. Doch die Auflehnung gegen diese Architektur reicht zurück in die Achtzigerjahre, als sich in der russischen Architektur eine Gegenbewegung formierte; die sogenannten Papierarchitekten. Eine beträchtliche Zahl junger russischer Architekten nahm damals erfolgreich an internationalen Wettbewerben teil, die zumeist von der Zeitschrift *The Japan Architect* organisiert wurden.[2] In ihren Arbeiten lehnten die Architekten die »Schöne Neue Welt« einer totalitären Moderne ab und plädierten stattdessen für eine romantische Welt voller Nostalgie, verklärten den Verfall und bemühten eine bedeutungsschwangere Metaphorik. Die internationale Architekturszene reagierte verblüfft. Zum ersten Mal seit der Ära des Konstruktivismus meldeten sich russische Architekten in der von postmodernen Themen dominierten internationalen Architekturdebatte wieder zu Wort. Als sich zehn Jahre später ein fundamentaler politischer Systemwechsel abzeichnete, rechnete alle Welt nicht von ungefähr mit einer neuen Architektur aus dem Osten – einer Renaissance, die in etwa mit der frischen Blüte der spanischen Architektur nach Francos Tod vergleichbar wäre. Diese Erwartungen haben sich nicht erfüllt – mit einer Ausnahme: In Nischni Nowgorod, einer großen Industriestadt 400 Kilometer östlich von Moskau, die früher Gorki hieß und im Westen vor allem als Verbannungsort des sowjetischen Dissidenten Andrej Sacharow bekannt wurde, entwickelte sich in den Neunzigerjahren eine neue Architektur-Strömung, die sich den Prinzipien der Vierten Revolution verschrieben hatte: Privatinitiative, Formenvielfalt und Gestaltungsfreiheit.

Das Wunder von Nischni Nowgorod

Dass diese Revolution ausgerechnet in der tiefen russischen Provinz stattfand, ist kein Zufall. Denn dort unterdrückte das zentralistische Sowjetregime vor allem im Bereich der Archi-

Temple-City
by I. Galimov, 1988 (left)
Stairway to Heaven
by M. Filippov, 1996 (right)
Stadt-Tempel,
Entwurf: I. Galimow,
1988 (links)
Stairway to Heaven,
Entwurf: M. Filippow,
1996 (rechts)

Garantiya Bank Building in
Nishny Novgorod, architects:
Alexander Kharitonov and
Yevgeny Pestov, 1995 (left)
Lukoil Office Building in
Nishny Novgorod, architects:
Valery Nikishin, Andrey
Roubtsov, Marina Sedova,
2000 (right)
Bankgebäude »Garantija«
in Nischni Nowgorod,
Architekten: Alexander Chari-
tonow und Evgenij Pestow,
1995 (links)
Bürogebäude »Lukoil« in
Nischni Nowgorod,
Architekten: Valeri Nikischin,
Andrei Rubtsow, Marina
Sedowa, 2000 (rechts)

tektur jeden abweichenden Impuls. Chruschtschows Vorstellungen von Industrialisierung und Standardisierung führten
dazu, dass außerhalb Moskaus nahezu alle Gebäude nach
vorgegebenen, in hauptstädtischen Planungsinstituten entwickelten Standardentwürfen errichtet werden mussten. Die
Aufgabe der Architekten vor Ort bestand ausschließlich darin, diese Standardentwürfe den jeweiligen Gegebenheiten
anzupassen. Als das kommunistische System mitsamt seiner
zentralistischen Wirtschaftsordnung zusammenbrach, nutz-
ten ehrgeizige Architekten die Gunst der Stunde und eröff-
neten ihre eigenen Büros. In Nischni Nowgorod entwickelte
sich sogar eine eigene Schule. Ihr Vordenker Aleksander
Kharitonow übernahm später die Leitung der Stadtpla-
nungsbehörde von Nischni Nowgorod.

Für die Stadtentwicklung bedeutete der ökonomische Wandel eine umfassende Umkehr. Zu Sowjetzeiten konzentrier-
te sich das Wachstum auf die städtische Peripherie, wo riesige Industriegebiete aus dem Boden gestampft wurden.
Unter den neuen Bedingungen einer kapitalistischen Markt-
wirtschaft hingegen gewann das jahrzehntelang vernachläs-
sigte Stadtzentrum rasant an Bedeutung. Nischni Nowgorod,
das in seinen zentralen Bereichen bis dahin zu einem Großteil aus verrotteten Holzbauten bestand, entwickelte sich zu
einem wichtigen Ort für Handel und Kommunikation. Die
längst überfällige Rekonstruktion des Zentrums wurde mit
den neuen Ansprüchen an die Stadt verknüpft; ein grundle-
gender Umbau- und Erneuerungsprozess begann. Die hölzernen Bauten wichen neuen Gebäuden, und die Architekten zündeten nach mehr als 30 Jahren erzwungener
Beschränkung auf schmucklose Betonkisten ein stilistisches
Feuerwerk. Und auch die neuen wirtschaftlichen Bedingungen kamen der lange unterdrückten schöpferischen Freiheit

der Architekten zugute. Dank billiger Arbeitskräfte, reicher
Bauherren und dem Fehlen jedweder Regulierung setzte
sich eine fast exzessive Architektur durch: Mit Stuck, Klinker
und Farbe wurden alle erdenklichen Wünsche wahr. In
gewisser Weise wurde der Eklektizismus des 19. Jahrhunderts noch einmal durchgespielt, allerdings mit dem bedeu-
tenden Unterschied, dass sich der aktuelle Wiedergänger
nicht allein auf die Historie bezog, sondern auch in der zeitgenössischen Architektur seine Vorbilder suchte. Neben
einer Palladio-Villa und einem Bankgebäude im Stil des Art
Nouveau wurde so ein Bürohochhaus frei nach Portzamparc
platziert, während direkt gegenüber eine neo-modernisti-
sche Shopping Mall entstand. Ihren Höhepunkt feierte die
Architektur Nischni Nowgorods in der zweiten Hälfte der
Neunzigerjahre. Ihr Ende als Architektur-Hauptstadt Russlands markiert der Tod von Alexander Charitonow, der im
Jahre 2000 bei einem Autounfall ums Leben kam. Ohne seinen charismatischen *Spiritus rector* konnte sich das schil-
lernde Baugeschehen in Nischni Nowgorod nicht mehr
gegen die wachsende Bedeutung Moskaus behaupten.[3]

Das post-sowjetische Moskau

Doch wenn Nischni Nowgorod in den Neunzigerjahren die
Architekturhauptstadt Russlands war – was passierte während dieser Zeit in Moskau? Als ökonomisches und kulturel-
les Zentrum der ehemaligen Sowjetunion hätte Moskau
eigentlich die besten Voraussetzungen gehabt, als bedeutende Adresse einer neuen, post-totalitären Architektur zu reüs-
sieren. Doch genau das geschah nicht. Und paradoxerweise
ist die zentrale Stellung Moskaus der entscheidende Grund
dafür. Die Moskauer Architekten mussten im Zuge des Sys-

Dom Mucha Residential
Building in Samara by
Leonid Kuderov, 1995 (left)
Residential Building in
Samara by Leonid Kuderov,
2002 (right)
Wohngebäude »Dom
Mucha« in Samara, Architekt:
Leonid Kuderow, 1995 (links)
Wohngebäude in Samara,
Architekt: Leonid Kuderow,
2002 (rechts)

temwechsels, anders als ihre Kollegen in der Provinz, zunächst beträchtliche Einbußen ihrer Macht hinnehmen. Leiteten sie früher Bauvorhaben in der ganzen Sowjetunion, beschränkte sich ihr Einflussbereich nun allein auf Moskau. Darüber hinaus war Moskau eine vergleichsweise wohlhabende Stadt, die sich ein riesiges und zentral kontrolliertes Planungs- und Baukombinat nach sowjetischem Vorbild leisten konnte, während in vielen anderen Städten solche Strukturen durch kleinere Architekturbüros und einzelne Bauunternehmen ersetzt wurden. In Moskau wurde die Vierte Revolution daher auf die gleiche Weise in Angriff genommen wie alle anderen vorher: das Paradigma der Moderne wurde auf Anordnung von oben durch ein anderes abgeschafft. Parole: Historizismus. Symptomatisch für diese Art und Weise steht das wichtigste Architekturereignis im Moskau jener Jahre: der Bau der Erlöserkathedrale. Sie entstand als exakte Kopie des 1883 unter Zar Nikolai I. errichteten Sakralbaus, der 1931 von Stalin zerstört wurde, um Platz für den nie vollendeten, verhassten Sowjetpalast zu schaffen. Für die neuen Planungen der Nachwendezeit kamen nicht, wie man naiv hätte erwarten können, die in den Achtzigerjahren international anerkannten Papier-Architekten zum Zuge, sondern jene Planer aus den städtischen Baubehörden, die vordem die berüchtigten sowjetischen Betonkästen realisierten. Sie hatten sich rasch neu orientiert und gerierten sich nun als Protagonisten des klassischen Bauens.

Auch die Proteste von politischen Aktivisten der Perestroika gegen den Abriss der historischen Stadt prallten an der allmächtigen Bürokratie einfach ab. In Wirklichkeit bedeutete die Einführung der Demokratie eine Stärkung des bürokratischen Apparats, der nach wie vor einen beträchtlichen Einfluss auf den Planungsprozess geltend macht. Am besten zeigt sich das demokratische Niveau der Entscheidungsprozesse in dem Umstand, dass der sogenannte »gesellschaftliche Rat«, der die Meinung sowohl der Öffentlichkeit wie auch der »kreativen Intellektuellen« zu neuen städtischen Entwicklungen ventilieren soll, in Wirklichkeit vollständig unter dem Diktat von Bürgermeister Jurji Luschkow steht. Denn er – so die lakonische Rechtfertigung – wurde schließlich vom Volk gewählt und repräsentiert demzufolge auch dessen Ansichten. Gleichzeitig verbinden die städtischen Behörden mit vielen Projekten auch vitale wirtschaftliche Interessen.

Dies gilt nicht nur für öffentliche Gebäude wie Theater, Museen, Sportstätten usw., sondern auch für Einkaufszentren, Wohn- und Bürogebäude. Viele Architekten haben mit einer Situation zu tun, in der Bauherr, Genehmigungsbehörde und nicht selten auch noch die Baufirma zu einer einzigen, großen städtischen Holding gehören (zu der natürlich auch der Architekt selbst oft gehört): ein kommunistisches Modell, das Willkürentscheidungen aus wirtschaftlichen oder politischen Interessen viel Spielraum bietet.[4] Während in vielen Ländern gerade Aufträge der öffentlichen Hand eine ideale Möglichkeit bieten, interessante Architektur zu realisieren, ist in Moskau das Gegenteil der Fall: Je stärker ein Projekt mit den Kommunalbehörden assoziiert ist, desto schlechter ist die Architektur. Qualität findet man hingegen bei privaten Investoren. Natürlich nicht bei allen: Jene, die auf ihre Beziehungen zur städtischen Regierung setzen, mühen sich im Allgemeinen, dass ihre Projekte auch dem Bürgermeister gefallen. Dies gilt besonders für den Projektentwickler Don-Stroi, den »Triumf Palas« errichtet hat – das höchste Wohnhaus Europas im Stil der Stalinistischen Wolkenkratzer aus den Fünfzigerjahren. Es gibt auch Pro-

English Quarter Residential Complex in Moscow by Mikhail Belov, Project 2005
Wohnquartier »Englisches Viertel« in Moskau, Architekt: Michail Below, Projekt 2005

jektentwickler, die einen anderen Ansatz verfolgen und ihr Angebot vornehmlich auf Büros für Privatfirmen sowie Wohnungen für Russlands neue Oberschicht beschränken. Sie arbeiten mit bestimmten Moskauer Unternehmen, die in der Lage sind, qualitativ anspruchsvolle und zeitgemäße Architekturdienstleistungen zu erbringen. Leute wie Kiselow und Partner, Asadow Studio, Rezerv, ABD, Michail Khasanow und Ostoschenka starteten in den Neunzigerjahren aus dem Nichts und haben sich mittlerweile als große private Architekturbüros fest etabliert. Der Stil ihrer Arbeit entspricht der Professionalität, mit der sich diese Büros auf dem Markt etabliert haben: eine kontextbezogene Moderne, die ohne die Frivolitäten der Postmoderne und jenen für internationale Architektur typischen experimentellen Ehrgeiz auskommt. Das interessanteste Büro ist wahrscheinlich Ostoschenka unter der Leitung von Aleksander Skokan. Das Büro heißt wie der Stadtbezirk, in dem die bereits erwähnte Erlöserkathedrale steht und wurde noch zu Zeiten des alten Planungssystems gegründet, als jeder Stadtbezirk in der Verantwortung eines bestimmten Architekten lag. Zu Beginn der Neunzigerjahre hatte Skokan eine umfassende Strategie für die städtische Erneuerung jenes Bezirks ausgearbeitet, für den er bis dahin zuständig war. In der Tat finden sich dort die interessantesten Architekturprojekte; viele davon von Skokan, in jüngster Zeit auch oft von jüngeren Architekten.

Innenarchitektur

Die Entwicklung dieser großen privaten Architekturbüros wurde in den Neunzigerjahren von der Herausbildung und Etablierung eines neues Berufszweiges begleitet: dem des Innenarchitekten. Hintergrund dieses Trends ist der Um-

stand, dass alle neuen, für die neureichen Russen errichteten Wohngebäude ohne Innenraumkonzept entstehen.[5] Dabei handelt es sich weder um ein technisches noch ideologisches Spezifikum sondern um eine Wirklichkeit des Marktes. Als Mitte der Neunzigerjahre die ersten Wohnhäuser für die so genannte Elite angeboten wurden, stellten die Projektentwickler fest, dass die neuen Bewohner als erstes sämtliche Wände in den Wohnungen abreißen und ein neues Innenraumkonzept nach ihren individuellen Wünschen entwickeln ließen. Daher war es einfach billiger, die Wände gar nicht erst hochzuziehen. Doch weil die Käufer keine Ahnung hatten, wie eine 200 bis 300 Quadratmeter große, leere Fläche zu bespielen sei, gab es plötzlich die Nachfrage nach Innenarchitekten. Vor allem junge Architekten entdeckten hier eine Nische, in der sie für gutes Geld die Probleme einer wohlhabenden Klientel lösen konnten. Dies bedeutete für die Berufsgruppe der Architekten eine Spaltung in »ob'emschiki« und »interierschiki«. Ein typischer »ob'emschik« (wörtlich: jemand, der mit leerem Raum zu tun hat) ist älter als 40, hat in der Sowjetunion studiert, im alten System gearbeitet und verfügt nun über gute Kontakte zu den Behörden. Der Maßstab seiner Entwürfe ist selten detaillierter als 1:100. Ein typischer »interierschik« ist bedeutend jünger, arbeitet für private Auftraggeber und hat gute Kontakte zu Möbelhändlern und Einrichtungsspezialisten. Oft untersteht ihm auch eine eigene Bautruppe.

Resümierend lässt sich feststellen, dass die interessantesten architektonischen Projekte der Neunzigerjahre aus dem Bereich Innenarchitektur kamen, die dem Zugriff der Bürokratie und der Großbauindustrie sowjetischen Zuschnitts entzogen war. Die jungen Innenarchitekten hatten ihre berufliche Laufbahn zu einer Zeit begonnen, als Informatio-

Villa Project by architects gr.a+d, 2006

Villa, Architekten: gr.a+d, Projekt 2006

nen über das internationale Architekturgeschehen langsam zugänglich wurden, während die ältere Generation den Großteil ihrer Erfahrung in einer Ära der Abschottung gesammelt hat, als Informationen aus der kapitalistischen Welt praktisch nicht zu bekommen waren. Dieser Informationsvorsprung der jungen Architekten zusammen mit ausgesprochen solventen Bauherren, die bereit sind, eine gewaltige Summe in die individuelle Gestaltung ihrer privaten Wohnungen und Häuser zu investieren, bot ungeheure Möglichkeiten für Entwurf und Realisierung auch der ungewöhnlichsten Ideen. Viele der eigens angefertigten Möbel und Einrichtungsgegenstände in den Häusern dieser Klientel wären im Westen Europas unbezahlbar.

Die nächste Generation

Die interessanten Entwicklungen der vergangenen Jahre gehen auf den Wandel sowohl der Architekten als auch der Bauherren zurück. Innerhalb des Berufsstandes ist festzustellen, dass die Reservate der »ob'emschiki« zusehends von einer neuen Generation Architekten erobert werden, die wiederum aus zwei Fraktionen besteht: Zum einen gibt es da jene jungen Architekten, die ihre Erfahrungen in einem der um 1990 gegründeten, neuen großen Büros gesammelt haben und nun ein eigenes Unternehmen aufbauen; zum anderen gibt es die »interierschiki«, die über die Arbeit als Innenarchitekten für private Häuser und Wohnungen allmählich zu Aufträgen für Wohn- und Geschäftsbauten in der Stadt gekommen sind. Diese Architekten haben im Vergleich mit der älteren Generation von »ob'emschiki« mehrere Vorteile: sie müssen für die Qualität der freiberuflichen Architekten keine Lanze mehr brechen – das haben bereits die

Vorgänger für sie getan – und sie verfügen dank ihrer Tätigkeit als Assistenten, ausführende Architekten oder praktische Innenarchitekten über reichlich Praxiserfahrung am Bau. Ihre Kompetenzen werden von Projektentwicklern stark nachgefragt, die ähnlich wie die Architekten Erfahrungen gesammelt haben, viel gereist sind und verstanden haben, wie Architektur als Marketinginstrument funktioniert. In Moskau, wo es eine quantitativ beachtliche Kundengruppe gibt, die bereit ist, riesige Summen für ein exklusives Grundstück zu bezahlen (bis zu 15.000 Dollar pro Quadratmeter), strebt jeder Projektentwickler auf den Markt für Luxusapartments. Diese Situation führte auch zu einer gestiegenen Nachfrage nach ausländischen Architekten. So hat sich der Projektentwickler Capital Group einen Namen mit Projekten gemacht, die unter der Federführung von Erik van Egeraat, Zaha Hadid, Behnisch und Behnisch entstanden; aber auch Rem Koolhaas, SOM, Norman Foster und KPF arbeiten gegenwärtig an Projekten in Moskau.

In ihren Arbeiten beziehen sich die jungen »ob'emschiki« direkt auf die jüngsten internationalen Trends und setzen sich dadurch auch von ihren nicht ganz so aktuellen älteren Kollegen ab. Zu erwähnen sind hier vor allem Aleksej Kozyr (Arch Ch Studio), Aryapetow und Golovanow, Anton Nadtochi und Vera Butko (Atrium), Project Meganom, Sergej Skuratow und die Architektengruppe DNK.

Russische Architektur?

Obwohl (oder weil) die neue Generation in die internationale Architekturszene integriert ist, kann sie mit ihrer Arbeit den Anspruch eines besonderen Ansatzes derzeit noch nicht einlösen. Einer der Gründe dafür dürfte sein, dass es in

Hodynskoye Pole Development in Moscow by MNIIP Mosproyekt-4, 2001-2008
Stadtentwicklungsprojekt auf dem alten Flughafengelände »Chodinskoje Polje«, MNIIP Mosprojekt-4, 2001-2008

Russland in den vergangenen 15 Jahren keine wirkliche Architekturdebatte gab – alle waren damit beschäftigt, sich mit ihren Büros den neuen wirtschaftlichen Gegebenheiten anzupassen. Eine wichtige Ausnahme allerdings bildet Jewgeni Ass, der gern auch als einziger »europäischer« Architekt Russlands bezeichnet wird, und der mit seinen Publikationen und seiner wissenschaftlichen Lehre einen enormen Einfluss auf die jüngere Architektengeneration in Moskau hat. Um eine Architektur zu finden, die definitiv und erklärtermaßen »russisch« ist, muss man zurück zu den Papier-Architekten gehen. Obwohl die meisten dieser Generation inzwischen zum planerischen Tagesgeschäft übergegangen sind, beschäftigen sich einige mit der Weiterentwicklung jener Konzepte, die sie vor nunmehr 20 Jahren begannen. Nach wie vor ist das große Thema ihrer Arbeit der Umgang mit zeitgenössischer Architektur nach dem Desaster der sowjetischen Plattenbau-Moderne. Die Fundamentalisten, an deren Spitze die Moskauer Architekten Michail Fillippow und Ilja Utkin stehen, sind Verfechter der ewiggültigen klassischen Architektur und kommen mit ihrer Überzeugung den britischen und amerikanischen Adepten des Historismus wie Krier und Stern nahe. Allerdings ist ihr Ansatz melancholischer und betont die Verfalls-Qualität klassischer Architektur. Diese Position ist Stärke und Schwäche zugleich. Auf dem Papier sieht Verfall immer schön aus; die gebaute Realität bleibt diesen ästhetischen Reiz jedoch immer schuldig. Dennoch sind diese Arbeiten auch ein Ausdruck einer echten post-sowjetischen Melancholie, die sie darüber hinaus auch kraftvoller erscheinen lässt als ihre bürgerlichen Pendants aus dem Westen.

Daneben gibt es noch jene Architekten, die sich weniger auf die klassischen Aspekte des Verfalls, sondern auf die Unvoll-

kommenheit beziehen. Sie schöpfen ihre Inspiration hauptsächlich aus der kommunistischen Vergangenheit, gleichwohl nicht in ihrer offiziellen Lesart als rationales, logisches und arbeitsteiliges System. Sie beziehen sich vielmehr auf eine neben der offiziellen kommunistischen Menschengemeinschaft existierende Parallelwelt der Datscha, jenes aus Resten und Ausschuss der kommunistischen Industrieproduktion selbstgebauten Landhäuschens. Es ist die Welt privater Partys mit endlosen Diskussionen, der Möglichkeit (und Notwendigkeit) einer systemfernen Zuflucht innerhalb des Systems.[6] Die Ästhetik dieser Welt entspricht dem Surrealismus des *objet trouvé*.[7] Dieses Phänomen hat Sergej Malachow untersucht, der mehr als 200 dieser provisorischen Gebäude aus Residuen der Industrieproduktion sammelte und sie nun als Entwürfe präsentiert: mit Zeichnungen, Modellen und einer Geschichte, die er zur Erklärung dieser Artefakte erfunden hat. Ein anderer Architekt, der sich von dieser Unvollkommenheit inspirieren lässt, ist Alexander Jermolajew, Gründer des architektonischen Formentheaters. Er fand diese Qualität in den Traditionen der Holzarchitektur, die typisch für den Norden Russlands ist. Seine Schüler Savinkin/Kusmin zählen zu den erfolgreichsten Architekten der Gegenwart. Es war eine Arbeit von ihnen, die in internationalen Fachmagazinen als erstes russisches Projekt seit den Siebzigerjahren publiziert wurde. Als weiterer Repräsentant dieser Richtung gilt die Gruppe Art-Blya, die in ihren Arbeiten eine kindliche Naivität exponiert. Der entscheidende Vorreiter ist jedoch Alexander Brodski. Seine Arbeiten – temporär, roh und unfertig – bringen das Wesen dieser Architektur der Unvollkommenheit kongenial zum Ausdruck, die ihrerseits eine Kritik der sowjetischen Moderne und gleichzeitig auch der modernen Architektur des Wes-

tens ist. Natürlich sind seine Entwürfe vor allem romantisch und auf lange Sicht vermutlich unrealisierbar; sie halten den Kriterien der Nachhaltigkeit ebenso wenig stand wie der Prüfung ihrer Wirtschaftlichkeit. Das Gleiche gilt wahrscheinlich auch für Russland. Es wird sich ändern. Die Frage ist nur, ob es ein Wandel zum Besseren sein wird.

1 1954 hielt Chruschtschow vor dem Bau- und Architekturkongress der Sowjetunion eine Rede über moderne Strategien in der Architektur. Die englische Übersetzung dieser Rede wurde erstmalig publiziert in: Microrayon – Post-soviet housing districts (Project Russia 25), Moscow/Amsterdam 2002.

2 Für einen vollständigen Überblick dieser Wettbewerbe vgl.: Battlefield Russia. International architectural competitions. (Project Russia 29), Moscow/Amsterdam 2004.

3 Für einen Überblick über die Architektur in Nischni Nowgorod vgl.: The Nishni Novgorod School (Project Russia 4), Moscow/Amsterdam 1998.

4 Eine Analyse dieses Prozesses bietet der Aufsatz Capitalist Realism. (Project Russia 24), Moscow/Amsterdam 2002.

5 The Free Plan (Project Russia 20), Moscow/Amsterdam 2001.

6 Der Kommunismus konnte aufgrund seines utopischen Charakters nicht funktionieren. Vieles blieb einfach unerledigt. Im Vergleich dazu ist eine kapitalistische Gesellschaft viel totalitärer. So berichtete ein Architekt aus Sankt Petersburg: »Als ich zum ersten Mal in den Westen kam, war ich überrascht, wie ideologisch es dort zuging. Jeder wusste immer genau, was richtig war.«

7 vgl. Countryside. Between bohemia and bourgeoisie (Project Russia 21), Moscow/Amsterdam 2001.

Kurort Ski Resort Project Development by Mikhail Khazanov, 2004 (left)
Railroad Covering Project, Belorussky Station in Moscow by Alexander Asadov, 2006 (right)
Künstliches Ski-Resort »Kurort«, Studie: Michail Chazanow, 2004 (links)
Überbauung der Bahngleise am Weißrussischen Bahnhof in Moskau, Studie: Alexander Asadow, 2006 (rechts)

Neue Architektur in Russland

Neue Architektur in Russland

Philipp Meuser

Als Zar Peter I. vor über 300 Jahren mit Sankt Petersburg eine neue Hauptstadt gründete und zu ihrer Erbauung in der Folgezeit berühmte Baumeister aus ganz Europa einlud, erwies er sich als Herrscher mit Weitblick. Architekten u. a. aus Italien, den Niederlanden und Deutschland errichteten in der neuen Ostsee-Metropole ein städtebauliches Ensemble, das bis heute Besucher aus der gesamten Welt anlockt. Freilich fiel die Entscheidung Peters des Großen eher aus pragmatischen denn aus baukulturellen Überlegungen. Doch durch diese wie auch andere politische Entscheidungen des Zaren rückte das Riesenreich im Osten deutlich an Europa heran. Auch die russische Baukunst wurde durch die ausländischen Ideen geradezu beflügelt. Bis weit in das russische Reich hinein sollte die Formensprache der neuen Hauptstadt wirken.[1]

Die Europäisierung von Sankt Petersburg durch den barocken Architekturimport hat den Formenkanon der russischen Baukunst insgesamt nachhaltig beeinflusst. Aber er blieb eben auch Episode und von rein staatsrepräsentativem Charakter. Die Architektur war in ihrer Pracht auffallender Indikator eines Landes, das zum Zeitpunkt der westeuropäischen Industrialisierung noch in einer Feudalstruktur mit den Säulen Zar, Kirche, Adel und den damit verbundenen, inzwischen aber überholten Spielregeln des Herrschens und Beherrschens verankert war. Erst die Oktoberrevolution von 1917 beseitigte dieses Gesellschaftssystem.

Wir halten uns vor Augen, dass sich die junge Sowjetunion von Anfang an zwischen den Stühlen von Tradition und Progression entwickelte. Eindeutig führte die Revolution Russland in einem gewaltigen Schub an die europäische Zeitrechnung. Dies jedoch im wörtlichen und im übertragenen Sinne: erstens durch die Abschaffung des Julianischen Kalenders zugunsten des in Resteuropa bereits seit 1582 gültigen Gregorianischen Kalenders und zweitens durch die Ermordung der gesamten Zarenfamilie in Jekaterinburg. Beides erfolgte 1918. Von hier aus gab es kein Zurück mehr. Mit der von der Revolution eingeleiteten europäischen Zeitrechnung sollte der städtebaulich vom Zarentum einst eingeleitete Anschluss an das moderne Europa nun auch gesamtgesellschaftlich vollzogen werden. Schließlich war die Oktoberrevolution nicht nur eine politische, sondern eben auch eine kulturelle Revolution. Die modernen Künstler, die gegen die »etablierte Kunstauffassung im Zarenreich rebellierten, fühlten sich jenen verbunden, die das ganze Gesellschaftssystem als überkommen ansahen. Kommunisten und Modernisten einte ein fast schicksalhafter Glaube an die Möglichkeiten von Technik und Wissenschaft, die menschlichen Verhältnisse grundlegend umzugestalten«.[2]

Die Abschaffung der Leibeigenschaft, die Zwangskollektivierung und die breit angelegte Alphabetisierung gehörten zu diesen Veränderungen des alltäglichen Lebens. Die Industrialisierung und Technisierung flankierten darüber hinaus den Aufbau des neuen politischen Systems, was nicht zuletzt in Lenins berühmtem Schlagwort gipfelte, Kommunismus sei die Summe aus Sowjetmacht und Elektrifizierung.

Sowjetische Avantgarde: neue Architektur für eine neue Gesellschaft

Begeistert stellte El Lissitzky, der Protagonist des russischen Konstruktivismus, 1929 in programmatischen Zeilen fest: »Die Geburt der Maschine ist der Anfang der technischen Revolution. Die Technik hat heute nicht allein die soziale und wirtschaftliche, sondern auch die ästhetische Entwicklung

revolutioniert und die Grundelemente des neuen Bauens bestimmt. Im Oktober 1917 beginnt unsere Revolution und damit ein neues Blatt in der Geschichte der menschlichen Gesellschaft. Die Grundelemente unserer Architektur gehören dieser sozialen und nicht der technischen Revolution an.«[3] Aus dieser Diktion ist der Einfluss des Malers und Kunsthistorikers Kasimir Malewitsch herauszulesen, der als einer der führenden Vertreter der russischen Moderne seine konstruktivistische Kunst als Ausdrucksform des revolutionären und technischen Zeitalters forcierte. Malewitsch war es auch gewesen, der den 1919 an der Kunsthochschule in Witebsk als Professor lehrenden Lissitzky für die konstruktivistische Bewegung gewonnen hatte. El Lissitzky leitete dann ab 1921 an der staatlichen Kunsthochschule in Moskau die Architekturabteilung, bevor er zeitweise ins westeuropäische Ausland ging. *Neues Bauen* und Kommunismus, das musste als logische Verbindung erscheinen, als Selbstverpflichtung des einen gegenüber dem anderen.

Daraus leitete Lissitzky 1929 folgenden gesellschaftlichen Auftrag der Architektur ab: »Die soziale Entwicklung führt zu der Aufhebung des Gegensatzes Stadt–Land. Die Stadt ist bestrebt, die Natur bis in ihr Zentrum hineinzubeziehen und durch die Industrialisierung das Land auf eine höhere Kulturstufe zu bringen. Wir müssen heute sehr sachlich, sehr praktisch und ganz unromantisch sein, um die übrige Welt einzuholen und zu überholen.«[4] Das erinnert nicht nur an die Proklamationen des Zentralkomitees der KPdSU, sondern auch in groben Zügen an die Postulate der deutschen Avantgarde, die in der Weimarer Republik, wenn auch unter weniger dramatischen Umbruchserscheinungen, die Morgenröte einer lichten, demokratischen, einer neuen Gesellschaft erblickten. Diese Gesellschaft hatte sich eines alten muffigen Geschichtsmantels entledigt und für deren Neuaufbau sich selbst als Architekten ernannt. »Neue Gehäuse für eine neue Gesellschaft« zu errichten, wie Hans Scharoun 1947 formulierte, das war es, was die Vertreter der Frühmoderne in Deutschland in den Zwanzigerjahren ebenso umgetrieben hatte, wie deren russische Kollegen in der jungen Sowjetunion. Russland hatte in jenen Jahren des gesellschaftlichen Umbruchs den Anschluss an eine künstlerische Internationale geschafft, die sich jetzt nur noch wirtschaftlich manifestieren musste.

Die Protagonisten der europäischen und hier insbesondere der deutschen Moderne garantierten dabei nicht nur architektonische und städtebauliche Unterstützung für das Gelingen der kulturellen Revolution, sondern auch gesellschaftsmoralische Rückendeckung hinsichtlich der alles entscheidenden Frage der Besitzverhältnisse: »Die schlimmste Fessel bleibt das unsittliche Recht des privaten Eigentums am Boden. Ohne die Befreiung des Bodens aus dieser privaten Versklavung kann niemals ein gesunder, entwicklungsfähiger und im Sinne der Allgemeinheit wirtschaftlicher Städtebau entstehen«, schrieb nicht Lenin, nicht Stalin, sondern Walter Gropius 1931 und stellte in einem Nachsatz fest: »Diese wichtigste Grundforderung hat allein und ohne Einschränkung die UdSSR erfüllt und damit den Weg zum modernen Städtebau freigemacht.«[5] Unmissverständlich machte der Gründer des Staatlichen Bauhauses Weimar aus der von ihm postulierten Vorbildrolle der Sowjetunion ebenso wenig einen Hehl wie er in und mit dem Buch *Neues Bauen in der UdSSR* gleichzeitig »die Arbeit von Ernst May als Organisator des Bauwesens und als praktischer Städtebauer in Sowjetrußland« zu würdigen gedachte. War also für das revolutionäre Russland die architektonische Moderne Vor-

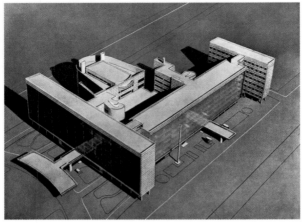
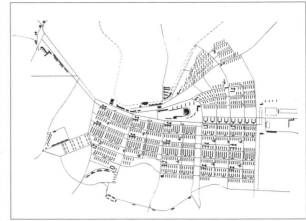

bild und Anlass zu einem regelrechten Anschauungstou-
rismus im Westen, so war umgekehrt für die Vertreter insbesondere der deutschen Pioniere der neuen Sachlichkeit
Russland ein gesellschaftspolitischer Vorreiter für die Boden-
reform in Deutschland. Ein Versuch, den politisch entmach-
teten Adel 1926 per Volksentscheid auch besitzrechtlich zu
entthronen, scheiterte jedoch an der erforderlichen 50-Pro-
zent-Hürde.

Die am 30. Dezember 1922 verfassungsmäßig gegründete
Sowjetunion, der 1918 die Gründung der Russischen Sozialistischen Föderativen Sowjetrepublik als neuer Kernstaat
vorausgegangen war, wurde zu einem Experimentierfeld
internationaler Architekten. Darunter waren Ernst May,
Charles Édouard Jeanneret-Gris alias Le Corbusier, Bruno
Taut und selbst US-Amerikaner wie etwa der Industriearchitekt und Erbauer der Ford-Werke, Albert Kahn. Dies gipfelte
in der grotesken Situation, dass die Architektenelite des
kapitalistischen Westens zumindest in Teilen ostwärts zog,
um Aufbauhilfe in einem neuen Staat zu betreiben, dessen
Führung von Anfang an keinen Hehl aus der Zerstörung der
kapitalistischen Welt gemacht hatte. Auch wenn angesichts
des Ausbleibens der schnell erwarteten Weltrevolution erst
einmal auf »friedliche Koexistenz« (Lenin) und auf die Vor-
bildfunktion des Sowjetstaates durch die Verwirklichung des
kommunistischen Gesellschaftsmodells im eigenen Land
(Stalin) gesetzt wurde, so war die Weltrevolution und mit ihr
der gerechte Krieg gegen den »europäischen Imperia-
lismus« (Lenin) nicht aufgehoben, sondern vorerst nur
aufgeschoben.

Die gesellschaftliche Aufgabe für den inneren Aufbau laute-
te: Anschluss an den technischen Standard der westlichen
Welt. Für diesen wirtschaftlichen Gewaltakt stand in der

Sowjetunion die so genannte »Neue Ökonomische Politik«
(NÖP) in Gestalt einer Industrialisierung und Mechanisie-
rung des gesamten Wirtschaftslebens vom Fließband bis
zum Acker. Entsprechend zitierte die »Bauwelt« Ernst May,
damals Stadtrat in Frankfurt, vor seinem Aufbruch zu neuen
Ufern an der Moskwa wie folgt: »Neue Städte müssen gebaut werden, andere umgebaut werden. Die interessanteste
und schwerste Aufgabe wird sein: Die Schaffung ganz neuer
Städte. Diese Städte werden in erster Linie der Sitz der
Eisen- und Stahlindustrie sein, die neu geschaffen werden
soll.«[6] May reiste am 1. September 1930 mit einem 21-köpfi-
gen Team nach Moskau.

Sozialistischer Realismus:
neue Städte im alten Format

Ernst May hatte an einem Wettbewerb für den Aufbau des
Schwerindustriekombinats Magnitogorsk teilgenommen,
das im ersten Fünfjahresplan (1929-33) als Modellstadt und
Vorbild vieler weiterer Retortenstädte dienen sollte. Magnitogorsk, das war im Prinzip eine Werksiedlung westlicher
Prägung, nur eben ins Riesenhafte gesteigert; eine Pionier-
stadt an der östlichen Seite des südlichen Urals. Die andere
Herausforderung lag in der Erweiterung vorhandener Städte, mit dem Ziel, die armseligen Agglomerationen des Indus-
trieproletariats in sicheren Wohnraum zu verwandeln sowie
die Stadt auf die völlig neuen Bevölkerungsströme vorzube-
reiten. Moskau war hierfür modellhaft und galt spätestens
nach der Einweihung der Metro im Jahr 1935 als sozialistische Welthauptstadt.

Zugleich wurden ab 1931 die Grenzen des »weltpolitischen
Experiments«, wie May den Aufbau der Sowjetunion

Palace of the Soviets
in Moscow by Boris Jofan,
Vladimir Shuko und Vladimir
Gelfreich, project 1943-45
Palast der Sowjets in Moskau,
Architekten: Boris Jofan,
Wladimir Schtschuko und
Wladimir Gelfreich, Projekt
1943-1945

bezeichnete, im Städtebau immer deutlicher. Damals forderte Stalins bevorzugter Stadtplaner und dessen rechte Hand im Zentralkomitee, Lasar M. Kaganowitsch, »die alten Städte zu rekonstruieren und die neuen – wie Magnitogorsk – gemäßigt modern zu gestalten.«[7] Kaganowitsch hatte damit die Leitlinie im sowjetischen Städtebau umrissen, die 1934 geradewegs in Andrej Schdanows Verkündung des »Sozialistischen Realismus« als sowjetpatriotische Geschmacksdirektive mündete. Damit war es mit der Freiheit des kreativen Kulturgeistes vorbei, und somit war auch der Wirkungsspielraum der modernen Avantgarde beendet, deren Architekten der politischen Zeitläufte wegen bis dahin kaum Zeugnisse hinterlassen hatte.

Ähnlich wie in Deutschland hatten die Protagonisten der Frühmoderne gemessen an ihren hoch fliegenden Idealen wenig verwirklichen können. Das meiste davon blieben papierene Träume. Der Moderne war in der Sowjetunion noch weniger als in Deutschland gesellschafts- und kulturpolitisch nur ein Intermezzo vergönnt. Ähnlich wie in der stalinistischen Sowjetunion wurden auch im nationalsozialistischen Deutschland die Grundprinzipien der Moderne mit Traditionen eines so genannten Heimatstils vermengt und mittels traditionellen Städtebautheorien zu einem heroischen Ganzen gefügt, nach der Prämisse: rational in der Materialverarbeitung, aber geschmackvoll und gewaltig in der Darstellung. Auch hier sind die Parallelen zwischen Stalinismus und Hitlerismus entgegen der Thesen des Historikerstreits der Achtzigerjahre, wonach der Nationalsozialismus gegenüber dem Kommunismus das extreme Gegenteil gewesen sei, äußerst verblüffend. Vergleiche stalinistischer Hauptstadtplanung mit Speers Konzepten für den Umbau Berlins zur künftigen Welthauptstadt Germania zei-

gen frappierende Ähnlichkeit in Gestus und Aussagewillen bis hin zur ideologischen Definition von Architektur an sich. Diesbezüglich steht einfach nur fest, dass die Sowjetunion unter Stalin das Projekt der sozialistischen Stadt weitgehend verwirklichen und nach dem Zweiten Weltkrieg dann sogar bis zur Elbe exportieren konnte. In Berlin ist dafür die heutige Karl-Marx-Allee als deutschlandweit längstes Baudenkmal steinernes Zeugnis und zugleich Fragment einer stalinistischen Hauptstadtplanung an der Spree.

Die ablehnende Haltung gegenüber der funktionalen Sachlichkeit lag ursächlich auf der Hand. Eine Architektur der Moderne in Reinkultur und deren »städtebauliche Ausdruck einer in wirtschaftlich und geistig selbständige Individuen atomisierten bürgerlichen Gesellschaft« widersprach in der Sowjetunion den sozialen Voraussetzungen und wurde seitens der neuen Nomenklatura, die unter veränderten Vorzeichen (Hammer und Sichel plus roter Stern statt doppelköpfiger Adler und Krone) die Herrschaftsprinzipen des Zarenreiches übernommen hatte, als mit dem Selbstverständnis des neuen Staates unvereinbar erklärt. Das kommunistische Russland ist so gesehen mit einer Firma vergleichbar, die ihre Belegschaftshierarchie neu ordnet und sich ein neues Label gibt. In der Unternehmensführung aber bleibt sie autoritär und pflegt einen aggressiven Staatskapitalismus.

Der »Sozialistische Realismus« war die säkulare Antwort auf alle dem Volk bis dahin geraubten Gewissheiten – inklusive der religiösen. Die Künstler hatten sich darum fortan als »Ingenieure der menschlichen Seele« (Schdanow) zu verstehen. »Verachtet Eure alten Meister nicht!«, war der populäre Ausspruch, mit dem der wesentlich für die sowjetische Kulturpolitik verantwortliche und einflussreiche Kultur- und Literaturwissenschaftler Anatoli W. Lunatscharski die neue

Linie begründete. Die Beobachtungen entsprachen denen von Bruno Taut, der 1929 über die Lage der Architektur in Russland festhielt: »Der Zweck der russischen Kunst ist, den unsichtbaren Atem des Vaters durch Fühlbares und Sichtbares auszudrücken. In Russland spielt sich das Suchen nach der Quelle in sehr dramatischen Formen ab, doch sieht man an Wettbewerben und ihren Ausgängen, wie immer erneut zwischen der Gestaltung des Zwecks und dem Durst nach Schönheit gerungen wird.« Bruno Taut nennt beispielgebend den Wettbewerb der Lenin-Bibliothek in Moskau, bei dem sich die Jury gegen einen Glasbau und für einen traditionellen Bau entschieden hatte, um »die Arbeit des Akademikers« darzustellen und »dabei bewusst Opfer in der praktischen Anlage«[8] habe bringen müssen. Geradezu überraschend postuliert Taut als Vertreter der neuen Sachlichkeit: »Die Aufgabe der russischen Architektur wird darin liegen, die neuen Einsichten mit der tatsächlichen Erdverbundenheit des Russentums in Harmonie zu bringen.«

Nichts anderes schwebte den Geschmackskommissaren im Zentralkomitee mit ihrer Losung vom »Sozialistischen Realismus« vor. Die daraus folgende gestalterische Gratwanderung kommentierte 1933 spöttisch die in Frankfurt erscheinende Zeitschrift *Die Neue Stadt*: »Man ehrt die Klassik, rechtfertigt den Klassizismus (Lunatscharski) und möchte gleichzeitig Le Corbusier, den Poeten des Konstruktivismus nicht ganz missen. Überdies Ökonomik und Standardisierung um jeden Preis! Man möchte das eine und muss das andere; eine allgemeine Unsicherheit ist das Resultat.«[9] Der scheinbare Widerspruch offenbart eine Dialektik, die in der Kunstdoktrin des »Sozialistischen Realismus« dennoch eine wenn auch eigenartige Synthese fand. Gemäßigt modern bauen hieß etwa, dass Ernst May[10] den Generalplan für die

neue Industriestadt Magnitogorsk plante und der amerikanische Industriearchitekt Kahn die Gebäude baute.

Rekonstruktion, das hieß, dass traditionsorientierte Stadtplaner wie der Kölner Kommunist Kurt Meyer, die unter Oberbürgermeister Konrad Adenauer entwickelten Pläne für Köln nun auf sozialistische Verhältnisse in Moskau schablonierte. Das KPD-Mitglied Meyer[11] verließ Köln 1930, nachdem Adenauer diesen als künftigen Stadtbaumeister zum parteipolitischen Stillhalten hatte verpflichten wollen. Hans Schmidt kommentierte die Situation der Protagonisten der Moderne 1932 in Sowjetrussland, nachdem die modernen Entwürfe im Wettbewerb für den Moskauer Sowjetpalast in der Jury durchgefallen waren, wie folgt: »Es ist nicht einmal verwunderlich, wenn dieselben jungen Architekten, die jahrelang auf Watmanpapier das Vorbild Le Corbusiers mit Glasfassaden und Dachgärten zu Tode ritten, heute auf demselben Watmanpapier unter Leitung der alten Meister der Architektur Fassaden mit klassischer Schönheit entwerfen.«[12] Eine verständliche Reaktion der Akteure, die erkannten, dass sie, die sich doch als künstlerische Vorhut einer politischen Avantgarde sahen, nicht mehr gefragt waren. Der aufstrebenden Moderne hatte eine autoritäre Parteidoktrin in der jungen Sowjetunion die Basis entzogen. Andererseits mobilisierte die neue Kunstdoktrin die Schaffenskraft der alten einheimischen Architektenschaft aus der Zarenzeit.

Vor diesem Hintergrund entstanden unter Stalins Herrschaft Gebäude, die – ungeachtet ihrer Wirtschaftlichkeit – Wegmarken einer gemäßigten Moderne bildeten. Bis heute ist diese stalinistische Architektur kaum als ernst zu nehmender Beitrag einer internationalen Debatte anerkannt. Aus Unkenntnis kommt eine Bewertung selten über den Spott »Zuckerbäcker-Stil« oder »diktatorische Geschmacksverir-

rung« hinaus. Eine seriöse Einordnung in die Baugeschichte des 20. Jahrhunderts steht nach wie vor aus, auch wenn Harald Bodenschatz und Christiane Post mit ihrem 2003 erschienenen Standardwerk *Städtebau im Schatten Stalins* einen viel versprechenden Anfang gemacht haben. Dort lassen beide in ihrem Vorwort wissen, dass die Ignoranz der westlichen Bauhistoriker der Bedeutung der stalinistischen Architektur für den Städtebau kaum gerecht werde. Dasselbe gilt für die architektonische Entwicklung. Provokativ ließe sich die These aufstellen, die heutige russische Architektur in Fortführung ihres sowjetischen Erbes sei in Europa die am stärksten auf Traditionen aufbauende Baukunst.

Kalter Krieg: Architektur zwischen
serieller Wirklichkeit und handgezeichneter Vision

Der russische Bauhaus-Ableger des Konstruktivismus sowie der sowjetische Funktionalismus als dessen Nachkriegsspielart einer westlichen Moderne, der unter Nikita Chruschtschows Leitmotiv »höhere Qualität bei niedrigeren Kosten« ab Mitte der Fünfzigerjahre einsetzte, könnten demnach als erfolglose Entwicklungen gewertet werden, die zunächst vom Stalinismus und heute vom neo-russischen Regionalismus abgelöst wurden. Das greift jedoch zu kurz. Der sowjetische Funktionalismus war eine spartanische Variante des Konstruktivismus – eine sozialistische Spielart des westlichen International Style, mit dem pragmatischen Zweck, möglichst preiswert möglichst viel Wohnraum zu schaffen und zugleich als künstlerische Ausdrucksform eine kulturelle Einheit nach innen zu zementieren. Zwischen Minsk und Wladiwostok entstanden fortan nahezu identische Bauten, deren Genehmigung in Moskau erteilt und zentral auch mit

einer Seriennummer versehen wurde. Die Rationalisierung im Planen und Bauen – eine Idee ihrer Zeit in Ost wie in West – führte in der Sowjetunion zum Verschwinden des Bauhandwerks. Als Westeuropa auch aus wirtschaftlichen Gründen zur konventionellen Bauweise zurückkehrte, war die serielle Bauweise in der Sowjetunion Gefangener ihrer selbst geworden. Die Architektur war auch nach außen ein Mittel künstlerischer Selbstdarstellung im Ringen um die Herrschaft über eine im Kalten Krieg erstarrte, sich aber unter dem modernen technischen Zivilisationsdruck abseits aller politischen Klüfte rasant vereinheitlichende Welt. Plötzlich galt die Moderne mit den sattsam bekannten Motiven des rationalen Bauens bis hin zur industriellen Massenfertigung von Architektur als staatstragend und wurde in dieser Weise ähnlich wie im Westen bis zur groben Verhässlichung überstrapaziert. Russland als Kernland einer politischen Welthälfte hatte den Westen einmal mehr zum Maßstab genommen.

Die poststalinistische Sowjetunion erstarrte im Laufe der Ära Leonid Breschnews in ihrem nüchternen Funktionalismus, der die »westlichen Desaster der Containerarchitektur noch übertroffen«[13] hatte, um nach 1991 wiederum alles daran zu setzen, im Zeitraffer die versäumt geglaubten westlichen Kulturphasen nachträglich zu durchleben. Dieses Psychogramm einer zu spät gekommen geglaubten und stets um sich selbst kreisenden Nation ist auch uns Deutschen ja nicht fremd. Nach dem Zerfall der Sowjetunion ist es nun der Neotraditionalismus, der als eine der Hauptströmungen der zeitgenössischen russischen Architektur auszumachen ist. Dies hat verschiedene Gründe.

Im Zuge der von Michail Gorbatschow verkündeten politischen Kurskorrektur zu Perestroika und Glasnost (Verände-

Large Panel Housing, Series 137, St Petersburg, 1980s

Großplattenbau-Komplex der Serie 137, entwickelt in Sankt Petersburg in den Achtzigerjahren

rung und Transparenz), wagte sich eine Architektenschaft an Bauprojekte, die jahrelang zuvor in Utopien und Fantasien, ihre Architektur nur auf Papier verwirklicht hatten. Als Reaktion auf den kreativen Stillstand und als Protest gegen einen »politisch erstarrten Staat und eine entsprechend erstarrte Architektur, deren Liaison eine fest im Sattel sitzende Partei-Architektenschaft jeden Tag bestätigte« (Klotz). Eine Art bürokratischer Selbstbedienungsladen war entstanden, der von Amts wegen linientreuen oder fügsamen Architekten gleichsam Aufträge im Abonnement garantierte, bei gleichzeitiger Ausschaltung menschlicher Fantasie.

Dagegen rebellierten jene, die am Bauen gehindert waren oder unter dem Verdacht einer »Fortschrittsfeindlichkeit« nicht handeln konnten. Diese Architekten verließen entweder das Land oder zogen sich gleichsam in die kreativen Hinterzimmer und Nischen der Gesellschaft zurück. Frei von jeder Bevormundung blühten die Fantasien und verewigten sich in teilweise skurril erscheinenden Bildern vom Bauen, von der Stadt. Das einzige Tabu, das diese Architekten leitete, war, dass es kein Tabu gab. Alles war möglich, und so begegneten sich in den zu Papier gebrachten Architekturen russischer Konstruktivismus der Zwanzigerjahre, Klassizismus des 16. Jahrhunderts à la Giovanni Battista Piranesi, der preußische Klassizismus eines Schinkel oder die Frühmoderne eines Adolf Loos. Epochen begegneten und verschränkten sich wie selbstverständlich. Zugleich offenbarten sich dabei in der Lehrtheorie verankerte Widersprüche und Gegensätze als organische Entwicklungslinien. Plötzlich zeigte sich, dass die mit vorgefassten Bildern besetzten Stilepochen Gemeinsamkeiten aufweisen. In den Fantasien der Papierarchitekten verschwammen diese Elemente zu einem neuen Ganzen oder nahmen für sich als Reinkultur zeitge-

mäße Formen an. N. Bronsowas, M. Filippows und W. Petrenkos Zeichnungen, die in ihren Bildern und Entwürfen primär Einflüsse aus dem Stilkatalog und Utopien der italienischen Renaissance erkennen lassen. M. Labasow und A. Tschelsow hingegen verschmolzen Kubismus und orientalische Stilmuster miteinander. Andere lieferten konkrete Entwürfe, wie etwa Michail Below, der unter dem Titel »Die Straße des Architekten« eine Rekonstruktion der Schusev-Straße in Moskau in der Manier italienischer Renaissancearchitektur ersehnte. Auch die mittelalterlichen Vorbilder waren im Grunde häufig so etwas wie Papierarchitekten. Zumindest dann, wenn sie malten und in ihren Motiven die architektonischen Ideen auslebten wie Raffaellos »Die Schule von Athen« als Ausschnitt aus einem Fresko in der Stanza della Segnatura im Vatikan belegt. Bei den russischen Papierarchitekten führte dieses Ausleben zuweilen selbst in unseren an den Formenkatalog postmoderner Schnuckeligkeit gewöhnten Augen an den Rand eines von jedem Zwang befreienden Kitsches.

Um die Eigenart der Papierarchitektur zu erfassen, die etwa aus der Gruppe NER in den Sechzigerjahren entstanden war, die nur zum Zweck theoretischer Erörterung projektierte, muss zwischen Utopie und Fantasie unterschieden werden. »Das utopische Denken, das sich in der Theorie und Praxis der europäischen Architektur des 19. und 20. Jahrhunderts und im Bauwesen der UdSSR entwickelt hatte, verneinte den Pluralismus.« Denn einem utopischen Projekt als Bestandteil von einer Weltverbesserung wohne auch der Wille inne, es zu verwirklichen. »In der Fantasie liegt ebenfalls eine mögliche Vision der Welt, im Unterschied zur Utopie hat die Fantasie aber nicht den Anspruch, diese Vision sei in der Wirklichkeit ein Schlüssel zur Lösung dringlicher

Vodka Pavillon by Alexander Brodsky near Moscow, 2004 (left)
Chess Residential Complex in Nizhny Novgorod by Yevgeny Pestov, 2005 (right)
Wodka-Pavillon bei Moskau, Architekt: Alexander Brodski, 2004 (links)
Wohngebäude »Karo« in Nischni Nowgorod, Architekt: Jewgeni Pestow, 2005 (rechts)

menschlicher Probleme«, brachte es der russische Architekturhistoriker Alexander G. Rappaport auf den Punkt.[14] Genau darin unterscheiden sich die Papierarchitekten der Achtzigerjahre von den Konstruktivisten des frühen 20. Jahrhunderts: Letztere sahen als Utopisten in der bolschewistischen Revolution die Chance, der neuen Gesellschaft auch eine passende künstlerische Kulisse verleihen zu können. Alles, was dem Geschmacksdiktat dieser Konstruktivisten widersprach, wurde bekämpft. Das war im Lager der europäischen Moderne nicht anders. Aus der Nervosität der Zeit heraus verständlich, machte sich selbst dort das Wesen einer totalitären Architektur bemerkbar, die eigentlich nur darauf wartete, politisch patentiert und abgesichert zu werden und die Weimarer Republik darin als Garanten erblickte, obgleich sie eine staatliche Observation gar nicht nötig hatte. Denn selbst in der ranzigen Politikkultur des wilhelminischen Deutschlands am Vorabend des Ersten Weltkrieges war aus schöpferischer Eigendynamik und überzeugenden besseren, das heißt zeitgemäßen Ideen, mehr Veränderung möglich als gemeinhin immer noch angenommen wird. Aber die Vorstellung, eine Utopie in einer total durchplanten Umwelt umzusetzen, gab es bereits im 18. Jahrhundert. Für sie wurden »jedoch erst im 20. Jahrhundert die technischen und politischen Voraussetzungen geschaffen« (Rappaport). Von derlei hatten sich die Papierarchitekten der Achtzigerjahre längst emanzipiert. Fakt ist, sie allesamt waren verhinderte Architekten, was sich wiederum nach 1991 für viele schlagartig änderte. Alexander Brodski oder Michail Below gehören seither zu denen, die plötzlich entwerfen, um zu bauen und somit aus dem gedachten in das konstruktive »Alles ist möglich« eingetreten sind. Einkaufszentren mit Fassaden, die Bildvorlagen aus dem Bauhaus-Repertoire gleichen und elegant sachliche Bauten stehen neben verspielten Häusern, die oftmals das authentisch Alte in der Stahlbetonfassade vorgaukeln, das dafür vorher wegplaniert wurde.

Kapitalistischer Realismus: Architektur im neuen Russland

»Altbauten verschwinden noch schneller als zu Sowjetzeiten«, beklagt Nikolai Malinin, und an ihrer Stelle entstünden »historisch angehauchte Neubauten. Die Rekonstruktion machte Platz der Restauration«[15] – ganz nach der Devise »Abriss mit anschließender Wiederherstellung« und habe demzufolge ihr Aufgabenfeld überschritten, das sich nur auf Orte beziehen kann, an denen vorher nichts oder nur Unpassendes stand. Was passend und unpassend ist, das entscheiden aber inzwischen an Stelle des Zentralkomitees lokale Autoritäten, die sich diesbezüglich wie kleine Feudalherren oder Politkommissare gebärden. Zu diesen Protagonisten gehört der Moskauer Oberbürgermeister Jurij Luschkow, der über seine Frau als Geschäftsführerin ein milliardenschweres Immobilienimperium aufgebaut hat, und die Gestaltung stadtbildprägender Orte diktiert. »Immer persönlich bei den Sitzungen des Öffentlichen Stadtplanungsrates dabei, äußert er sich zu fast jedem Projekt und ist Vertreter von recht klaren ästhetischen Prinzipien: Im Zentrum bauen wir nur historisch, Glas nur in den Randbezirken, Nein zu glatten Fassaden.«[16] Das alles ist an sich nicht verwerflich, aber die persönlich-autoritäre Direktive, die jene der Staatspartei ersetzt, hat sich zur Zensur verschärft und vermengt sich zugleich mit Korruption, denn »der Architekt muss für jede Innovation zahlen (aus der Brieftasche des Bauherren, versteht sich)«, dann sei auch manches abseits der persön-

The Cathedral of Christ the Savior in Moscow by Mosproyekt-2, 1997

Christus-Erlöser-Kathedrale in Moskau, Planung: Mosprojekt-2, 1997

lichen Geschmacksverordnungen möglich, die im Übrigen auch ein städtebauliches Leitbild ersetzen.

Anders verlief diese Entwicklung beispielsweise in Berlin. Dort sei es laut der Moskauer Architekturkritikerin Irina Chipova dank eines schon in den Achtzigerjahren von Josef Paul Kleihues im Zuge der Internationalen Bauausstellung entworfenen Masterplans einer »langfristigen städtebaulichen Entwicklung Berlins« gelungen, nach dem Mauerfall von 1989 beide Teile der Stadt erstaunlich schnell harmonisch zusammenwachsen zu lassen. Während man es in Berlin schaffte, ästhetische Fragen des Einzelgebäudes zur Architektur der Stadt zu machen, sei im Moskau der postsowjetischen Zeit von Stadtplanung nichts zu sehen. Gebaut werde nach Empfinden und wenn es stimmig ist, sei dies eher dem Zufall geschuldet. Im Unterschied zu sozialistischen Zeiten gebe es nicht mal ansatzweise eine Vorstellung davon, wie die Stadt als Zivilisationsorganismus zu funktionieren habe. Daran liege die Ambivalenz des eifrigen Bemühens, im städtebaulichen Detail in Gestalt verspielter Architektur gleichsam eine gefühlte Nestwärme zu erzeugen. Das einzelne Objekt sei wichtig, das große Ganze eher beliebig. Die Architektur ersetze den Städtebau. Und dafür setze Moskau seit 1991 Maßstäbe. Dazu gehört es, unverwechselbare optische Fixpunkte in einer auch ästhetisch rationalisierten Stadtökonomie zu setzen, die von den Gesetzen des Marktes gesteuert ist. Ein Baustein dafür ist der Kirchenbau. Zu den prominentesten Beispielen des sakralen Rekonstruktionsprogramms zählt der Wiederaufbau der Christus-Erlöser-Kathedrale 1997 anlässlich der 850-Jahr-Feier der Stadt Moskau. An prominenter Stelle, wo einst der Sowjetpalast errichtet werden sollte, aber statt dessen ein Schwimmbad entstand, ließ Oberbürgermeister Luschkow eine Kopie der

früheren Kathedrale errichten. Nun steht sie da wie eh und je, so als hätte das Gotteshaus nie zu den jenen achtzig Prozent Sakralbauten gehört, die unter Stalins Befehl abgerissen wurden. Täuschend echt in der Gestalt, ist das Gebäude allerdings mit einer Parkgarage im Untergeschoss lukrativ vermarktet. Denn in Russland werde nach dem Gesetz des Geldes geplant, für schön befunden und entschieden, wie Malinin spitz anmerkt.

Dass die Christus-Erlöser-Kathedrale in der öffentlichen Meinung darum nicht einhellig begrüßt wurde, hängt mehr von undurchsichtigen Machenschaften des Immobilienhandels ab als vom Geschmacksempfinden der Bevölkerung. Neben dem Handel mit Rohstoffen zählt das Immobiliengeschäft zu den lukrativsten Wirtschaftsbereichen im neuen Russland. Und dies immer noch, obgleich der Studie einer internationalen Wirtschaftsprüfungsgesellschaft zufolge die durchschnittliche Jahresrendite auf dem Moskauer Immobilienmarkt seit der Wirtschaftskrise Ende der Neunzigerjahre auf 30 Prozent im Jahr 2004 gesunken ist. Der Immobilienmarkt ist zwar nervös geworden, aber immer noch ein goldener Boden verglichen mit den Verhältnissen im übrigen Europa, wo sich Investoren seit geraumer Zeit mit Jahresrenditen zwischen vier bis fünf Prozent zufrieden geben müssen. Mit den enormen Renditen auf dem russischen Immobilienmarkt verknüpft sich aber nicht zwingend eine gute Qualität im Bau.

Dies lässt sich auf drei Faktoren zurückführen: auf die Bauherren, das allgemeine Misstrauen in die Architekten und die naiven Wohnungskäufer. »Die Bauherren in Moskau sind geizig, ängstlich und uneitel. Sie sparen bei allem: bei Baumaterialien, Technologie, Bauarbeitern, Architekten. Die meisten Bauherren vertrauen den Architekten nicht, sie

Stolnik Apartment building in Moscow by Art-Blya, 2003
Wohngebäude »Stolnik«,
Architekten: Art-Blya, 2003

bevorzugen die, die alle Formalitäten am schnellsten erledigen.« Doch dieser Trend schwindet ebenso wie das Kartell aus Banken, Politik und Immobilienmaklern. Dafür dürfte der normalisierende »Einbruch« der Renditen der beste Beweis sein.

Inzwischen sieht Malinin denn auch eine Wende hin zu mehr Qualität, zu einfallsreicher Architektur mit zeitgemäßer Sprache an Stelle von Adaptionen zwischen Klassizismus, Jugendstil und den Stilblüten einer zwanzig Jahre verspäteten europäischen Postmoderne. Schließlich habe sich nach der Wirtschaftskrise 1998 eine neue »Investorenklasse gebildet, die eingesehen hat, dass das Geld nicht nur in Nutzfläche, sondern auch in Architektur« investiert werden sollte. Zum anderen hätten die Papierarchitekten ihre kreative Unbefangenheit nicht überzeugend in gebaute Substanz umzusetzen vermocht. Malinin, ein ebenso scharfer wie scharfzüngiger Beobachter seiner Stadt Moskau, will den qualitativen Wandel an den ausgewählten Baumaterialien und dem wachsenden Einfluss der neuen Architekten-Generation der Dreißigjährigen bemerkt haben, was angesichts der Tatsache, dass es »Architektur hier erst seit 15 Jahren« gebe und demzufolge der »Architektenberuf schwer vererbbar« sei, eben schon erstaunlich ist. Ein weiteres Indiz seien die ausländischen Architekten, die immer mehr Wettbewerbe in Russland gewinnen. Als gebaute Belege für diese Wende hin zur Moderne gelten unter anderem das »Copper House« von Sergei Skuratow oder der High-Tech-Bau »Stolnik« vom Architekturbüro Art-Blya.

Streiten lässt sich über diese Wahrnehmung trefflich, stellt doch der Autor ebenso klar, dass die Architektur auf gesellschaftliche Bedürfnisse antwortet, die er wie folgt skizziert: »Während der Durchschnitts-Moskauer das alte Moskau

liebt, lehnt er die neue Architektur entschieden ab.« Gründe hierfür sieht er in der Geschichte sowie darin, dass die neue Architektur jahrzehntelang die Stadt entstellt habe, außerdem in den Ressentiments der Bewohner, die registrieren, dass jene, die Geld haben, sich gleichsam in das Gewand nobel-sachlicher Architektur hüllen, und Moderne sich folglich als Stil der Bourgeoisie darstellt. Andererseits besteht ein Bedürfnis nach gefühlter Ruhe, Ordnung und Stabilität. Im Bereich der Repräsentationsbauten befriedigt niemand dieses soziale Volksempfinden geschmackssicherer als die russisch-orthodoxe Kirche mit ihrer jahrhundertelang unangefochtenen Bildsprache. Sie verfügt über ein bekanntes, anerkanntes und unverwechselbares künstlerisches Repertoire, das auch nach jahrzehntelanger Sowjetherrschaft vorurteilsfrei ebenso problemlos wie eifrig abrufbar ist, wenn es um nationale Identität und Selbstvergewisserung geht. So umstritten die Christus-Erlöser-Kathedrale in Moskau auch sein mag, so sehr ist sie ein Meilenstein der neuen russischen Architektur und zugleich ein Zeichen für die Unbefangenheit von Politik und Architektur, ein Haus zu rekonstruieren, das über 50 Jahre im Stadtbild nicht existent war. Es geht bei den Kirchenbauten in erster Linie um Bilder, um den schönen Schein. Ausnahmen bestätigen allenfalls die Regel. Über 90 Prozent der Neubauten der russisch-orthodoxen Kirche entsprechen dem Formenkanon aus der Zeit der Zaren. Sei es in Moskau, Jekaterinburg, Samara oder irgendwo in Sibirien – die neuen Gotteshäuser sind kaum von historischen Bauten zu unterscheiden, wären da nicht die neuen Fassaden-Materialien oder die Kunststoff-Profile in den Fenstern.

Erstaunlich ist hierbei, dass vor allem die Architekten, die zu Sowjetzeiten mit funktionalistischen Großbauten gut im

Geschäft waren, bei heutigen Kirchenentwürfen auf die historischen Typologien zurückgreifen. Damit haben wir heute ein ähnliches Phänomen wie nach dem Erlass der Kunstdoktrin im Jahre 1934, als zaristische Architekten an ihre vergangene Arbeit anknüpften und Schmuckvolles für die neue Sowjetunion bauten. Ein anderes Phänomen ist die Renaissance der stalinistischen Architektur, die gleichfalls auf die beschriebenen Bedürfnisse eine vortreffliche Antwort gibt und auch eine politische Entsprechung in der Wiederwahl Wladimir Putins findet, der führend im Auslandsressort des sowjetischen Geheimdienstes KGB tätig war und nun unter dem zaristischen Doppeladler das neue Russland führt.

Mit Putins Zustimmung ist in der russischen Hauptstadt der »neostalinistische Stil« wieder aufgeblüht, ohne dass sich ein unmittelbarer Zusammenhang zwischen Bauweise und Zentralisierung der Macht konstruieren lässt. In Moskau, das unverkennbar von Stalins Architektur bestimmt wird, ist die Renaissance dieses Stils eigentlich nicht verwunderlich. Es wohnt ihm sogar eine städtebauliche Logik inne, wenn es darum geht, wieder ein in sich geschlossenes Stadtbild zu schaffen. Nach einem Entwurf des Projektentwicklers Don Stroi ist darum 2006 in Innenstadtnähe die »achte Schwester« der stalinistischen Hochhäuser entstanden. Bei dem Wohngebäude mit dem Namen »Triumf Palas« handelt es sich um das höchste seiner Art in Europa – erbaut im neostalinistischen Stil.

Das wäre, übertragen auf Berlin, etwa so, als baute man die ehemalige Stalinallee einfach Richtung Osten weiter – allerdings nicht als kollektiven Arbeiterpalast der politischen Elite sondern als hochexklusive Wohnimmobilie einer neuen Geldelite. Aber dieser Komplex sagt viel über eine Gesellschaft aus, in der abseits der schlichten Volksgemüter auch Käufer von Luxusappartements das Stalinsche Haus mit hohen Decken, breiten Fensterbänken, großen Räumen, Balkons und Balustersäulen im Kopf haben. Denn jeder wusste, was es heißt, in solchen Häusern zu wohnen, und viele Russen sind auch heute noch fest davon überzeugt, dass es sich darin am besten leben lasse.

Hinzu kommt, dass ein Großteil der russischen Immobilienentwickler gerade im Wohnungsbau der Nachfrage am Markt gerecht werden, indem sie einen populären Geschmack bedienen. Und der besteht im post-sowjetischen Russland, wo noch über drei Viertel der Menschen in seriellen Plattenbauten wohnen, in verspielten Formen und nicht in abstrakter Einfachheit. Lediglich dort, wo sich junge Architekten über den Mainstream hinwegsetzen und aufgrund einer Ausbildung in Europa oder durch einen intensiven Blick in die internationalen Zeitschriften puristische Gebäude gestalten, die einer Schweizer oder spanischen Schule entspringen, fehlt das klassische Vokabular von Erkern, Gesimsen und Ornament. Allerdings stellen die Projekte der nächsten Generation noch eine Ausnahme dar. Der Hang zum Bekannten und Bewährten ist typisch für eine Gesellschaft, die sonst nur Umbrüche und Ungewissheiten kennt. Schließlich haben Städtebau und Architektur seit Stalin in Russland keine vergleichbare Qualität mehr erfahren. Stalinistische Architektur ist daher so etwas wie eine Mischung aus Ersatz-Schinkel und der bei uns noch als solide und gleichwohl ästhetisch eingestuften Frühmoderne und somit durchaus vergleichbar mit den Trends, die etwa ein Hans Kollhoff in seiner rational-expressionistischen Backsteinarchitektur in Berlin mit den Attributen würdevoll, steinern, elegant besetzt. Der Trend zur Rekonstruktion ist aber keine Moskauer Marotte.

Auch in Sankt Petersburg, das eine nahezu intakte barocke und klassizistische Innenstadt besitzt, ordnet sich die neue Architektur schonend in den Bestand ein, will sagen: Die Architekten, die an sensiblen Orten im Zentrum bauen, werden von der Baupolitik angehalten, sich konservativ der Aufgabe Alt und Neu zu stellen. So etwa wurde 2004 das Verwaltungsgebäude der Russischen Zentralbank am Fontanka-Kanal (Architekten: Wladimir Grigoriew u. a.) fertig gestellt, dessen Vorderfassade mit strukturierenden Gesimsen, vorstehenden Erkern und floralen Schmuckelementen kaum von den knapp 100 Jahre alten Nachbargebäuden zu unterscheiden ist. Allerdings präsentiert sich die Fassade in der Seitenstraße alles andere als neotraditionell: im kühlen Stahl-Glas-Gewand. Immerhin ist dies ein Versuch der architektonischen Revolution. Dass Dominique Perrault mit einem kristallartigen Glasbau Anfang 2003 den Zuschlag für die Erweiterung des Mariinsky-Theaters erhielt, ist daher kaum mehr als eine die Regel bestätigende Ausnahme.

Beim Blick auf die Fülle der Projekte, die im neuen Russland entstanden sind, trennt sich schnell die Spreu vom Weizen. Ebenfalls in Moskau steht das Wohngebäude Patriarch, das 2002 nach einem Entwurf von Sergei Tkachenko fertig gestellt wurde. Das für die neue Geld-Elite errichtete Haus steht am Rande des Patriarchen-Teichs, in einem schon zu Sowjetzeiten vornehmen Wohnviertel im Zentrum der Stadt. Mit seiner ausgesprochenen Vielfalt an Farben und Formen stellt es einen beispiellosen Stilmix dar. Die neobarocke Fassade türmt sich nach oben hin zu einem verschachtelten Etwas, das seinesgleichen sucht. Lediglich ein Zitat gibt dem Haus einen anspruchsvollen Abschluss: Über der letzten Etage ragt eine verkleinerte Kopie des nie realisierten Tatlin-Turms in den Moskauer Himmel. Dass die Inkunabel aus

den frühen Jahren des Konstruktivismus eigentlich mehrere hundert Meter hoch werden sollte, scheint weder die Architekten noch die Bewohner zu stören. Auch nicht, dass die ornamentreiche Fassade und die utopische Stahlkonstruktion einem architektonischen Geist entspringen, der gegensätzlicher kaum sein könnte.

Russland spiegelt somit ein Phänomen wider, das in der gesamten Welt zu beobachten ist und unter immer anderen Namen die Fachwelt in rege Diskussionen verstrickt. Sei es der New Urbanism in Nordamerika oder seine europäischen Ableger, die sich inzwischen in Verbänden organisieren, oder sei es das chinesische Verlangen nach europäischer Identität im Wohnungs- und Städtebau – allgegenwärtig zitieren die neuen Traditionalisten altbewährte Formen und Rezepte, setzen sich gegen die anonyme Architektursprache zur Wehr, die die Globalisierung mit sich gebracht hat. Zugleich versucht Russland auch gegenüber den ehemaligen Unionsstaaten, die ihrerseits nach traditionellen architektonischen Ausdrucksformen in einer technisch genormten Welt setzen, ein eigenes Profil in der Kunst zu entwickeln. Daher kann erst jetzt im Zuge einer kulturellen Regionalisierung im Raum der ehemaligen Sowjetunion folgerichtig auch von einem russischen Regionalismus, gar einem russischen Post-Globalismus gesprochen werden.

Derartige Extreme wie vor allem in Moskau kennt die Architektur in der Region nicht. Um den neuen russischen Regionalismus in seiner Reinheit zu betrachten, lohnt sich gerade eine Fahrt in die Wolga-Region. So etwa sind in Nischni Nowgorod, Perm oder Samara Wohn- und Geschäftshäuser entstanden, die sich um ein stilistisches Anknüpfen an den Jugendstil bzw. Art Déco bemühen. Wie selbstverständlich stehen diese Gebäude im Stadtbild und geben den in der

Fontanka Bank Building in St Petersburg by Vladimir Grigoryev, 2004 (left)
Mariinsky Theatre Extension Project in St Petersburg by Dominique Perrault, Competition First Prize 2003 (right)
Verwaltungsgebäude der Russischen Zentralbank am Fontanka-Kanal in Sankt Petersburg, Architekten: Wladimir Grigoriew u. a. (links)
Erweiterung des Mariinsky-Theaters in Sankt Petersburg, Architekt: Dominique Perrault, Wettbewerb 1. Preis, 2003 (rechts)

Sowjetzeit teilweise arg verunstalteten Städten ein wenig Identität zurück. In diesem Sinne hat die russische Architektur gerade in der Region ihre ausdrucksvollsten Beispiele hervorgebracht. Zu den außergewöhnlichsten Bauten zählt hierbei das Bankgebäude Garantija in Nischni Nowgorod (Seite 122), das 1995 von dem Architektenduo Evgenij Pestow und Alexander Charitonow fertig gestellt wurde. Zur Straße präsentiert sich eine Putzfassade, deren ovale Fenster und filigrane Keramikdetails an die Art-Déco-Zeit der ausgehenden Zaren-Dynastie erinnern. Ebenfalls Mitte der Neunzigerjahre entstanden in Perm ein Wohn- und Geschäftshaus nach Entwürfen von Mendel Futlik (Seite 130) sowie in Samara das »Dom Mucha« (»Haus Maus«) nach Entwürfen von Leonid Kuderov. Beide Gebäude zitieren wie selbstverständlich Motive aus dem Art Déco und verbinden sie mit der funktionalistischen Sprache einer modernen Architektur. Während in Moskau ein gewisser Pluralismus internationaler Stile und Strömungen vorherrscht, reduziert sich die Vielfalt in den regionalen Zentren auf eben jene neo-traditionellen Formen sowie auf die leider überall in der Welt entstehenden verspiegelten und ebenso eisigen Kisten, hinter denen sich Hotels, Shopping-Malls oder Business-Center verbergen. Hinsichtlich des Regionalismus kann die russische Architektur auch zur europäischen Avantgarde gezählt werden. Aber vor allem die Neotraditionalisten müssen sich im internationalen Diskurs daran messen lassen, inwieweit die neue russische Architektur durch Reduzierung auf Stilfragen und Marktgerechtigkeit einen Beitrag zur ideologischen Erneuerung der Gesellschaft leisten kann. Noch ist die Nachfrage nach neuen Gebäuden nicht gesättigt. Sobald aber der Markt von konkurrierenden Angeboten geprägt ist, wird sich die architektonische Qualität als Trumpf in der Vermarktung

entpuppen. Dann werden sich auch die utopischen Quadratmeterpreise, die im Moskauer Wohnungsbau teilweise auf über 10.000 Euro angestiegen sind, auf europäisches Niveau einpendeln. Bis dahin zeigt sich der postkommunistische Kapitalismus weiterhin von seiner extremen Seite. In einem Land wie Russland, das trotz seines unendlichen Reichtums an Bodenschätzen noch zu den Transformationsstaaten gezählt werden muss, ist die Suche nach Identität daher längst noch nicht abgeschlossen.

1 Vgl. Kristin Feireiss/Hans-Jürgen Commerell (Hg.):
   B.A.U. Berliner Architektur Union. Ausstellungskatalog
   Berlin/Moskau 2003. Vgl. auch: Philipp Meuser: Russischer
   Regionalismus. In: Baumeister 08/04 (August 2004)

2 Jan Pehrke: Der Künstler-Ingenieur, in: Jungle World,
   13. Januar 1999.

3 El Lissitzky: Der Unterbau. In: El Lissitzky 1929. Rußland:
   Architektur für eine Weltrevolution. Braunschweig 1989

4 El Lissitzky: Zukunft und Utopie. In: El Lissitzky (1929)

5 Walter Gropius: Was erhoffen wir vom russischen Städt-
   bau? In: Hartmut Probst/Christian Schädlich: Walter
   Gropius. Ausgewählte Schriften. Berlin 1988

6 Stadtrat Mays Russlandpläne. In: Bauwelt, Heft 36/1930

7 Harald Bodenschatz/Christiane Post (Hg.): Städtebau im
   Schatten Stalins. Die internationale Suche nach der
   sozialistischen Stadt in der Sowjetunion 1929-1935.
   Berlin 2003.

8 Bruno Taut, Rußlands architektonische Situation.
   In: El Lissitzky (1929)

9 X.Y.: Zu den Auseinandersetzungen über Rußland.
   In: Die neue Stadt. Heft 12-1933

10 Ernst May verließ nach Ablauf des ersten Fünfjahresplans
   1933 wieder die Sowjetunion und wirkte von 1934-1954
   als Farmer und Architekt in Kenia. In Nairobi hinterließ er
   Spuren einer modernen Architektur und war ab 1954 in
   Deutschland als Stadtplaner mit dem Wiederaufbau und
   Ausbau deutscher Städte befasst (Mainz, Wiesbaden,
   Bremerhaven) sowie bis 1961 Planungsleiter der Neuen
   Heimat (u.a. Siedlung Neue Vahr in Bremen).

11 Als Stadtplaner machte Kurt Meyer zunächst in sowjetischen
   Gremien eine steile Karriere und wurde im Zuge der »Großen
   Säuberung« innerhalb der Parteikader Ende der Dreißige-

jahre inhaftiert und 1944 in einem sowjetischen Lager
ermordet. Vgl. dazu auch Susanne Schattenberg: Stalins
Ingenieure. Lebenswelten zwischen Technik und Terror in den
1930er-Jahren, München 2002.

12 Hans Schmidt: Die Sowjetunion und das neue Bauen.
   In: Die neue Stadt. Heft 6/7-1932

13 Heinrich Klotz (Hg.): Papierarchitektur. Neue Projekte aus
   der Sowjetunion. Ausstellungskatalog Frankfurt/Main 1989

14 Alexander G. Rappaport: Sprache und Architektur des »Post-
   Totalitarismus«. In: Heinrich Klotz (Hg.): Papierarchitektur.
   Neue Projekte aus der Sowjetunion. Ausstellungskatalog
   Frankfurt/Main 1989

15 Nikolai Malinin: Eine Hauptstadt ohne Gesicht. In: Moskau-
   Berlin. 1950-2000. Architektur. Ausstellungskatalog Moskau
   2004

16 Irina Chipowa: Das geteilte Berlin. Kampf und Einheit der
   Gegensätze. In: Moskau-Berlin. 1950-2000. Architektur.
   Ausstellungskatalog Moskau 2004

Residential building in
Moscow by Sergey Skuratov,
2004
Wohngebäude in Moskau,
Architekt: Sergei Skuratow,
2004

Appendix

Architects Architektenverzeichnis*

* Die Nennung erfolgt nach den Regeln der englischen Schreibweise.

Photographic Credits Abbildungsnachweis

All other illustrations and photographs are from the archives of the *Project Russia* architectural journal or were provided by the architects and/or planners.

Alle anderen Abbildungen und Fotos stammen aus dem Archiv der Architekturzeitschrift *Projekt Rossija* oder direkt von den Architekten und Planern.

Urban Context	■	Städtischer Kontext
Rural Context	▣	Landschaftlicher Kontext
Private Funding	€	Private Finanzierung
Public Funding	Руб	Öffentliche Finanzierung
Office Building	🖈	Bürobau
Residential Building	🛏	Wohnungsbau
Sport Venue	✿	Sportstättenbau
Transport Infrastructure	🚗	Verkehrsbauwerk
Art Museum	🎨	Kunstmuseum
Restaurant	☕	Restaurant
Discotheque	♫	Diskothek
Shopping Centre	🛒	Einkaufszentrum
School	🎒	Schulbau
Theatre	🎭	Theater
Security	🔑	Sicherheit
Ecclesiastic Building	✝	Sakralbau

Die Deutsche Bibliothek lists this publication in the *Deutsche Nationalbibliografie*; detailed bibliographic data is available on the internet at *http://dnb.ddb.de*

Die Deutsche Bibliothek verzeichnet diese Publikation in der *Deutschen Nationalbibliografie*. Detaillierte bibliografische Daten sind im Internet über *http://dnb.ddb.de* abrufbar.

ISBN 3–938666–10–2

© 2006 by DOM publishers
www.dom-publishers.com

Editors Lektorat
Cornelia Dörries, Uta Keil, Ansgar Oswald

Translation Übersetzung
Meredith Dale, Nina Hausmann (English)
Irina Shipova (Russian)

Layout Grafik
Atelier Kraut

Thanks to Danksagung
Elena Gonzales, Alexander Loshkin, Alexey Muratov,
Daniela Pogade, Simone Voigt, Marina Zvegintsova

Project partners Projektpartner
Project Russia | A-FOND publishers, Amsterdam/Moscow
The Schusev State Museum of Architecture, Moscow
Goethe-Institut Moskau

Барт Голдхорн • Филипп Мойзер

Капреализм

Новая архитектура в России

Архитектура после коммунизма

Барт Голдхорн

Революционно! Все по-новому! Все совершенно иначе! Огромный выбор! Свобода! Эти слова неслучайно используются в рекламных целях – их привлекательность универсальна и действенна. Перемены и революция – это слова с позитивным подтекстом, что явно ощущалось в России в начале девяностых годов. И весь мир замер в ожидании великого расцвета культуры и подъема экономики в огромной стране, освободившейся от ига коммунизма. С этого времени прошло 15 лет. И достаточно только включить телевизор, чтобы убедиться, что Россия по сей день борется с проблемами, оказавшимися значительно сложнее, чем изначально предполагалось. Это относится не только к экономике или обществу, но и к архитектуре и градостроительству. Российские города будут еще десятилетия нести в себе печать семидесятилетнего правления коммунизма. В этом их принципиальное отличие от городов в других странах Центральной Европы с коммунистическим прошлым, которые более легко преодолели его последствия. Это объясняется множеством причин. В России индустриализация началась намного позже, чем в Центральной Европе, а коммунизм – раньше. До революции большинство русских городов – за исключением Москвы и Санкт-Петербурга – было застроено деревянными зданиями. От этого времени мало что уцелело. Поэтому в сегодняшних городах практически невозможно найти следы древней истории, хотя в некоторых случаях она составляет более тысячи лет. Физическая структуря российского города, наблюдаемая нами сегодня, закладывалась в годы коммунизма. Поэтому коммунизм это не просто слой, который можно было бы стереть, для того, чтобы обнаружить под ним «подлинный» город. И это не «историческое недоразумение», которое хочется как можно скорее забыть. Не множество монументов, лозунгов и политических символов в общественном пространстве определяют коммунистический характер российского города, а то, что этот город создавался в условиях общества, функционировавшего по коммунистическим принципам – отсутствие частной собственности, незначительная разница в доходах большей части населения, централизованное распределение жилья, типологизированное индустриальное строительство. И даже в этом определяющей была не идеологическая надстройка, а ее практическое воздействие на повседневность. Законы, выглядевшие как непотопляемые воплощения коммунистической идеологии, повлекли за собой непредвиденные последствия и нередко – диаметрально противоположенные тому, что от них ожидалось. Я обозначил эти механизмы как «советский парадокс». Потому что в архитекту-

ре и градостроительстве бывшего Советского Союза все происходило не жестко и рационально, а хаотично и аморфно.

Четвертая революция.

Непредсказуемые воздействия идеологических принципов обнаруживаются повсеместно. Рем Колхас, бывший в Москве в семидесятые годы и попавший в нее вновь после долгого перерыва, наиболее четко сформулировал причину, по которой этот город вызывает столько восхищения у многих западных архитекторов: самое замечательноео в сформированном советской системой российском городе это радикальность его замысла.[1] Никаких спекуляций земельными участками, никакого неконтролируемого рынка – только архитектура, базирующаяся на строгой идеологии. Тоталитарное проектирование – собственно, мечта любого архитектора. Идеологическое содержание архитектуры проявляется наиболее остро именно в тот момент, когда политическая власть провозглашает смену парадигмы. На протяжении советской эры произошло три таких революции. Конструктивистская революция двадцатых-тридцатых годов хотела за счет модернистского эксперимента стереть все следы буржуазной эклектики дореволюционного времени. Стилинистская революция же, наоборот, заменила современные постройки конструктивизма поти барочно перегруженной нео-классикой и пропагандировала возвращение к традиционному градостроительству. Революция Хрущева прокляла декор и насадила почти повсеместно модернистские формы: огромные типологизированные постройки из производимых индустриальным методом элементов.[2] И была четвертая революция. Она произошла после 1990 года и по радикальности не уступала своим предшественницам. Она произошла не по указу сверху, а явилась в первую очередь реакцией архитектуры на развал социализма, проявившегося в Советском Союзе самым сильным образом, и оказавшим значительное влияние и на Западную Европу. Так как и там социально-демократические принципы проектирования, преобладавшие в градостроительстве после второй Мировой Войны, вытеснили капиталистические проявления.

Бумажная архитектура.

Все четыре революции примерно одинаковы в своем кардинальном отрицании предшествующей эпохи. Так, для четвертой революции характерно преодоление советского модернизма, инициированного Хрущевым в шестидесятые годы. Однако это настроение уходит корнями еще в восьмидесятые годы, когда в русской архитектуре сформировалось критическое движение так называемых бумажных архитекторов. Значительная часть молодых русских архитекторов в это время с большим успехом участвовала в международных конкурсах, в большинстве случаев организованных японской газетой «The Japan Architect».[3] В своих работах архитекторы отвергали «прекрасный новый мир» тотального модернизма и вместо этого погружались в романтический мир, полный ностальгии, упивались эстетикой распада и разрушения, а также многозначительной метафоричностью. Интернациональная архитектурная сцена реагировала на все это с нескрываемым восторгом. Впервые со времен конструктивизма русские архитекторы заявили о себе в международном архитектурном дискурсе, в котором превалировала в то время постмодернистская тематика. Когда спустя десять лет обозначилась фундаментальная смена политической системы, весь мир неспроста ждал возрождения восточноевропейской архитектуры – по ассоциации с расцветом испанской архитектуры после смерти генерала Франко. Эти ожидания не оправдались. За одним только исключением – только в Нижнем Новгороде – крупном индустриальном городе, расположенном 400 км восточнее Москвы, называвшемся раньше Горьким и известным на Западе как место ссылки А.Сахарова, – в 90-е годы сформировалось новое архитектурное движение, руководствовавшееся принципами четвертой революции: частная инициатива, разнообразие форм, свобода художественного выбора.

Чудо Нижнего Новгорода

В том, что эта революция произошла в глубокой русской провинции, нет ничего удивительного. Потому что централизованный советский режим подавлял там до этого любой творческий импульс. Представления Хрущева об индустриализации и стандартизации привели к тому, что за пределами Москвы практически все здания должны были возводиться согласно разработанным в столичных проектных институтах стандартным образцам. Задача архитекторов на местах состояла исключительно в том, чтобы эти стандартные образцы приспособить к местным условиям. Когда же коммунистическая система, включая ее централистский принцип хозяйствования, пошла ко дну, честолюбивые архитекторы воспользовались моментом и открыли свои собственные бюро. В Нижнем Новгороде сформировалась даже собственная школа. Ее основатель – Александр Харитонов, ставший позднее

главным архитектором Нижнего Новгорода. Для развития города экономические преобразования означали существенные перемены. В советские времена строительство концентрировалось на периферии города, где на пустырях вырастали гигантские индустриальные районы. В новых условиях рыночной экономики центр города, на протяжении десятилетий пребывающий в запустении, вновь приобрел былое значение. Нижний Новгород, центральная часть которого состояла до этого времени преимущественно из обветшалых деревянных домов, вновь приобрел значение как центр коммуникации и торговли. Давно назревшая необходимость в реконструкции центра получила новую направленность, нацеленную на новые требования; начался основательный процесс перестройки и обновления. Деревянные строения уступали места новым зданиям, и архитекторы – после более чем 30 лет вынужденной работы с бетонными коробками – создали настоящий стилистический фейерверк. Новые экономические условия также содействовали творческому раскрепощению. Благодаря дешевой рабочей силе, богатым заказчикам и упущениям в существующих нормативах, произошло утверждение почти эксцессивной архитектуры – штукатурка, клинкер и краски позволяли реализовывать любые желания. В какой-то мере эклектика XIX века получила свое второе рождение, хотя в данном случае образцы для подражания находились не только в прошлом, но и в современности. Рядом с палладианской виллой и зданием банка в стиле «ар нуво» располагается офисный комплекс в духе Портзампарка, в то время как прямо напротив возводился нео-модернистский шоппинг-молл. Своего расцвета архитектура Нижнего Новгорода достигла во второй половине 90-х годов. Со смертью Александра Харитонова, в 2000 году погибшего в автокатастрофе, Нижний Новгород перестает быть архитектурной столицей России. Без его харизматического влияния, бурное строительство в Нижнем уже не могло конкурировать с возрастающим значением Москвы.[4]

Пост-советская Москва

Если Нижний Новгород я девяностые был архитектурной столицей России, то что же происходило в это время в Москве? Как экономический и культурный центр бывшего Советского Союза у Москвы были все предпосылки стать важным адресом для новой, пост-тоталитарной архитектуры. Но именно этого и не произошло. И парадоксально, но именно центральное положение Москвы было тому главной причиной. Московские архитекторы – в отличие от их кол-

лег в провинции – должны были сначала понести значительные потери во власти. Если раньше они руководили проектами по всей стране, то теперь их влияние сконцентрировалось только на Москве. При этом Москва являлась относительно благополучным городом, который мог себе позволить гигантский и централизовано контролируемый проектный и строительный комбинат по советскому образцу, в то время как в других горадах подобные структуры заменялись малыми архитектурными бюро или отдельными строительными предприятиями. В Москве четвертая революция была воспринята так же, как и все предыдущие – модернистская парадигма указанием свыше будет заменена другой. Ключевое слово: историзм. Симптоматичным для такого метода восприятия является главное архитектурное событие тех лет – возведение Храма Христа Спасителя. Он был построен как точная копия созданного при Николае 1 в 1883 году храма, который был при Сталине - в 1931 г.- снесен для того, чтобы освободить место для никогда не построенного Дворца Советов. К новым проектам пост-перестроечного времени пришли не пользовавшиеся в восьмидесятые годы мировой славой архитекторы-бумажники (как наивно полагали на Западе), а архитекторы из государственных учреждений, которые до этого реализовывали печально известные советские бетонные коробки. Они очень быстро сориентирововались и выступили теперь как протагонисты классической архитектуры.

Протесты политически активных слоев общества времен перестройки против сносов в историческом центре при столкновении со всемогущей бюрократией также оборачивались провалом. В реальности введение демократии означало усиление бюрократического аппарата, который как и прежде оказывал значительное влияние на архитектурный процесс. Нагляднее всего степень демократичности в принятии решений проявляется в том, что так называемый «общественный совет», который должен был бы направлять мнение как общественности, так и «творческой интеллигенции», к новому развитию города, на самом деле полностью подчиняется мэру Юрию Лужкову. Потому что он – в качестве скромного оправдания – был избран народом и представляет, соответственно, его взгляды. Одновременно городские власти представляют во многих проектах собственные экономические интересы.

Это относится не только к общественным зданиям - театрам, музеям или спортивным залам, но и к торговым центрам, жилым и офисным зданиям. Многие архитекторы сталкиваются с ситуацией, когда Заказчик, согласовательная инстанция, а нередко еще и строительная фирма, принадлежат единому крупному государственному холдингу (к которому часто принадлежит и сам архитектор): коммунистическая модель, при которой личные интересы в области экономики или политики предоставляют большую свободу действия.[5]

Частные заказчики – частные бюро

В то время как во многих странах именно государственные заказы предоставляют идеальные возможности для реализации интересных архитектурных решений, в Москве сложилась прямо противоположная ситуация: чем прочнее связан проект с государственными инстанциями, тем хуже его архитектура. Качество же, напротив, можно обнаружить в проектах частных инвесторов. Конечно же, не во всех: те, кто заинтересован в хороших отношениях с властями, прилагают все усилия для того, чтобы проект понравился мэру. Это относится прежде всего к такому инвестору как «Дон-Строй», построившему «Триумф-Палас» – самый высокий жилой дом в Европе – в стиле сталинских высоток пятидесятых годов.
Существуют однако девелоперы, преследующие и другие цели, ориентирущиеся прежде всего на офисы для частных фирм и жилье для состоятельной прослойки новой России. Они работают с определенными московскими бюро, которые в состоянии осуществлять высококачественные и современные архитектурные проекты. Такие бюро как «Киселев и партнеры», Мастерская А.Асадова, ТПО «Резерв», ABD, мастерская М.Хазанова или «Остоженка» стартовали в 90-е годы с нуля и за это время этаблировались как крупные частные архитектурные бюро. Стиль их работы соответствует профессионализму, за счет которого они добились успеха: ориентирующийся на контекст модернизм, чуждый фривольностям постмодернизма и характерной для международной архитектуры тяги к экспериментированию. Наиболее интересным бюро, пожалуй, является «Остоженка», возглавляемая Александром Скоканом. Бюро носит имя района, в котором находится уже упоминавшийся выше Храм Христа Спасителя, оно было основано еще во времена старых планировочных структур, когда каждый район находился в ведении определенного архитектора. К началу 90-х годов Скокан разработал обширную программу развития и обновления подведомственного ему района. И действительно на этой территории находятся самые интересные постройки Москвы – многие принадлежат самому Скокану, но в последнее время там все чаще стали появлятся здания молодых архитекторов.

Интерьеры.

Развитие этих крупных частных бюро связано с формированием и этаблированием новой профессиональной специализации – архитектура интерьеров. До этого было проще оставлять стены нетронутыми. Однако в силу того, что покупатели чаще всего не знали, как им оформить пустые пространства площадью в 200-300 кв.м, неожиданно возник большой спрос на оформление интерьеров. Прежде всего эту нишу открыли для себя молодые архитекторы, способные за хорошие деньги решить проблемы состоятельных клиентов. Это предопределило разделение профессиональной архитектурной среды на «объемщиков» и «интерьерщиков». Типичный «объемщик» (буквально: тот, кто создает пустые архитектурные объемы) – архитектор за сорок, учившийся в советские времена и работавший при старой системе, располагающий хорошими связями в инстанциях. Масштаб его проектов редко бывает более детальным, чем 1:100. Типичный «интерьерщик» обычно молод, работает на частных заказчиков и обладает хорошими контактами с поставщиками мебели и отделочных материалов. Зачастую ему подчиняется собственная строительная бригада. Обобщая, можно сказать, что наиболее интересные архитектурные проекты 90-х годов в области интерьеров возникли как противостояние вмешательству бюрократии и строительной индустрии советского образца.
Молодые «интерьерщики» начали свою профессиональную карьеру, когда постепенно стала доступна информация о мировых архитектурных процессах, в то время как старшее поколение накапливало опыт во времена изоляции, когда информация из мира капитализма была практически недоступна. Это преимущество в обладании информации молодого поколения в сочетании с исключительно платежеспособными заказчиками, которые готовы выложить изрядные суммы в индивидуальное оформление их частных квартир или домов, открыло практически безграничные возможности для разработки и реализации самых невероятных идей. Многое из индивидуально выполненных предметов мебели и обстановки в домах подобных клиентов были бы в Западной Европе финансово неосуществимы.[6]

Новое поколение.

Интересные процессы последних лет связаны с изменениями как в среде архитекторов, так и заказчиков. Внутри профессионального цеха стало ощутимо пополнение штата «объемщиков» новым поколением, которое, в свою очередь, тоже делится на две группы. К одной принадлежат молодые архитекторы, набравшиеся опыта в одном из основанных после 1990 года крупных новых бюро, и открывающих теперь собственные фирмы. К другому относятся «интерьерщики», которые постепенно перешагнули за рамки собственно интерьерных проектов частных домов и квартир и стали уже получать заказы на жилые и офисные здания в городской черте. По сравнению с предыдущим поколением «объемщиков» эти архитекторы располагают существенным преимуществом: они не должны самоутверждаться в качестве самостоятельно работающего архитектора. – это сделали за них старшие коллеги, кроме того они располагают большим практическим опытом, полученным во время работы в качестве ассистенетв, руководителей проектов или практикующих интерьерщиков. Их компетенция пользуется сегодня большим спросом со стороны заказчиков, которые тоже располагают определенным опытом, много ездят по миру и успели понять, что архитектура является важным инструментом маркетинга. В Москве сегодня насчитывается значительное число заказчиков, готовых заплатить огромные суммы за эксклюзивный участок (до 15 000 долларов за квадратный метр), каждый девелопер стремится к возведению жилья класса «люкс». Эта ситуация привела и к спросу на привлечение иностранных архитекторов. Так, крупная компания «Капитал Груп» выдвинулась за счет проектов, созданных Эриком ван Эгераатом, Захой Хадид или «Бениш и Бениш», сегодня для Москвы работают так же Рэм Колхас, СОМ, Норман Фостер и КПФ. В своих проектах молодые «объемщики» ориентируются на актуальные международные тенденции, и этим они отличаются от уже не совсем актуальных предшественников. Можно упомянуть Алексея Козыря, Левона Айрапетова и Никиту Голованова, Антона Надточего и Веру Бутко («Атриум»), «Проект Меганом», Сергея Скуратова и ДНК.

Русская архитектура?

Несмотря на то (или как раз именно потому), что молодое поколение интегрировано в международную архитектурную сцену, оно еще не может в своей работе претендовать на исключительность. Причиной тому является отсутствие в России последние 15 лет настоящих архитектурных дискуссий – все были поглощены приспособлением к новым экономическим условиям. Единственное существенное исключение составляет Евгений Асс, которого по праву можно назвать «европейским» архитектором в России. Благодаря своим публикациям и преподавательской деятельности он оказывает огромное влияние на молодое архитектурное поколение. Для того, чтобы найти архитектуру, которую можно определить и обозначить как «русскую», необходимо вернуться к явлению бумажной архитектуры. Хотя большинство из этого поколения уже давно перешли к ежедневной проектной рутине, некоторые по-прежнему развивают те концепции, с которых они начинали 20 лет назад. Как и прежде существенной темой их работы является отношение к современной архитектуре после катастрофального советского панельного строительства. Фундаменталисты, главой которых можно назвать московских архитекторов Михаила Филиппова и Илью Уткина, являются приверженцами вечно живой классики и в своих убеждениях они близки британским и американским апологетам историзма, таким как Криер или Стерн. Их позиция, правда, отличается большей меланхоличностью и подчеркивает упоение красотой распада классической архитектуры. Эта позиция является одновременно сильной и уязвимой. На бумаге этот распад всегда выглядит очень эффектно, однако в виде построенной субстанции вряд ли способен убедить. В то же время эти работы – выражение подлинной пост-советской меланхолии, за счет чего они обладают большей силой, чем буржуазные западные аналоги.

Наряду с этим существуют и архитекторы, которые концентрируются не на классических аспектах распада, а на несовершенстве. Они черпают вдохновение преимущественно в коммунистическом прошлом, хотя при этом не в его официальной версии как рациональной, логической и работающей системе. В гораздо большей степени их занимают существующие наряду с официальным коммунистическим обществом параллельные миры дачи – загородного дома, построенного из остатков и отбросов коммунистического промышленного производства. Это мир домашних посиделок с бесконечными дискуссиями, который позволял совершать побег из системы, не покидая ее. Эстетика этого мира соответствует сюрреалистскому «objet trouveé». Этот феномен исследовал Сергей Малахов, который собрал более 200 образцов этих временных зданий из останков промышленной продукции и представил их в виде проектов – с чертежами, моделями и описаниями, которые он придумал для этих артефактов. Другой архитектор, вдохновившийся этим несовершенством – Александр Ермолаев. Основатель театра архитектурных форм, он открыл качество традиционной деревянной архитекутры, характерной для русского севера. Его ученики – Кузьмин и Савинкин сегодня являются одними из самых успешных архитекторов. Это их проект был опубликован во многих международных архитектурных изданиях как первый российский проект, опубликованный с 70-х годов. Еще одним представителем этой линии является бюро «А-Б», демонстрирующее в своих работах абсолютно детскую наивность. Но безусловным лидером в этой группе является, конечно же, Александр Бродский. Его работы – временные, сырые, незаконченные – являются конгениальным выражением этой архитектуры несовершенства, и одновременно они – критика как советского модернизма, так одновременно и современной западной архитектуры. Конечно, его проекты прежде всего романтичны и в большинстве своем не созданы для реализации, им чужды критерии долгосрочности, равно как и экономичности. Это, пожалуй, можно отнести и к России в целом. Но это будет меняться. Вопрос только, будет ли это изменение к лучшему.

[1] В 1954 году Хрущев произнес речь на строительном и архитектурном конгрессе СССР о современных стратегиях в архитектуре. Она была опубликована в журнале «Проект Россия» № 25, Москва-Амстердам, 2002

[2] Более полный обзор этого конкурса в журнале «Проект Россия» № 29, Москва-Амстердам, 2004

[3] Более полный обзор архитекутры Нижнего Новгорода в журнале «Проект Россия» № 4, Москва-Амстердам, 1998

[4] Анализ этого процесса – в журналах «Проект Россия» № 24, Москва-Амстердам, 2002 и «Проект Россия» № 20, Москва-Амстердам, 2001

[5] Коммунизм не мог функционировать в силу своего утопического характера. Многое оставалось неосуществленным. По сравнению с ним капиталистическое общество является гораздо более тоталитарным. Так, один из петербуржских архитекторов поделился со мной своими наблюдениями: «Когда я впервые оказался на Западе, меня поразило, насколько он идеологизирован. Каждый знал совершенно точно, что именно правильно».

[6] См. так же «Проект Россия» № 21, Москва-Амстердам, 2001

Современная архитектура в России

Филипп Мойзер

Когда Пётр Первый более 300 лет пригласил для строительства основанной им новой столицы Санкт-Петербурга известных зодчих со всей Европы, он проявил себя как дальновидный политик. Архитекторы – в том числе, из Италии, Голландии и Германии – возвели на берегах Финского залива градостроительный ансамбль, который до сих пор привлекает туристов со всего мира. Правда это решение Петра Первого имело скорее прагматические нежели архитектурно-художественые основания, однако благодаря ему гигантская империя приблизилась к Европе – как географически, так и в культурном отношении. Русское зодчество было буквально окрылено западными идеями. Архитектурный язык новой столицы должен стал эталоном для развития городов во всей империи, вплоть до глубинки.[1]

Европеизация Санкт-Петербурга путем «импортирования» архитектуры барокко существенно повлияла на каноны русского зодчества в целом. При том, что этот эпизод имел скорее государственно-репрезентативную подоплеку. Роскошная архитектура больше всего подходила стране, которая к моменту индустриализации Западной Европы все еще стояла на якоре феодальной системы с ее вертикалями власти «царь – церковь – дворянство» и связанными с этим правилами управления и господства. Только Октябрьская революция 1917 года смогла устранить эту иерархическую структуру.

У нас перед глазами был пример того, как молодой Советский Союз с самого начала своего существования развивался, пытаясь соединить несоединимое – традиции и прогресс. Революция вытолкнула Россию на рельсы европейского летоисчисления – в прямом и переносном смысле. Это проявилось, во-первых, в отмене Юлианского календаря и переходе на григорианский, действующий во всей Европе с 1582 года, и, во-вторых, казнью всей царской семьи в Екатеринбурге. Оба эти события произошли в 1918 году. С этого момента пути назад не существовало. С переходом страны на европейскую систему летоисчисления начатое некогда Петром Первым приближение к Европе в области архитектуры должно было распространиться и на другие сферы общественной жизни. В конечном итоге Октябрьская революция оказалась не только политической, но и культурной революцией. Современные художники, «бунтовавшие против установленного при царе подхода к искусству, чувствовали себя сторонниками тех, кто считал всю эту социальную систему наследством царской эпохи. Коммунистов и модернистов объединяла почти фатальная вера в возможности науки и техники, которые могли существенно изменить отношения между людьми».[2]

Отмена крепостного права, принудительная коллективизация и поголовная ликвидация безграмотности как раз и были этими изменениями в повседневной жизни. Индустриализация и механизация маркировали создание новой политической системы, что в свою очередь было выражено в ленинском лозунге «коммунизм это есть советская власть плюс электрификация всей страны».

Советский авангард: новая архитектура для нового общества

Эль Лисицкий, один из важнейших представителей русского авангарда, в 1929 году в своей программе воодушевленно провозгласил: «Создание машины – это начало технической революции. Техника сегодня произвела переворот не только в социальном и экономическом, но и в эстетическом развитии и определила основы новой архитектуры. В октябре 1917 года началась наша революция, а с ней и новая страница в истории человечества. Основные элементы нашей архитектуры относятся к этой социальной, а не технической революции».[3] В этих идеях чувствуется влияние художника и философа Казимира Малевича, который, будучи одним из ведущих представителей русского модернизма, развивал собственное направление в искусстве как выражение нового времени - времени революций и технического прогресса. В 1919 году в Витебской школе искусств Малевич привлек профессора Лисицкого своими взглядами. С 1929 года и до отъезда на Запад Эль Лисицкий заведовал кафедрой архитектуры в Московской государственной школе искусств. «Новое строительство» и коммунизм должны были возникнуть в логической связи между собой, как индивидуальное социалистическое обязательство одного перед другим.

Исходя из этого, Лисицкий в 1929 году вывел следующую социальную задачу архитектуры: «Социальное развитие приводит к устранению контраста между городом и деревней. Город стремится вплоть до самого центра включить в себя природу и одновременно за счет индустриализации вывести деревню на более высокий уровень культуры. Сегодня мы должны быть очень материалистичными, практичными и неромантичными, чтобы догнать и перегнать весь остальной мир».[4]

Это напоминает не только лозунги ЦК КПСС, но и отчасти постулаты немецкого авангарда, который в Веймарской республике видел зарю светлого будущего – демократического, нового общества. Это общество скинуло обветшалую мантию истории и провозгласило себя строителем новой жизни. Строить «новые дома для нового общества», как сказал Ханс Шарун в 1947 году, – это было именно то, что занимало представителей немецкого авангарда в двадцатые годы, точно так же, как их русских коллег в молодом Советском Союзе. В те годы общественного перелома Россия присоединилась к мировому авангардному процессу, и ей оставалось только подкрепить это экономически. Представители европейского и особенно немецкого авангарда гарантировали при этом не только поддержку в области архитектуры и градостроительства для осуществления культурной революции, но также и социально-моральную поддержку в отношении неизбежного вопроса о частной собственности. «Тяжелыми оковами остается безнравственное право собственности на землю. Без освобождения земли от рабства частной собственности не сможет возникнуть здоровое, способное к развитию и экономически оправданное градостроительство» – писал не Ленин и не Сталин, а Вальтер Гропиус в 1931 году и заключал в дополнении: «Это важное основополагающее требование выполнил Советский Союз - в одиночку и безоговорочно, и тем самым расчистил путь к современному градостроительству».[5] Основатель веймарской школы «Баухаухауз» откровенно восхищался образцовой ролью Советского Союза, а в книге «Новое строительство в СССР» он оценил работу Эрнста Мая «как организатора строительства и активного проектировщика Советской России». Для революционной России Запад привлекал возможностью обмена идеями и опытом, для западных же архитекторов - особенно, для немецких, - Россия была общественно-политическим провозвестником земельной реформы в Германии. Попытка лишить права владения землей уже лишенное к этому времени политического могущества дворянство, согласно всенародному решению 1926, все-таки сорвалась, не собрав необходимых для этого пятидесяти процентов голосов.

30 декабря 1922 конституционно утвержденный Советский Союз, которому предшествовало основание в 1918 году Российской Социалистической Федеративной Советской Республики как основы нового государства, стал полем для экспериментов архитекторов со всего мира. Среди приехавших сюда были Эрнст Май, Ле Корбюзье, Бруно Таут и даже американец Альберт Кан, архитектор промышленных предприятий, построивший знаменитые заводы Форда. Гротескность ситуации заключалась в том, что архитектурная элита капиталистического Запада переместилась на Восток, чтобы оказать помощь в строительстве нового государства, руководство которого с самого начала не скрывало стремления к разрушению капиталистиче-

ского мира. Даже когда в связи с запаздыванием планируемой мировой революции, остановились на «мирном сосуществовании» (Ленин) и на образцовой функции Советского Союза через воплощение в жизнь коммунистической модели общества в собственной стране (Сталин), мировая революция, а с ней и справедливая война против европейского империализма (Ленин) не были отменены, а были всего лишь отсрочены. Общественная задача внутреннего строительства провозглашала переход на технические стандарты Западного мира. За этот акт экономического насилия отвечала так называемая «Новая Экономическая Политика» (НЭП), которая скрывалась под маской индустриализации и механизации всей экономики от конвейера до поля. На эту тему Эрнст Май, который в то время еще был городским советником во Франкфурте, перед тем как податься на берега Москвы-реки, цитировал «Bauwelt»: «Нужно строить новые города, а старые перестраивать. Самой интересной и сложной задачей является создание совсем новых городов. Города в первую очередь должны стать центрами металлургии, которую тоже надо будет создать заново».[6] 1 сентября 1930 года Май отправился в Москву с командой, состоящей из 21 человека.

Социалистический реализм: новые города в старом формате

Эрнст Май принял участие в конкурсе на строительство металлургического комбината в городе Магнитогорске, который в первую пятилетку (1929-33) должен был стать моделью и образцом для последующего строительства многих других новых городов Советского Союза. Раньше Магнитогорск был рабочим городком европейского типа, который разросся до гигантских размеров; он стал городом-пионером на восточной стороне южного Урала. Другое требование заключалось в расширении уже существующих городов с целью переселения промышленного пролетариата из убогих бараков в более благоустроенную жилую среду, а так же подготовки городов к большим притокам населения. Москва в этом смысле стала моделью для подражания, а после открытия метро в 1935 году она стала считаться мировой социалистической столицей.

С 1931 года границы «мирового политического эксперимента», как Май называл строительство Советского Союза, стали в области градостроительства более четкими. Тогда Лазарь Каганович, почитаемый Сталиным градостроитель и его правая рука в Центральном Комитете, требовал «перестраивать старые города, а новые, такие как Магнитогорск, строить умеренно современ-

ными».[7] Тем самым Каганович очертил основную линию советского зодчества, которая была озвучена в 1934 году в провозглашении Андреем Ждановым «социалистического реализма» как советско-патриотической директивы вкуса. На этом закончилась свобода творческого духа, и сильно ограничилось пространство для игр современного движения, архитекторы которого, вследствие политических обстоятельств, почти не оставили после себя очень мало свидетельств.

Так же как и в Германии, сторонники авангарда поняли, что свои смелые идеи они вряд ли смогут осуществить. Многое осталось лишь запечатленными на бумаге мечтами. В общественном и культурно-политическом плане авангарду в Советском Союзе было позволено еще меньше чем в Германии, его краткий взлет был всего лишь интермеццо. Так же, как и в сталинском Советском Союзе, в национал-социалистической Германии основные принципы авангарда были перемешаны с чертами так называемого национального стиля и при помощи традиционных теорий градостроительства объединены в единое целое, руководствуясь лозунгом : «рациональность в обработке материала, красота и смелость в воплощении». Но даже здесь параллели между сталинской и гитлеровской культурами - в противовес тезисам историков восьмидесятых годов, которые видели в них полную противоположность, — являются ошеломляющими. Сравнения сталинского проектирования столицы со шпееровской концепцией превращения Берлина в будущую мировую столицу Германия обнаружили поразительное сходство в форме и содержании, вплоть до идеологического определения понятия архитектуры. В связи с этим становится понятно, что Советский Союз под руководством Сталина был в состоянии осуществить проект социалистического города и после Второй Мировой войны экспортировать его вплоть до берегов Эльбы. Карл-Маркс-аллее в Берлине – самый протяженный архитектурный ансамбль в Германии, являющийся материализованным свидетельством сталинского архитектурного стиля на Шпрее.

Негативная позиция по отношению к функционалистской архитектуре была вполне понятна. Архитектура модернизма в ее чистом виде - с «градостроительным отражением общества, раздробленного на экономически и духовно самостоятельных индивидуумов», противоречила социальным предпосылкам в Советском Союзе и со времен новой номенклатуры, которая под новыми символами (серп и молот с красной звездой вместо двуглавого орла и короны) переняла принципы правления царской империи, считалась несовместимой с самосознанием нового государства. Коммунистическую Россию в этой ситуации можно сравнить с фирмой, которая реорганизовала иерархию служащих и создала себе новый бренд. Но при этом в отношении руководства компания осталась авторитарной и продолжает проповедовать агрессивный государственный капитализм.

«Социалистический реализм» отвечал многим потребностям народа, подавлявшимся долгое время – в том числе, и религиозной. Поэтому архитекторы должны были, прежде всего, осознавать себя «инженерами человеческих душ» (Жданов). «Презирайте старых мастеров!» - таков был популярный лозунг, которым начал новую линию Анатолий Луначарский, значительный для советской политики деятель в области культуры, влиятельный искусствовед и литературовед. Наблюдения Бруно Таута подтверждали его теории, и 1929 году он высказался на тему положения архитектуры в России: «Целью русского искусства является выражение невидимого дыхания Бога в видимой и осязаемой форме. В России поиск источника происходит в очень драматической форме. По конкурсам и их результатам видно, как все еще по-прежнему происходит борьба между стремлением к функциональности и жаждой красоты». Бруно Таут приводит в пример конкурс на строительство библиотеки имени Ленина в Москве, в котором жюри из двух вариантов – остекленного здания и традиционного – сделало выбор в пользу последнего. Оно было вынуждено пойти на эту жертву для того, чтобы «обеспечить нормальную работу ученых в библиотеке».[8] По этому поводу Таут, будучи представителем функционализма, изумленно отмечает: «Задача русской архитектуры заключается в том, чтобы создать гармонию между новыми взглядами и реальной привязанностью русских к земле». Именно это и виделось стражам вкуса в Центральном Комитете при провозглашении ими социалистического реализма. Следующий по очереди творческий сдвиг был с иронией прокомментирован в 1933 году в газете «Новый город», издаваемой во Франкфурте: «Мы почитаем классику и оправдываем классицизм (Луначарский), и в то же время мы не хотим потерять Ле Корбюзье, как олицетворение современности, и помимо этого – экономия и стандартизация любой ценой! Мы хотим одного, а должны делать совсем другое; а результат этого – всеобщая нестабильность».[9] То, что кажется противоречием, обнаруживает диалектику, которая в доктрине искусства «социалистического реализма» создает своеобразный синтез. Умеренный модернизм означало то, что Эрнст Май[10] разработал генеральный план застройки нового промышленного города Магнитогорска, а американский промышленный архитектор Кан застраивал его зданиями. Реконструкция означала то, что такой традиционно ориентированный градостроитель как, например, кёльнский коммунист Курт Майер, переносил в Москве по шаблону планы, разработанные для Кельна еще в те времена, когда его мэром был Конрад Аденауэр. Член Коммунистической партии Германии, Курт Майер покинул Кельн после того, как Аденауэр попытался его - как будущего главного архитектора города – принудить к соблюдению партийно-политической линии.[11] Ханс Шмидт в 1932 году следующим образом прокомментировал ситуацию с представителями модернизма в Советской России, после того, как жюри объявило провальными авангардистские проекты московского Дворца Советов: «Это нисколько не удивительно, потому что те же самые молодые архитекторы, которые на протяжении долгих лет на ватмане без устали копировали образцы Ле Корбюзье с его остекленными фасадами и висячими садами, сегодня разрабатывают фасады классической типа, на том же ватмане и под руководством тех же старых мастеров архитектуры».[12] Это естественная реакция архитекторов, считавших себя передовиками политического авангарда, когда они осознали, что они уже больше не востребованы. У нацеленного на будущее модернизма в Советском Союзе авторитарная доктрина партии выбила почву из-под ног. С другой же стороны доктрина в области искусства мобилизовала творческие силы старого сообщества архитекторов, оставшихся еще с царских времен.

На этом фоне под руководством Сталина стали возводиться здания, которые, не смотря на экономичность, могли служить образцами умеренного модернизма. До сих пор эта сталинская архитектура едва ли признается в международных дебатах. Из-за незнания ее нередко называют, например, «кондитерским стилем» или «вкусовыми заблуждениями диктатуры». Ее также не включают в архитектурную историю XX века, даже, несмотря на то, что Харальд Боденшац и Кристиане Пост положили этому многообещающее начало своей изданной в 2003 году книгой «Градостроительство в тени Сталина». В ее предисловии авторы высказываются о том, что игнорирование западными историками этого периода едва ли воздает должное значению сталинской архитектуры в градостроительстве. То же самое касается и развития архитектуры. Провокационно звучит тезис о том, что сегодняшняя русская архитектура в своей приверженности советскому наследию является в Европе самой традиционалистской.

Холодная война: архитектура между серийной действительностью и версией handmade

Русский конструктивизм, так же, как и советский функционализм, являющийся репликой на послевоенный западный модернизм и введенный Никитой Хрущевым под лозунгом «высокое качество при низких затратах» в середине пятидесятых годов, можно оценить как безуспешные попытки – на смену одному пришел сталинизм, на смену другому - неорусский регионализм. Но это было бы слишком просто. Советский функционализм был спартанским вариантом конструктивизма, своеобразным социалистическим отражением западного интернационального стиля с прагматичной целью построить как можно дешевле как можно больше жилых помещений и в то же время, будучи формой выражения искусства, укрепить внутреннее культурное единство. От Минска до Владивостока строились почти одинаковые здания, которые согласовывались в Москве и централизованно получали серийные номера. Рационализация в проектировании и строительстве – идея, соответствующая своему времени как на Востоке, так и на Западе – привела в Советском Союзе к вымиранию архитектуры как профессии. В то время, как Западная Европа из экономических соображений вернулась к конвенциональному строительству, серийное домостроение в Советском Союзе стало заложником самого себя. Архитектура стала также важным средством политического противостояния в годы «холодной войны» - в борьбе за господство над миром, который под давлением современной технической цивилизации стал объединятся, несмотря на все политические разногласия. Внезапно модернизм с его столь популярными идеями рационального строительства стал ведущей государственной линией, и превратясь в массовое промышленное производство архитектуры, как на Востоке, так и на Западе, был растиражирован до полного безобразия. Советский Союз, будучи центральным государством половины политического мира, вновь стала ориентироваться на Запад.

Постсталинский Советский Союз эпохи Леонида Брежнева застыл в своем постном функционализме, который «превзошел западные ужасы контейнерной архитектуры»[13], чтобы потом, после 1991, опять все поставить на то, чтобы в спешке пережить кажущиеся упущенными пройденные на Западе фазы культуры. Такая психограмма нации, которая постоянно кружится вокруг самой себя и, которой все время кажется, что она ко всему приходит с запозданием, также не чужда и нам немцам. После распада Советского Союза неотрадиционализм был призван стать главным течением в современной русской архитектуре, и тому есть разные объяснения.

С провозглашением Михаилом Горбачевым курса на перестройку и гласность, архитектурное сообщество отважилось на проекты, которые долгое время до этого в воплощали только на бумаге. Это была реакция на творческий застой и протест против «политически застывшего государства, и с ним застывшей архитектуры, связь между которыми укреплялась партийными архитекторами (Клоц). Возникла разновидность бюрократической системы, которая послушным и преданным партийной линии архитекторам гарантировала как бы целые абонементы заказов, требуя при этом от них полного выключения творческой фантазии.

Против этого протестовали те, кто был лишен возможности строить, кто не мог работать, подозреваясь в «препятствии прогрессу». Эти архитекторы либо покидали страну, либо находили себе альтернативные ниши в обществе. Они отказывались от гротескных картин реального градостроительства, и фантазии бурно расцветали – свободные от всякого контроля. Единственное табу, которому подчинялись архитекторы, было отсутствие всякого табу. Все было возможно, и так встречались перенесенные на бумагу русский конструктивизм двадцатых годов, классицизм XVI века а-ля Джованни Баттиста Пиранези, прусский классицизм Шинкеля и ранний модерн Адольфа Лооса. Эпохи встречались и скрещивались друг с другом как само собой разумеющееся. При этом обнаружилось, что укрепившиеся в теории противоречия и антагонизмы всего лишь стадии органического развития. Внезапно стало понятно, что осажденные предвзятыми образами стилевые эпохи обнаруживают сходства. В фантазиях «бумажных архитекторов» эти элементы превращались в нечто новое, современные формы перенимались как чистая культура. В чертежах Н. Бронзова, М. Филиппова, В. Петренко, в их образах и проектах, прежде всего, чувствуются влияния стилей и утопий итальянского Ренессанса. М. Лабазов и А. Чельцов, напротив, сплавляли кубизм с восточными мотивами. Другие представляли конкретные проекты, как, например, Михаил Белов, который в проекте «Улица Архитекторов» мечтал реконструировать улицу Щусева в Москве в духе итальянского Ренессанса. Впрочем, даже образцы Средневековья часто были всего лишь чем-то вроде бумажной архитектуры. По крайней мере, тогда, когда художники создавали свои полотна, то в их мотивах в полной мере проявлялись архитектурные идеи, как, например, «Школа старины» Рафаэля сохранилась лишь в виде фрагмента фрески в Ватикане. У русских «бумажных архитекторов» это иногда доходило до крайностей и свободного от любого принуждения китча - что поражает даже нас, столь привыкших к разнообразию форм постмодернизма.

Чтобы понять своеобразие «бумажной архитектуры», возникшей из Группы НЭР в шестидесятые годы, которая проектировала только в целях теоретической дискуссии, нужно понимать различия между утопией и фантазией. «Утопическое мышление, которое развивалось в теории и практике европейской архитектуры XIX и XX веков и в строительстве бывшего Советского Союза, отрицало плюрализм». Утопический проект как составная часть улучшения мира, должен сопровождаться желанием воплощения его в жизнь. «В фантазии существует также возможная версия мира, в отличие от утопии у фантазии нет каких-либо притязаний, эта версия в действительности может стать ключом к решению срочных проблем человечества»[14], - этого вопроса коснулся историк архитектуры Александр Раппапорт. Именно этим отличаются «бумажные архитекторы» восьмидесятых от конструктивистов начала XX века: последние, будучи утопистами, видели в большевистской революции шанс дать новому обществу соответствующую маску искусства. Все, что противоречило диктату вкуса этих конструктивистов, уничтожалось. Однако, ситуация не была иной и в лагере европейского модернизма. По причине нервозности времени, стало ощутимым существование тоталитарной архитектуры, которая добивалась только того, чтобы быть политически окрашенной и защищенной, гарантом чего ей представлялась Веймарская республика, несмотря на то, что контроль со стороны государства ей был абсолютно не нужен. Даже в прогнившей политической культуре Германии времен Вильгельма накануне Первой Мировой войны по причине творческой динамики и более убедительных, соответствующих духу времени идей, было возможно больше изменений. Представление об осуществлении утопии в окружающем мире существовали уже в XVIII веке. «Однако технические и политические предпосылки для этого были созданы впервые только в XX веке» (Раппапорт).

«Бумажные архитекторы» восьмидесятых годов долгое время боролись за освобождение от этого. Остается фактом то, что все они были архитекторами, лишенными возможностей, что для многих изменилось существенно и внезапно после 1991 года. Александр Бродский или Михаил Белов с тех пор стали относиться к тем, кто проектируют, чтобы строить, и тем самым перешли из воображаемого в конструктивное «все возможно». Торговые центры с фасадами, похожими на архитектуру «Баухауза», и элегантные модернистские здания стоят сегодня рядом с перегруженными декором домами, которые часто скрывают свои старые железобетонные фасады.

Капиталистический реализм: архитектура новой России

«Старинные постройки сносятся еще в большем объеме, чем в советское время», - жалуется Николай Малинин, и на их месте возникают «исторически кричащие новые здания». «Реконструкция очистила место для реставрации», прямо следуя девизу „Снос здания с последующим его восстановлением", и, вследствие этого, перешагнула через свои задачи, которые до этого распространялись только на те места, где раньше ничего не было или стояло что-то непригодное.[15] «Пригодно» или «непригодно» определяют теперь заместившие бывшие органы Центрального Комитета местные начальники, которые в этом отношении ведут себя как мелкие феодалы и политические комиссары. Одним из таких решающих людей является мэр Москвы Юрий Лужков, который при участии своей жены в качестве руководителя крупного концерна основал миллиардную империю недвижимости и определяет, как должны выглядеть важнейшие места в городе. «Всегда лично присутствуя на всех заседаниях Общественного градостроительного совета, он выражает свое мнение почти по каждому проекту и является представителем чисто эстетических принципов: в центре мы строим только историческое, стекло – только на окраинах, никаких гладких фасадов». Само по себе это допустимо, но личностно-авторитарная директива, которая сменила предыдущую директиву партии, дошла до характера цензуры и одновременно предопределила коррупцию, так как «архитектор должен платить за любое новшество (разумеется, из кошелька заказчика)». В такой ситуации что-то, конечно, остается за пределами личных эстетических предпочтений, за счет чего происходят изменения в облике города.

Совсем по-другому это развитие проистекало, например, в Берлине. По словам московского архитектурного критика Ирины Шиповой, это удалось благодаря единой программе «долгосрочного градостроительного развития Берлина», который начал разрабатываться еще в восьмидесятые годы Йозефом Паулем Кляйхузом во время Международной Строительной Выставки.[16] Благодаря этой программе две, такие разные, части Берлина после падения стены в 1989 году поразительно быстро и гармонично смогли срастись в единое целое. В то время как в Берлине пытались свести вопросы эстетики каждого отдельного здания к архитектуре города, в Москве постсоветского времени вообще ничего не было слышно о городском планировании. Все строилось согласно интуиции и наугад, а если вдруг что-то удавалось, то только благодаря случаю. В отличие от социалистических времен, не было ни малейшего представления о том, как должен функционировать город как организм цивилизации. Этим объясняется амбивалентность поспешных стараний создать на уровне города уютность теплого гнезда за счет богато декорированной архитектуры. Важен только отдельный объект, а общее целое может быть каким угодно. Архитектура заняла место градостроительства, и в этом Москва, начиная с 1991 года, стала задавать масштаб всей стране. Важным моментом в этом стало создание ярких визуальных доминант в эстетически рационализированном облике города, управляемого прежде всего по законам рынка. Главным ходом на этом пути стало возведение церквей. К выдающимся примерам программы восстановления религиозных построек относится воссоздание Храма Христа Спасителя в 1997 году, в честь празднования 850-летия города Москвы. На историческом месте, на котором однажды должен был быть воздвигнут Дворец Советов, но вместо него был построен бассейн, мэр Москвы Юрий Лужков построил копию прежнего собора. Теперь храм выглядит так, как будто стоял здесь всегда, как будто он и не относился к тем восьмидесяти процентам церквей, которые были разрушены по приказу Сталина. Создающее ощущение подлинности здание все же снабжено платной подземной автостоянкой, потому что «в России строят по законам денег» – как иронично заметил Н.Малинин.

То, что Храм Христа Спасителя не встретил единодушного положительного отклика в сознании общественности, скорее связано с непрозрачными махинациями в сфере торговли недвижимостью, а не с эстетическими пристрастиями общества. Наряду с торговлей сырьем, сфера недвижимости относится к самым прибыльным областям экономики в новой России. И это все еще так, несмотря на то, что согласно исследованиям Международной экономической аудиторской организации средняя ставка годовой прибыли на рынке московской недвижимости со времен кризиса конца девяностых годов снизился к 2004 году до тридцати процентов. Рынок недвижимости стал очень напряженным, но он все еще по-прежнему остается золотым дном по сравнению с Европой, где инвесторы уже долгое время должны довольствоваться годовыми доходами от четырех до пяти процентов. При этом высокие проценты прибыли отнюдь не

означают высокого качества строительства. Это объясняется тремя причинами: заказчики, общее недоверие архитекторам и наивность покупателей. «Заказчики в Москве очень жадны, боязливы и не очень тщеславны. Они экономят на всем: на строительных материалах, технологиях, строительных работах и архитекторах. Большинство заказчиков не доверяют архитекторам, они предпочитают тех, кто быстрее всего может уладить любые формальности». Все же это постепенно исчезает, так же, как и пирамида, состоящая из банков, политиков и маклеров недвижимости. Нормализующий «обвал» доходов стал лучшим этому доказательством.

Между тем Н.Малинин все же видит изменения в сторону улучшения качества и форм архитектуры с современным выразительным языком вместо адаптации и смешения классицизма и модерна, запечатлеваемых в мертворожденных формах запоздавшего на двадцать лет европейского постмодернизма. В конечном итоге, после экономического кризиса 1998 года «образовался новый класс инвесторов, которые осознавали, что деньги необходимо вкладывать не только в полезные площади, но и в архитектуру». К слову, «бумажные архитекторы» не смогли убедительно перенести свою творческую независимость в реальный строительный процесс. Н.Малинин, будучи объективным наблюдателем своего города и острым на язык критиком, замечает качественные перемены в выборе стройматериалов и возросшее влияние нового поколения молодых архитекторов, что довольно удивительно в свете тех обстоятельств, что «архитектура появилась здесь только пятнадцать лет назад», вследствие чего, «профессия архитектора не может быть унаследованной». Вторым важным показателем является приток иностранных архитекторов, которые выигрывают все больше и больше конкурсов. Реальными доказательствами этих перемен являются среди прочего *Copper House* Сергея Скуратова или высокотехнологичное здание „Стольник" архитектурного бюро «А-Б» (Андрей Савин, Михаил Лабазов, Андрей Чельцов).

С этим мнением, конечно, можно поспорить, но автор ясно дает понять, что архитектура реагирует на общественные потребности, которые он обрисовал следующим образом: «По причине того, что среднестатистический москвич любит старую Москву, он решительно отвергает новую архитектуру». Причина этого кроется в истории, как, в прочем, и в том, что новая архитектура на протяжении долгих лет уничтожала облик города, и, кроме того, в обиде и зависти жителей, которые замечают, что те, у кого появляются деньги, сразу пытаются скрыться за стенами

респектабельных современных зданий, вследствие чего модернизм предстает стилем новой буржуазии. С другой стороны, ощущается потребность в тишине, порядке и стабильности. В области репрезентативных зданий ничто не удовлетворяет это народное чувство больше, чем русская православная церковь с ее веками сложившимся образным языком. Она располагает известным, признанным и незаменимым репертуаром искусства, который даже после нескольких десятилетий советского господства остается свободным от предрассудков и проблем и ревностно востребованным, если речь заходит о национальной идентичности и самосознании. Насколько Храм Христа Спасителя в Москве является спорным, настолько же он является вехой в истории новой русской архитектуры и в то же время знаком того, что, в независимости от политики и архитектуры, можно восстановить здание, которого более пятидесяти лет не было на портрете города.

В первую очередь при строительстве церквей речь идет о создании идеальной картины, существующей в народном сознании. И исключения только подтверждают правила. Более девяноста процентов новых зданий русских православных церквей отвечают канонам еще царских времен. Москва ли это, Екатеринбург, Самара или какой-нибудь городок в Сибири, новые храмы едва ли отличаются от исторических построек, в независимости, используются ли там новые фасадные материалы или пластиковые оконные рамы. Удивительно при этом то, что именно архитекторы, в советские времена преуспевавшие в возведении типовых панельных коробок, теперь активно берутся за проектирование церквей на основе исторических типологий. Сегодня в этом просматривается тот же феномен, что и в 1934 году, когда после обнародования новой художественной доктрины, архитекторы еще старой школы создавали прекрасное будущее для Советского Союза.

Другой феномен – это ренессанс сталинской архитектуры, которая отвечает описанным потребностям и также находит политическое созвучие в выборе на второй срок Владимира Путина, который долгое время занимал руководящую должность разведке КГБ, а теперь под царским двуглавым орлом руководит новой Россией. В годы правления Путина в российской столице расцвел «неосталинский стиль», особенностью которого является отсутствие непосредственной связи между архитектурными формами и централизацией власти. В Москве, которая без сталинской архитектуры просто не воспринимается, возрождение этого стиля отнюдь не удивительно. В нем присутствует своя градостроительная логика, если речь заходит о том, чтобы вновь создать завершенную картину города. По этой причине в 2005 году по проекту компании «Дон-Строй» в непосредственной близости от центра города возникла «восьмая сестра» сталинских высоток. Жилое здание под названием «Триумф Палас», построенное в неосталинском стиле, считается самым высоким в Европе. Если спроецировать это на Берлин, то ситуация выглядела бы так, как если бы бывшая Сталин-аллее была продлена в прежних формах, но уже не для рабочих и партийной верхушки, а как в высшей степени эксклюзивное жилье для новой финансовой элиты. Комплекс «Дон-Строя» довольно многое говорит об обществе, в котором давно оторвавшиеся от народа покупатели элитарного жилья по-прежнему мечтают о сталинских домах с высокими потолками, широкими подоконниками, просторными комнатами, балконами, колоннами и баллюстрадами. Ведь каждый в этой стране всегда понимал, что значит жить в таком доме, и потому многие до сих пор твердо убеждены в том, что ничего лучше просто не может быть. Большое значение имеет и то, что подобный популизм гарантирует конкурентоспособность для большинства девелоперов. И это происходит в постсоветской России, где три четверти населения до сих пор живет в панельных домах, при этом стараясь их как можно больше украсить и отнюдь не стремясь к абстрактной простоте. Только там, где молодые архитекторы минуют генеральную линию развития и, вследствие учебы в Европе или регулярного просматривания зарубежных журналов, создают пуристские здания, похожие на творения швейцарской или испанской школы, отсутствует классический словарь эркеров, карнизов и орнаментов. Правда, проекты молодого поколения составляют пока скорее исключение. Привязанность к знакомому и испытанному присуща обществу, которое до этого знало только переломы и нестабильность. В конечном итоге, градостроительство и архитектура России со времен Сталина больше не знали подобного качества. Нео-сталинскую архитектуру можно сопоставить со смешением псевдо-Шинкеля с архитектурой довоенного модернизма, в Германии по-прежнему ценящегося очень высоко, - именно на этом сделал себе имя Ханс Колхоф, рационально-экспрессивная кирпичная архитектура которого воспринимается как полная достоинства, благородства и элегантности.

Мода на реконструкцию – это, однако, не какой-то московский каприз. Также и в Санкт-Петербурге, где центр города безупречно сочетает в себе барокко и классицизм, новая архитектура старается вписаться в контекст. Архитекторы, которые строят в центре города, сдерживаются строительной политикой, и должны однозначно консервативно решать дилемму между стилизацией и современными формами. Так, например, в 2004 году на реке Фонтанке было простроено здание управления Центрального Банка России (архитекторы: Владимир Григорьев, Вадим Пономарев, Павел Васильев, Екатерина Железны), главный фасад которого с его скульптурными карнизами, выступающими эркерами и растительным декором едва ли отличается от соседних зданий, построенных почти сто лет назад. В то же время фасад, обращенный к боковой улице, является каким угодно, только не неотрадиционным: это холодная стена из стекла и стали. Это очередная попытка архитектурной революции. И то, что Доминик Перро в начале 2003 года спроектировал похожую на кристалл пристройку к Мариинскому театру, больше не является исключением, подтверждающим правило.

При взгляде на проекты, которые возникли в новой России, сразу можно отделить зерна от плевел. Так, например, в 2002 году в Москве было построено жилое здание «Патриарх», по проекту студии СПАР (С. Ткаченко, О. Дубровский, Е. Грицкевич и О. Скумс). Построенный для финансовой элиты дом стоит недалеко от Патриарших прудов - в уголке города, который еще в советское время был очень престижен. Своим кричащим разнообразием красок и форм он являет собой такое смешение стилей, которому нет аналогов. Фасад в стиле необарокко тянется ввысь, для того, чтобы завершиться блестящей модернистской цитатой: над последним этажом в московское небо устремляется уменьшенная копия непостроенной башни Татлина. То, что инкунабула из революционного раннего конструктивизма должна была быть выше на много сотен метров, кажется, не смущает ни жителей дома, ни архитекторов. Как не смущает их богатый орнаментами фасад и невероятные стальные конструкции, создающие в целом образ, который вряд ли мог бы быть более противоречивым.

Таким образом, Россия отражает феномен, который можно наблюдать во всем мире, и который под разными именами повергает весь профессиональный мир в размышления. Будь то новые урбанисты в Северной Америке или их европейские последователи, объединяющиеся в различные группировки, и даже если речь заходит о достижении европейской идентичности в градостроительстве и жилом строительстве в Китае – везде новые традиционалисты цитируют давно зарекомендовавшие себя формы и рецепты, оказывая сопротивление анонимному языку архитектуры, который принесла с собой глобализация. В то же время Россия пытается развить собственный профиль в искусстве, в отличие от бывших союзных республик, которые со своими традиционными средствами выражения соответствуют технически нормированному миру. Исходя из этого, в свете культурной регионализации на территории бывшего Советского Союза, теперь можно говорить и о российском регионализме.

Такого рода экспериментов, как в Москве, архитектура региона не знает. Чтобы понаблюдать русский регионализм в его чистом виде, стоит совершить поездку по Волге. Например, в Нижнем Новгороде, Перми и Самаре возникли жилые и общественные здания, которые стремятся к эстетическому родству со стилем модерн или Ар Деко. Эти здания совершенно естественно вписываются в общую картину города и возвращают хотя бы немного идентичности городам, которые в советские времена застраивались так грубо и однообразно. В этом смысле самые выразительные примеры русской архитектуры возникли в регионах. К самым необычным зданиям относится, например, здание банка «Гарантия» в Нижнем Новгороде, которое в 1995 году было построено архитектурным квартетом: Евгений Пестов, Александр Харитонов, Сергей Попов и Игорь Гольцев. К улице обращен оштукатуренный фасад с овальными окнами и филигранными керамическими деталями, которые напоминают о временах правления последней царской династии. Таким же образом в середине девяностых годов возникло жилое и офисное здание по проектам Менделя Футлика в Перми и «Дом-муха» по проекту Леонида Кудерова в Самаре. Оба здания, конечно же, цитируют мотивы Ар Нуво и соединяют их с функциональным языком современной архитектуры.

В то время как в Москве господствует определенный плюрализм интернациональных стилей и течений, архитектурное разнообразие в региональных центрах сводится к неотрадиционным формам и, к сожалению, к возникающим по всему миру зеркальным и железным коробкам, за фасадами которых размещаются гостиницы, магазины и бизнес-центры. В этом плане региональная русская архитектура может вполне быть причислена к европейского авангарду. Но, прежде всего, неотрадиционалисты в международной дискуссии должны брать в расчет то, насколько большой вклад сможет внести русская архитектура в идеологическое обновление общества путем сокращения многих проблем до вопросов стиля и рыночной свободы. Спрос на новые здания еще не удовлетворен. Как только рынок будет наполнен конкурирующими предложениями, качество архитектуры станет важным фактором торговли. Тогда и астрономические цены на квадратные метры жилья, которые в Москве местами уже перешагнули отметку 10 000 евро, стабилизируются до европейского уровня. А пока посткоммунистический капитализм раскрывает себя с совершенно экстремальной стороны. В такой стране, как Россия, которая, несмотря на свои сырьевые богатства, все же еще относится к развивающимся странам, поиск идентичности еще долго не будет завершен.

[1] Кристина Файерайс / Ханс-Юрген Коммерелль: Б.С.А. Берлинский Союз архитекторов. Каталог выставки Берлин / Москва 2003. При уч. Филиппа Мойзера: Русский регионализм. В журнале: Baumeister 08/04 (август 2004)

[2] Ян Перке: Художник – инженер, в журнале Jungle World, 13 января 1999.

[3] Эль Лисицкий: Основание. В: Эль Лисицкий 1929. Россия: Архитектура для мировой революции. Брауншвейг 1989.

[4] Эль Лисицкий: Будущее и утопия. 1929

[5] Вальтер Гропиус: Что мы ожидаем от русского градостроительства? В: Хартмут Пробст / Кристиан Шедлих: Вальтер Гропиус. Избранные сочинения. Берлин 1988.

[6] Планы Майя в России. В журнале: Bauwelt, выпуск 36 / 1930.

[7] Харальд Боденшац / Кристиане Пост: Градостроительство в тени Сталина. Интернациональный поиск социалистического города в Советском Союзе 1929-1935. Берлин 2003.

[8] Бруно Таут. Архитектурная ситуация а России. В: Эль Лисицкий (1929)

[9] К противоречиям на тему России. В: «Новый город». Вып. 12-1933.

[10] Эрнст Май по истечении первой пятилетки в 1933 году покинул Советский Союз и с 1934 по 1954 год был фермером и архитектором в Кении. В Найроби он оставил следы современной архитектуры. С 1954 года Май занимался в Германии реконструкцией и восстановлением городов (Майнц, Висбаден, Бремерхафен), до 1961 года он был руководителем движения «Новая Родина» (среди прочего возведение района Нойе Вар в Бремене).

[11] Будучи проектировщиком городов, Курт Майер сделал блестящую карьеру в советских структурах. Во время «большой чистки» в партийных рядах в тридцатые годы он был арестован и в 1944 году расстрелян. На эту тему Сюзанне Шаттенберг: Сталинские инженеры. Жизнь между техникой и террором в 1930-е годы. Мюнхен, 2002.

[12] Ханс Шмидт: Советский Союз и новое строительство. В: Новый город. Вып. 6/7 – 1932.

[13] Хайнрих Клоц: Бумажная архитектура. Новые проекты из Советского Союза. Каталог выставки. Франкфурт на Майне, 1989.

[14] Александр Раппапорт: Язык и архитектура «пост-тоталитаризма». В: Хайнрих Клоц: Бумажная архитектура. Новые проекты из Советского Союза. Каталог выставки. Франкфурт на Майне, 1989.

[15] Николай Малинин. Столица без лица. В: Москва – Берлин. Архитектура 1950-2000. Каталог выставки. Москва, 2004.

[16] Ирина Шипова. Разделенный Берлин. Борьба и единство противоположностей. В: Москва – Берлин. Архитектура 1950-2000. Каталог выставки. Москва, 2004.

Новый православный собор в Калининграде. 2006

Жилой комплекс в Москве
Сергей Скуратов

В данном проекте речь идёт о двух расположенных рядом жилых зданиях в Бутиковском переулке – разительно отличающихся друг от друга, но при этом созданных одним архитектором. Дом с закруглённым углом не только кирпичной облицовкой с вставками из светлого юрского камня, но и самой своей формой составляет яркий контраст с тремя малахитовыми кубами соседнего здания. Облицованный клинкером дом – перетекающий контраст, оптический переход внутри пятиэтажного жилого комплекса. По своему стилю он относится к так называемой контекстуальной архитектуре, в которой важную роль играют отношения между зданием и его окружением. Характерная черта контекстуального подхода к архитектуре – нейтральный облик её зданий. Снаружи дом №5 может быть как и офисным, так и жилым зданием: его качество заключается не в архитектурном стиле, а в том, что он не выбивается из окружающей его застройки. Главной контекстуальной темой здесь является контраст между старой и новой Остоженкой: здесь – применение юрского известняка как перекличка с построенным напротив домом Ю. Григоряна, там – тёмный кирпич как реминисценция красных кирпичных домов этого квартала. «Купер Хауз» показывает другой, противоположный подход: здесь главное – не окружение, а характер здания. Новое поколение элитных домов намерено не подражать, а впечатлять. И архитектура в этому отношении является важным средством для повышения ценности объекта. Сильно вытянутый корпус здания, выступающие консоли, покрытая патиной медь, застеклённые галереи – всё это должно свидетельствовать об эксклюзивности этого жилого объекта.

Жилой комплекс в Москве
Проект Меганом

Этот жилой комплекс состоит из двух зданий: четырехэтажного многоквартирного дома, огибающего дугой парк, находящийся на развилке Бутиковского и Молочного переулков, и расположенной позади него частной виллы, названной именем всего этого исторического квартала «Остоженка». Это действительно замечательный уголок в юго-западной части центра Москвы: в поле зрения находятся Башни Кремля, а по соседству – новый Храм Христа Спасителя. Над обращённым в сторону парка стеклянным партером следуют облицованный природным камнем трехэтажный бельэтаж и заглублённый аттиковый этаж. Заказчик скромно обозначает этот комплекс как недвижимость, которая «следует принципам качественной, соответствующей требованиям рынка архитектуре». Архитекторы, в свою очередь, говорят без пафоса о «хорошей архитектуре». Определяющий фактор – будущий покупатель: инвестор и архитекторы ориентируются на личность, свободную от советских комплексов и предрассудков. Этот пример достойно опровергает клише об эксклюзивном жилье в России как обязательно пышно декорированной безвкусице. Новые масштабы следуют европейским стандартам, которые включают в себя такие разумные критерии как хорошее расположение, комфорт и рыночная ликвидность. Вместо клаустрофильского девиза «Мой дом – моя крепость» современному частному жилью становится присуща открытость – о чем вполне свидетельствуют вестибюль и лифт, крытый бассейн и фитнесс-клуб, а так же внутренний двор и даже включенный в композицию прилегающий сквер.

Офисное здание в деревне Челобитьево
Евгений Асс

В унылой деревне с разнородной застройкой в пригороде российской столицы небольшая фирма своим простым офисным зданием показала, что хорошая, функциональная архитектура не обязательно должна быть безликой и безрадостной. В сложившемся парковом ландшафте на берегу ручья архитекторы построили вытянутое невысокое здание, которое своим простым обликом больше всего напоминает складской сарай. Проект предусматривал здание, в котором должны будут размещаться гаражи, офисы, помещения для приёмов и пребывания гостей, а также кабинеты правления. Соответственно этому постройка была разделена на три зоны. В южной части находятся отделенные от четырёх гаражей и технических помещений офисы сотрудников, а центральный тракт с главным входом был обустроен как приемная и коммуникативная зона. Здесь рядом с рецепцией располагаются кафе, гостинная с камином и баром, а также комната для курения. Современная деревянная мебель в этой части здания была также спроектирована архитекторами. Северная часть здания предназначена для правления. Компактный одноэтажный объем с обращенным к улице ефронтоном подкупает прежде всего своим внешним обликом: яркая раскраска кирпичной облицовки, охватывающая крышу и продольные фасады, придаёт простой оболочке динамику и неповторимость. Элегантное оформление прилегающего участка, а также размещённая у воды терраса создают впечатление продуманности этой архитектуры, созданной с большим вниманием к деталям.

Загородный дом в Горках-2
Проект Меганом

Рельефный участок, на котором построен дом, расположен на краю коттеджного поселка под Москвой. Главный фасад находящегося на нем здания множеством своих окнон смотрит не на улицу, а в сторону леса, и напоминает таким образом традиционный деревянный дом – избушку из русских сказок. Его план образует ступенчатую композицию из сужающихся призм. Фасад акцентировааан высоким, вздернутым кверху карнизом, опирающимся на деревянные столбы. Его нисходящую линию продолжает скат кровли. Часть корпуса отступает, образуя широкую террасу, которой соответствуют каменные террасы сада. Стена из битого камня образует не только цоколь дома, но и «заползает» местами до уровня второго этажа. В доме есть сауна, маленький бассейн, а также так называемая зона отдыха, которая является «противовесом» к двусветной гостинной. Хотя эта вилла с односкатной крышей и навесом сильно выделяется на фоне построенных в России за последние годы типовых зданий, но она тоже выглядит уж слишком образцово-показательной. Этот дом провоцирует ассоциации с архитектурой и комфортом европейских загородных домов, которые теперь в Москве становятся настолько популярны, что «строительный бум» вскоре завоюет последние незастроенные участки под виллы «новых русских», чем вполне может подорвать внутригородскую реставрационную программу мэра г. Москвы Юрия Лужкова, как написала Кристине Гамель о России в одном из художественных путеводителей.

Загородный дом под Москвой
Проект Меганом

В строительную типологию современных вилл следует ввести еще один тип: лесной дом. В конце концов почти каждая вторая дача в окрестностях Москвы, которая появилась в последние годы, окружена густым лесом. Архитекторы Григорян и Иванчиков из бюро «Меганом» также стремились сохранить растущие на участке сосны и, насколько возможно, включить их в проект. Дом и участок были разделены функционально. Двухэтажное, трехчастное по композиции бунгало окружено деревянным забором, который отмечает границу участка. Мощеный тротуар посреди ухоженного зеленого сада ведет к главному входу. Три основных объема – блок спален, блок гостиной и соединяющий их переход – образуют гибкую структуру плана при довольно жесткой композиционной схеме. Над бетонным основанием первого этажа возвышается полностью обшитый деревом основной объем, где размещены спальные комнаты. Форма и расположение окон повторяют форму балок деревянного фасада, динамичное чередование их вертикалей и горизонталей создают характерный геометрический узор фасада. Прозрачный фасад холла контрастирует с деревянной отделкой второго этажа, а также с бетонным цоколем. К переднему продольному корпусу присоединяется поперечный флигель, к нему еще один – короткий и к тому же смещенный продольный флигель, таким образом здание охватывают внутренний двор, в котором находится бассейн.

Загородный дом под Москвой
Эдуард Забуга

Три объема разной конфигурации, выполненные из меди, камня и дерева, вставлены друг в друга словно части хитроумной головоломки. В результате получился двухэтажный жилой дом, располагающий бассейном, обширной гостиной и эксплуатируемой кровлей. Участок находится в непосредственном соседстве с коттеджным поселком, и при возведении дома использовались ранее заложенные секции фундамента. Основной задачей архитекторов было создание дома, который бы не проецировал свою внутреннюю жизнь на внешнюю оболочку, но в то же время был бы открыт природному окружению, наполнен солнечным светом и воздухом. На рустованном фасаде со стороны улицы расположены два небольших окна. Дневной свет проникает сквозь большое окно над односкатной крышей, через стеклянную крышу бассейна, а также через застекленный вход на крышу. Композицию первого этажа определяет вытянутое пространство двусветной гостинной, маркированное двумя лестницами – одна, парадная, ведет в хозяйскую половину, вторая – в детскую часть. В отдельной части дома находится мастерская его владельца – скульптора. Она выделяется огромным окном, а также высоким полукруглым сводом, создающим удачное обрамление для рождающихся здесь скульптур.

Здание охраны в Горках-10
Арх 4

Дом охраны в Горках-10 — один из самых необычных проектов архитектора Алексея Козыря, который выделился в последние годы благодаря экспериментам с черным бетоном. Из-за нетрадиционного внешнего облика, а также многочисленных технических изысков, это здание стало одним из фаворитов архитектурной выставки «АрхМосква» в 2002 г. — одного из самых значительных архитектурных смотров в России. В принципе, данный архитектурный объем является не домом, а олицетворением функции, для которой он создавался. Аспект безопасности отражается в строгом разделении здания и его скрытой симметрии: простой антрацитного цвета куб, поставленный на белые опоры, напоминает элемент детского конструктора. Его фасад членится лишь вертикальными щелями окон, и дверью, к которой ведет открытая лестница. Это только видимая часть всего здания. Еще один куб, в котором размещены трансформаторы, спрятан в земле. Справа расположено бунгало владельца участка, его фасад своими двумя круглыми окнами напоминает лицо с очками, сквозь которые хозяин может наблюдать, действительно ли охрана сторожит его владения или она спит.

Торговый центр в Москве
Сергей Киселев/ Группа ДНК

Здание расположено около станции метро «Аэропорт» на Ленинградском проспекте. В этой северо-западной части центра строительство торгового комплекса должно было решить как сугубо практическую, так и важную градостроительную функцию. В то время как с правой стороны — если ехать из центра — фронт улицы сформирован в основном пяти- девятиэтажными домами преимущественно сталинского времени, то ее левую сторону определяют крупные постройки времен управляемого государством прогресса и физического закаливания — комплекс бывшей государственной компании «Аэрофлот», в честь которого названо метро, а так же различные учебные и спортивные здания. Состоящий из нескольких кубических объемов торговый центр пространственно охватывает площадь Эрнста Тельмана. Вынесенный вперед почти до края улицы, поставленный на легкие опоры боковой корпус с динамичной наклонной линией фасада своим эффектным жестом как бы приглашает вовнутрь. Светлокоричневый кирпич чередуется с тонированным, зеленоватым стеклом и металлом, что придает внешнему облику ясность членений. Элементом, оптически связующим различные части здания являются опоясывающие его по горизонтали металлические профили, объединяющие все части композиции в единое целое. Оказавшийся на фоне торгового центра памятник Эрнсту Тельману приобретает таким образом эффектную кулису, гарантирующую его достойное существование в пост-советской России. В коллективном сознании с этой статуей связано представление о бесклассовом обществе, которое невольно проецируется и на торговое здание: во время покупок все равны. Хотя и не каждый это замечает.

Офисное здание в Москве
Группа ДНК

Никто не ожидал в этой части Москвы градостроительного чуда. Что примечательного может произойти между высотными жилыми домами и индустриальными постройками? И тем не менее, здесь, на бесхозном пустыре с руинами старого детского сада возникло офисное здание класса «А», придавшее безжизненному и затрапезному облику улицы Вавилова абсолютно иное звучание. Проект представляет собой рефлексию на тему консервативной деловой архитектуры Ханса Коллхофа. То, что эта очевидная апелляция не выглядит здесь как экзотика и не провоцирует дешевый триумф, происходит за счет исключительно профессиональной и сдержанной трансформации этих форм в московский контекст. Здание ниже своих соседей и своим коричневатым кирпичным фасадом выгодно отличается от грязно-серого окружения. Однообразие его горизонтально вытянутого объема компенсируется пропорционально ритмизованными фасадами, обладающими за счет пилястр пластичностью. Скульптурный характер куба подчеркивается сильно вырезанными плоскостями балконов, а также заглублениями фасада. В аттиковом этаже разместились репрезентативные помещения. Внутренняя структура здания определяется прежде всего трезвыми соображениями экономичности. В соответствии с современными запросами здание располагает свободными планами, рациональным техническим оборудованием и прагматичным членением внутренних помещений. Это офисное здание являет собой образ московского капитализма в классическом одеянии.

Ресторан на Клязьме
Тотан Кузембаев

Новый ресторан с прилегающим к нему жилым комплексом для гостей расположен на берегу озера и своими выразительными формами стал эффектным акцентом на этом протяженном участке берега, зрительно объединяя стоящие здесь разнородные небольшие постройки. Здание ресторана маркирует границу между уже существующим пляжем по одну его сторону и большой пристанью, а так же конным манежем, спроектированным Евгением Ассом, по другую сторону от него. Экспрессионистское здание Тотана Кузембаева продолжает классическую линию «пляжной архитектуры» и представляет собой деревянную постройку на ножках, напоминающую эллегический ресторан «95 градусов» Александра Бродского. В солнечные дни картина ярко-красного домика у голубого озера на фоне такого же голубого неба, желтого песка и зеленых деревьев выглядит как колористический конструктивистский этюд. Это впечатление не является случайным. Архитектор в своих стилистических предпочтениях совершенно открыто апеллирует к русскому авангарду и одному из его интереснейших направлений – конструктивизму. Главенствующая роль большого крыла ресторана подчеркивается выстроенностью иерархической композиции малых объемов. Динамика этой композиции создается открытым проитвопоставлением - прямоугольный фасад ресторана и загзагообразные линии расходящихся диагональных опор, устремленные в небо крыши – и глубоко посаженные в землю входы и веранды. Эта архитектура обладает одновременно легкостью и приземленностью - что превращает ее в достойный внимания объект между землей и небом.

Клуб под Москвой
Архитектурная мастерская XYZ

Данное здание относится к стрельбищу и находится в кратере карьера, песчаные отвалы которого образуют искусственный ландшафт, в который органично вписано расположенное рядом озеро. Здание клуба «Лисья нора» - своеобразные ворота в этот закрытый мир. Сооружение вмещает в себя офисы для персонала, технические службы стрельбища, представительские помещения, магазины и ресторан. Три блока объединяются открытыми террасами. Застекленные переходы соединяют друг с другом деревянные корпуса здания, окрашенные в ярко-красный цвет. Зрительное единство фасадов по-разному оформленных частей комплекса, выстроенных слева и справа от одноэтажного среднего корпуса, подчеркивает также функциональное единство деревянной постройки. Средний корпус, который в плане является центром развернутой под тупым углом композиции, выделяется крытой верандой, к которой ведет открытая лестница. Здесь наверху находится ресторан – таким образом визуальный центр притяжения становится центром притяжения функциональным.

Панельная вилла под Новосибирском
Анатолий Андрющенко

Вышедший на пенсию пилот-вертолетчик Анатолий Андрющенко построил себе в поселке Ордынское под Новосибирском пятиэтажный дом из готовых бетонных панелей. Для этого предприимчивый пенсионер создал в собственной мастерской комбинат для производства железобетонных плит. Дом выглядит абсолютно гротескно не только в силу используемых для его строительства материалов и форм, но и самих методов его возведения. В его формах можно опознать что-то схожее с приграничным замком с капеллой. Капеллой в данном случае служит полукружие абсиды. Но сегменты бетонных плит доказывают удивительную близость между орнаментикой массовой строительной продукции и современной архитектуры, а так же близость к традиционному ремесленному творчеству. Это строение воспринимается еще более абсурдно, так как окружено деревенскими домами и сараями, на фоне которых оно выглядит как инопланетянин. Интерес же это здание представляет в силу органичности сочетания индустриального строительства с индивидуальными решениями. Андрющенко, до этого не имевший строительного опыта, попытался воспроизвести строительный процесс и производство бетонной продукции так, как он себе это представлял. С помощью одной единственной матрицы, с помощью дополнительных вставок и вырубок, он сумел создать болле двадцати пяти различных готовых элементов. Разнообразие форм, о котором проектные институты и строительные комбинаты могли бы только мечтать. Вес и размеры каждой плиты были им расчитаны так, что для строительства ему не понадобились никакие дополнительные механизмы и приспособления кроме собственных рук.

Летняя школа в Ошевенске
Мастерская ТАФ

Летняя школа в Ошевенске Архангельской области была основана для будущих дизайнеров, архитекторов и художников. Они приезжают сюда, чтобы проникнуться духом места, еще сохранившим свойства подлинной народной культуры, тематизировавшимся в ландшафте, постройках, предметах быта и одежде. Для приехавших здание школы должно стать подобием учебного пособия, сконцентрировавшим в себе основные свойства типичных построек прошлого. Оно должно быть функциональным, демонстрировать знакомство с традициями современной архитектуры и в то же время выглядеть так, как будто стояло здесь вечно.

Главными принципами его оформления можно назвать три параметра. Прежде всего, это эскизность его архитектуры на всех уровнях. Она начинается с неформального проектирования, без разработки рабочей документации, продолжается принятием решений о том, какой ствол куда класть, в процессе строительства и заканчивается ручной обработкой дерева при оформлении интерьеров или окон. Не обладая исключительными способностями к импровизации, подобный проект невозможно было бы осуществить. Второй параметр проектирования — минимальные размеры окон при максимальном использовании естественного освещения интерьеров. И третья особенность заключается в асимметричности плана, ориентирующегося на изгиб реки, и создающего ощущение, что этот дом стоит здесь уже более 200 лет и пережил за это время не одно потрясение. Язык современной архитектуры и материалы, не типичные для этого места, здесь оказались бы никем не поняты. И прежде всего, они бы не выдержали суровой зимы, которая больше полугода определяет жизнь этого региона.

Клуб «Кокон» в Москве
Владимир Кузьмин/Влад Савинкин

Клуб «Кокон» является наверно одним из наиболее необычных интерьеров, созданных в последние годы в Москве . Его название заключает в себе его архитектурную программу. Дискотека на Проспекте Мира разместилась в трехэтажном павильоне, постмодернистские фасады которого – с полированным гранитом, сталью и стеклом – воспринимаются довольно холодными и отстраненными. Для прогрессивной Москвы этот стиль уже давно устарел. Круглые окна, открывающие вид в интерьер, прорезают кубический объем, навевая ассоциации со швейцарским сыром. Вытянутые, изогнутые и деформированные круглые проемы увлекают взгляд в биоморфную среду, а как будто размытые водой или ветром внутренние оболочки пробуждают любопытство. Входы и проемы образованы – как и в настоящих пещерах – круглыми и волонообразными отверстиями в органично выступающих поверхностях стен и нишах, и создается иллюзия, что над этими формами природа трудилась не одно столетие для того, чтобы теперь здесь могли обниматься влюбленные парочки, в то время как «Кокон» сотрясается от музыки и ритмов. Биоморфные формы дискотеки и в особенности деревянные конструкции фирмы «Биоинъектор» являются оболочкой для неожиданных пространств. Это непременная зона Chill-Out, деревянные цилиндрические столики которой контрастируют с находящимися рядом стеклянным столам и стульям, стоящими как кубики льда на блестящем полу. От подвала до крыши здесь размещается множество помещений и пространственных зон, вопиюще контрастирующих друг с другом. Единственное, что их объединяет – это как будто вручную вылепленная деревянная пещера-оболочка.

Жилой дом во Внуково под Москвой
Владимир Кузьмин/Влад Савинкин

Было бы преувеличением сказать, что эстетика этого загородного дома основана только на любви архитекторов к традициональному деревянному зодчеству. Когда Кузьмин и Савинкин начали его проектировать, срубы уже находились на участке. Привезенные из республики Мари Эл разобранные старая школа и несолько домов послужили материалом для создания этого архитектурного шедевра. По мнению архитекторов, в конструкции дома должен отражаться характер его владельца. В данном случае – это энергичный и деятельный бизнессмен, предпочитающий необычные решения и идеи не только в деловой, но и в частной жизни, что предоставляло архитектором достаточно свободы для воплощения их фантазий. Они создали необычную конструкцию, в которой несколько готовых изб поставили на металлические и бетонные сваи и соединили друг с другом. Эта конструкция дополняется вертикалями труб, лестницами и световыми колодцами. Архитекторы с уважением отнеслись к «предыдущей» жизни используемых ими фрагментов домов, подчеркнув нюансы их деревянных поверхностей и найдя для них новые композиционные сочетания. В то же время, это не помешало им использовать дополнительные «индустриальные» элементы – такие как галиванизированные стальные опоры и перфорированный металлический забор. Пространственное разнообразие – типичное для традиционных русских деревянных домов, создается здесь не только за счет игры с перспективами, но и за счет использования самых различных, в том числе, и прозрачных материалов.

«Музей плавсредств» под Москвой
А-Б (Арт-Бля)

Воспринимающиеся несколько сюрреалистично плавательные средства являются объектами, которые сделали дети в мастерской Михаила Лабазова. Однако эти разноцветные объекты несопоставимы с привычными лодками. Почти целый год маленькие плавучие средства размещались на нижнем этаже расположенного на соседней пристани ресторана «95 градусов» (архитектор Александр Бродский). Для того, чтобы вдохнуть в них жизнь, Михаил Лабазов спроектировал эту деревянную конструкцию на берегу реки Клязьмы.

Новый «Музей плавсредств» повторяет в малом формате вечную тематику музейных построек: искусство само по себе неформально, конструкция выставочного здания должна быть формализирована и типологизирована. Строгая и элегантная деревянная конструкция музея находится в напряжённом контрасте с разноцветными корабликами. Членение выставочного пространства на ярусы делает экспозицию очень рациональной. Частично висящие, частично стоящие экспонаты защищены выступающим над водой навесом, который таким образом соединяет архитектуру и природу, искусство и воду.

Загородный дом «Морковь» под Москвой
А-Б (Арт-Бля)

Загородный дом, построенный под Москвой и окрещённый архитекторами как «Морковь», трудно классифицировать, и можно описать как архитектурное чудачество. Его невозможно включить в рамки существующих типологий и стилей, он выпадает из привычного архитектурного контекста. Но если рассматривать «дом-морковь» в контексте творчества архитектурной группы «Арт-Бля», то этот проект становится более чем понятным. Идентификация здания лежит не в рамках архитектуры как таковой, а в логике самих архитекторов. В рамках этой идентификации можно обнаружить три основных принципа: архитектура как акт искусства, акт искусства как продолжающийся во времени процесс и процесс - как создание синтетического продукта в пространстве. Однако искусство в этом случае – не эстетическая категория, а метод создания формы. Архитектура трактуется как коллективная деятельность актеров. При таком подходе заказчик становится соавтором, который переживает муки не только экономического порядка, но и муки художественного творчества. Характерно, что архитекторы бюро «А-Б» весьма неохотно предоставляют детальные планы для публикации, – она для них является уделом строителей. Для архитекторов обычным считается общаться с заказчиком и коллегами на языке картин и эскизов. Художник-керамист Евгений Рыбин, известный своими экспериментами с цветом и материалом, оформил капители колонн, а строители собрали бесконечную мозаику из керамических плиток непосредственно на строительной площадке.

Жилой дом «Стольник»
А-Б (Арт-Бля)

И это называется жилым домом? Здание в Малом Левшинском переулке действительно не соответствует привычными представлением о престижном жилье в центре Москвы. С самого начала дому пришлось подвергнуться многочисленным нападкам, связанным с его самонадеянной «инаковостью», и основывающихся на том, что нормальный дом так выглядеть не может. Критики правы. Жилой дом «Стольник» в самом центре Москвы, недалеко от легендарного Арбата, на фоне представительных доходных домов и вилл конца XIX – нач. XX века и даже скромных построек советского времени выглядит как случайно здесь приземлившийся неопознанный летающий объект. Его экспрессивные формы, блестящие, холодные материалы и эффектная поза, в которой он застыл в городском пространстве являются без сомнения чем-то новым. Архитекторы сознательно отказываются от исторических реминисценций и реализуют свои фантазии, навевающие ассоциации с Фрэнком Гери или Хансом Холляйном. Это в теории. На практике же здание послушно вписывается в привычные для этого места градостроительные масштабы. Его высота не превышает установленных здесь отметок, и участок застройки не превышает привычных измерений. Здание образует со стоящим по соседству пятиэтажным домом послевоенного времени единый ансамбль, подчеркивая тем самым интровертный характер Малого Левшинского переулка. Собственно, как своим урбанистичным уличным фасадом, так и скрывающимся в глубине участка двором, этот дом вполне соответствует градостроительным принципам, определявшим жилое строительство в Москве в предыдущие десятилетия.

Ресторан «95 градусов» под Москвой.
Александр Бродский

Недалеко от «Музея плавсредств» находится ресторан «95 градусов» – простая деревянная конструкция, похожая на причал, с символическим названием: ровно 95 градусов составляет угол ее вертикалей. Внутренняя структура более чем на две трети прозрачного здания напоминает интерьер корабля. Банкетная комната доминирует в общей композиции за счет цветового решения: расположенная высоко «палубная рубка» – ржаво-железная. Кухня на «средней палубе», отделённая от главного помещения и обшитая гофрированным волнистым железом, снабжена впечатляющим ячеистым стеклянным фасадом, который определяет облик здания со стороны берега. Одновременно тему прозрачности продолжает открывающийся к воде нижний уровень, создавая взаимосвязь между природой и архитектурой. Этот мотив развивается также и в неровном покрытии крыши, которая дополнительно защищена прозрачным пластиковым тентом. Корабельный характер постройки дополнительно подчёркивается такими деталями, как лестницы-трапы или наклонные балки в виде мачт.

Павильон для водочных церемоний
Александр Бродский

Александр Бродский уже давно мечтал построить павильон для водочных церемоний. Два обстоятельства способствовали тому, что он смог осуществить эту мечту: снос Бутиковской фабрики на Остоженке и ежегодно проводимый фестиваль «Арт Клязьма». Организаторы фестиваля предоставили А.Бродскому участок земли на опушке леса, а старая фабрика обеспечила его материалом - оконными рамами, изготовленными в 1917 году, которые в руках художника превратились в универсальный строительный материал. Окна представляют собой в этом здании как его конструкцию, так и основной фасадный материал. Несмотря на большую поверхность остекления, яркий свет не нарушает интимности процесса принятия напитка - стекла замазаны белой краской, и потому плохо пропускают свет. Днем свет пробивается сквозь закрашенное стекло, вечером же в домике зажигаются свечи и он как волшебный фонарь светится в темноте. На этот свет слетаются все поклонники водочной церемонии, которая одновременно проста и торжественна: два человека стоя пьют водку, находясь в полном единении с самими собой и друг с другом. Интимность церемонии усугубляется отказом от традиционного третьего участника. Отношение архитектора к ритуалу можно без труда распознать во внешнем облике строения: оно стоит на возвышении и обращено не к земле, а к небу.

Баня на Клязьминском водохранилище
Александр Бродский/Ярослав Ковальчук

Купальня на берегу Клязьминского водохранилища – не совсем похожа на русскую баню, которая по традиции должна быть маленькой, тёмной и очень горячей. Это не соответствовало бы представлениям заказчика, который вознамерился построить на искусственном озере на юге Москвы развлекательный клуб для отдыха. Клиентами клуба стали бы обитатели многочисленных дач и вилл, которыми изобилует местный ландшафт. В отличие от соседнего ресторана «95 градусов» здание поставлено непосредственно на землю, а не на опоры. Оно состоит из деревянных стволов прямоугольного сечения и окружено изящными обходными галереями. Помимо чисто функциональной, галереи играют также важную конструктивную роль, поскольку они объединяют различные части фасада друг с другом. Тонкие вертикальные подпорки и горизонтальные скобы галерей создают устойчивую конструкцию, в которую заключен главный объём здания. Благодаря этим внешним конструкциям стало возможным отказаться от конструктивных элементов, традиционных для подобных построек. За счет выстраивания объема здания «снаружи вовнутрь» оно выглядит не таким массивным и грузным, как это могло бы быть при таких размерах. Только второй этаж, на котором размещаются гардероб, туалет, парная и душ выполнен монолитно. Сердцем проекта без сомнения является застеклённый эркер с круглым плавательным бассейном. Он словно парит над искусственным прудом и придаёт бане почти медитативный характер.

Строительные леса под Москвой
Группа «Обледенение архитекторов»

Идея проекта «Строительные леса в лесу» возникла у его авторов, членов группы «Обледенение архитекторов», в 1999 году - после того, как они увидели старый тополь, который врос в решетку окна дома журналистов на Суворовском бульваре. Было обнаружено, что взаимодействие природы с искусственными объектами (в данном случае с памятником архитектуры) не является противоречием. Напротив, как предположили молодые архитекторы, на базе противоположного проникновения достигается равноправие элементов. Эта идея была успешно осуществлена в августе 2000 года в рамках фестиваля современного искусства на территории пансионата «Клязьма». В расположенном на холме и ограниченном песчаным пляжем водоема березовом лесу, была возведена металлическая пятнадцатиметровая конструкция, охватывающая ствол и крону дерева. Возникла динамичная композиция, меняющая свой облик в зависимости от природного цикла дерева и погоды. По ночам конструкция освещалась - десятки электрических лампочек, подчвечивающих металлическую конструкцию придавали этому сооружению нечто мистическое. Предполагалось, что деревья со временем поглотят трехмерную металлическую сетку – тогда возник бы органический симбиоз – единственный в своем роде смешанный лес из берез и строительных лесов.

Жилой дом «Куча» в Нижнем Новгороде
Александр Харитонов/Евгений Пестов

Некоторые считают этот дом, насчитывающий от 4 до 7 этажей и построенный рядом со стадионом в окружении преимущественно одноэтажной застройки 18 века, недоразумением и нагромождением несовместимостей. Это не очень справедливо. Вернее было бы охарактеризовать это явление как проявление основного стремления новой русской архитектуры быть во что бы то ни стало оригинальной, ограниченное здесь рамками сложившейся строгой регулярной застройки. Над темным оштукатуренным цоколем первого этажа, накрытого по всему периметру металлическим козырьком, высятся четыре этажа центральной части здания, гладкие фасады которого покрыты светлой штукатуркой и имеют регулярные оконные членения. Над ними же начинается игра с выступами и углублениями, эркерами и нишами. Эта разноэтажная надстройка - от одного до трех этажей - выполнена из чередующихся полос светлого и темного кирпича, что отчасти перекликается с фактурой тоже полосатого цоколя. Создается ощущение, что на крыше обычного дома приземлился небольшой поселок из разноэтажных коттеджей. Постмодернистский характер этой архитектуры, с легким влиянием Марио Ботты, абсолютно очевиден. Здесь явно угадывается попытка объединить эстетические противоречия сложившейся застройки в одном здании - скромной застройки 70-х годов с такой же простой по сути, хотя и более интересной архитектуры 18-19-го веков.

Торговый центр «Этажи»
Виктор Быков

Не считая двух исключений, до недавнего времени магазины в Нижнем Новгороде располагались в бывших жилых домах, гостиницах или спортсооружениях, приспособленных для новых, коммерческих целей. Упомянутыми исключениями являются два универмага, сооруженные в 30-е годы в городе, насчитывающем около 1,4 миллиона жителей, который был переименован в 1932 г. в честь родившегося здесь Максима Горького, а после 1990 г. вновь обрел своё первоначальное название. С этого времени потребительские запросы крупного индустриального центра, в котором среди прочего выпускаются автомобили „Волга", сильно изменились. Торговый центр „Этажи"– ответ на эти изменения, он определяет характер новой коммерческой архитектуры. Располагается магазин на углу улиц Белинского и Ижорской – в одном ряду со старыми винными складами и оперой. Пятиэтажное здание с бросающимся в глаза стеклянным фасадом обладает ярким, узнаваемым обликом. Стеклянный фасад-экран позволяет еще с улицы увидеть, как функционирует здание внутри: эскалаторы, панорамный лифты и подобный зависшему в помещении дирижаблю зал игровых автоматов. Цилиндрическая пристройка перенимает у главного фасада его поэтажное членение – металлические ленты переходят здесь в узкие ленты окон, прорезающие глухой металлический фасад, которые затем перетекают в фасады трехэтажной пристройки. Конструктивная схема главного фасада, образованная лентами сплошного остекления, немного напоминает здание высшей школы строительства и художественного конструирования „Баухауз" в Дессау, что зримо свидетельствует о пристрастии архитекторов к архитектуре довоенного модернизма.

Торговый комплекс «Сити»
Александр Харитонов/Евгений Пестов

С конца 80-х годов Нижний Новгород стал архитектурной столицей региона, переживаемый им архитектурный расцвет связан прежде всего со стилистическими предпочтениями архитектуры модерна и конструктивизма. Доказательством второго служит этот торговый центр, возведенный в Канавино, на участке между Мещерой и Березкой – в рамках градостроительной программы, предусматривающей застройку пустырей в этом районе вплоть до Кавинского рынка. После реконструкции рынка район стал заполнятся торговыми площадями и магазинами. Торговля стала проникать сначала в первые этажи существующих зданий, что оживило район, но не изменило характер его застройки. Эта ситуация изменилась с появлением торгового комплекса. Он построен над уже существовавшим ювелирным магазином, стоявшим у выхода из подземного перехода. Перед архитекторами стояла задача построить крупный объем с четко структурированными фасадами, расчитанными на рекламные щиты, с верхним светом, а возможно и стеклянной крышей, и уличной площадью, которую можно было бы использовать для рыночной торговли. В результате появилось здание, внешний облик которого выдает в нем скорее традиционный универмаг, а не шоппинг мол. Этому способствует прежде всего остекление первого этажа. Над ним высится закрытый абстрактный куб с вырезанными в нем окнами и полыми стальными конструкциями, повторяющимися так же в виде надстроек на крыше. Геометрический рисунок и цветовая гамма фасадов являются узнаваемыми цитатами из Пита Мондриана.

Офисное здание «Громкоговоритель»
Александр Харитонов/Евгений Пестов

„Вот она - настоящая архитектура!"- вероятно воскликнул бы немецкий историк Карл Шлёгель, увидев „Башню-громковоритель". Здание однозначно можно признать за дом эпохи немецкого югендштиля, и Шлёгель, наверняка, тотчас перебрал бы в памяти примеры аналогичных построек, созданных работавшими в этом стиле Альбертом Гесснером, Паулем Гельднером или Отто Кауфманном. Все это говорит об убедительности этого здания, для создания которого архитекторы перебрали целую палитру от историзма до конструктивизма, чтобы сразу четырьмя строениями закрыть зияющую рану в исторической застройке. Центром притяжения здесь является угловая башня с овальным окном на границе между гладкой и кассетированной частями фасада, увенчанная причудливым колпаком крыши, напоминающем громкоговоритель. На самом деле еще больше эта крыша похожа на крышку кофейника. Сравнение с громкоговорителем кажется довольно надуманным и скорее беспомощным по отношению к архитектуре, которая спустя более ста лет доказывает, что она явно ничего не утратила в своей стилеобразующей динамике вопреки всему за это время построенному. Стиль модерн был и остается частью поэтики и жизнеощущения, и потому так легок и стремителен переход от ассиметричной орнаментики и цветочных контуров к соседней скругленной башне во внутреннем дворе, с ее вертикальными оконными навесами, и оттуда – к следующему зданию на краю улицы, которое подхватывает этот фасадный мотив в немного измененной форме и преносит его в смежный дом с двускатной крышей.

Банк «Гарантия» в Нижнем Новгороде
Александр Харитонов/Евгений Пестов

Здание правления пенсионного фонда банка «Гарантия» свое самоопределение как «финансовая гарантия вечной молодости» выражает в архитектурных формах стиля модерн. Стилеопределяющим элементом, объединяющим все части здания является лента цокольного этажа. Однако эффектным центром здания несомненно является опирающийся на две фантазийные колонны портик, несомая стена которого перетекает наверху в нависающий карниз боковых скругленных частей фасада. Симметричность композиции фасада подчеркивают овальные окна. Не менее эффектно выглядит и боковая башня с такими же органическими, перетакающими друг в друга формами. В целом комплекс из трех объемов воспринимается как пластически материализованная поэзия, связь с реальностью которой возвращает вычеканенная на полу у входа надпись «Банкомат». В любом случае, от избыточных растительных форм уличных фасадов в интерьере здания уже не остается и следа.

Жилой дом «Квадраты» в Нижнем Новгороде
Евгений Пестов

Офисно-жилое здание является градостроительным завершением квартала в историческом центре города. Архитекторы Александр Харитонов и Евгений Пестов, являющиеся так же авторами всех остальных нижегородских зданий, рассмотренных в этой главе, видели своей задачей создать переход от исторического центра к застройке советского времени и одновременно придать улице масштаб и направление развития. Современный архитектурный язык здания на углу Студеной и улицы Горького является тактической игрой с призраками прошлого. Его геометрически ясные формы и рациональный, лишенный декора облик продолжают традиции социалистического строительства, однако они преодолевают его безликость и абстрагированность. Двухэтажный, охватывающий все здание цоколь с длинными бойницеобразными окнами и срезанным углом входа определяет масштаб улицы на уровне пешеходов и выглядит как терраса, вынесенная перед четко структурированным фасадом. Этот фасад воспринимается как композиция из перекрывающих друг друга геометрических фигур. Эти клетчатые узоры образованы черным и красным кирпичом и белой штукатуркой, они не только оживляют фасады, но и придают им пластичность. Оптические эффекты подчеркиваются игрой оконных проемов – двумя неожиданно возникшими окнами на углу и прорезавшим карниз крыши окном пентхауса. Фасад со стороны улицы Горького членится по вертикали сильно вынесенным вперед треугольным выступом лоджий.

Жилой дом в Перьми
Мендель Футлик

По сути, этот дом – с его мощной надстройкой-аттиком, причудливыми формами и орнаментикой в духе стиля модерн – абсолютно инороден той среде, в которой он построен, и со своей градостроительной задачей заполнения пустоты на пересечении двух улиц тоже не очень справляется. Потому что между ним и последующими домами по-прежнему остаются незаполненные пространства. В то же время, это был наверно единственный возможный ход создать угловой акцент в этой стилистически выверенной, но достаточно однообразной градостроительной ситуации. Это особенно важно для города, жизнь которого основана на металлургии, и который существует с 1723 года скорее как рабочее поселение, чем город. Потому что Пермь – город без центра. И когда отсутствует среда, подобное здание создает важный акцент – с его скругленными балконами над расположенным на углу парадным подъездом, серыми и зелеными лентами кафельной плитки, облицованным черным мрамором цоколем, скульптурами и рельефами растительного характера. Здесь достигнуто стилистическое единство, в том числе и благодаря высоким потолкам и тонкой отделке подъездов с их круглыми венчающими окнами. Вот только венчающая угол башня-надстройка производит странное впечатление. У нее явно было какое-то назначение, но сейчас из нее торчат только два электропровода, ожидающих своего подключения. Возможно, изначально здание планировалось как офисное или даже медицинское, а в результате используется как жилое.

Торговый центр в Перьми
Виктор Тарасенко/Евгений Колчанов

Новый торговый центр на южном берегу Камского водохранилища, в расположенном в западном Предуралье индустриальном городе остротой своих форм напоминает кинжал. Его стальная конструкция и стеклянные фасады, эффектно светящиеся изнутри в темноте, скорее навевают мысли о железнодорожном вокзале, чем о магазине. Еще одна особенность этого центра – его стальные опоры, на которых высится основной объем здания. Большинство торговых и офисных площадей центра, занимающего 550 кв.м, находятся на уровне второго этажа, вынесенного над выходом из подземного перехода. Таким образом, благодаря этому из магазинов можно без проблем спуститься в туннель при любой погоде. Торговый центр располагает двумя входами. С северной стороны посетители попадают по пандусу на первый этаж молла, с южной – лестницы ведут к главному входу. Южная часть комплекса сконструирована так, что она служит навесом для ожидающих транспорта пассажиров. На архитектурном смотре «Зодчество» 2001 комплекс был отмечен как «лучшая архитектурная работа года».

Стадион «Локомотив» в Москве
Моспроект 4

Принадлежащий одноименному клубу новый стадион «Локомотив» на 30 тысяч зрителей был построен по международным стандартам – согласно нормам Европейского Футбольного Союза (UEFA) и международного футбольного союза (FIFA). Он включает шесть этажей с тремя ярусами трибун. Нижний ярус объединяет 20 рядов, верхний – 17 рядов, между ними располагается узкая остекленная трибуна с рестораном и 60 фирменными лоджиями. Смонтированные на промежуточном перекрытии нагреватели обеспечивают приятную для зрителей температуру в 15 градусов. Даже трава подогревается и проветривается – она здесь точно такая же, как на стадионе «Сантьяго Бернабео» Мадридского «Реала». В этом образцовом для России стадионе, напоминающем амстердамскую «Арену» и финансируемом московской железной дорогой, царит комфорт мирового уровня. Ярусы трибун по коротким сторонам разбиты на четыре сектора, а по длинным – на пять секторов с отдельными входами. Это создает обозримость и способствует безопасности. Ров шестиметровой ширины и трехметровой глубины, окруженный барьером и полосой безопасности, создает дистанцию между полем и трибунами. Входы на игровое поле располагаются в четырех скругленных углах арены. За счет выполненной из стекла и стали крыши и вынесенных полукруглых козырьков на длинных фасадах, арена похожа на большую устрицу – особенно, когда в темноте ее контуры подсвечиваются прожекторами. Конструкция крыши держится на вантах, закрепленных на двух, расположенных снаружи здания Г-образных мачтах. Крыша накрывает стадион, не затемняя его и не создавая тени, так как этот покров, охватывающий 230 000 кв.м., почти на 90% пропускает свет.

Дворец ледового спорта в Крылатском
Моспроект 4

Долгое время русские фигуристы тренировались за рубежом, в том числе, и в Германии. С появлением нового ледового стадиона необходимость в таком кочевничестве отпала. Среди множества возможных мест выбор для строительства стадиона пал на Крылатское. С одной стороны, это довольно переферийное расположение – на Западе Москвы, на границе между Филевским парком и жилым микрорайоном 80-х годов. В то же время, это место было выбрано еще для проведения олимпийских игр 1980-го года. Недалеко от изгиба Москва-реки располагается учебное стрельбище, гребной канал и велотрек. Ледовый стадион дополняет олимпийскую деревню своей органической архитектурой. Дальнейшие постройки последуют, если Москва выиграет право на проведение олимпийских игр в 2012 году. Так же как и в футбольном стадионе, здесь применяется вантовая конструкция, придающая облику стадиона сходство с морским животным. Крыша, накрывающая арену, составляет по ширине 117 метров и перекрывает площадь в 297 000 кв.м. Она заканчивается за пределами здания и держится на стальных канатах, закрепленных на наклонных мачтах. Издалека конструкция похожа на вантовый мост. Под этой огромной крышей находятся наряду с трибунами и необходимой стадиону инфраструктурой функционально структурированное для хокеистов и конькобежцев ледовое поле площадью 12 000 кв.м с 400-метровыми и 250-метровыми ледовыми дорожками. Благодаря функциональному членению ледовой поверхности, здесь могут одновременно тренироваться, не мешая друг другу, до 300 спортсменов.

Комплекс с аквапарком в Ясенево
Сергей Кислев

Для того, чтобы попасть в спортивно-развлекательный комплекс, надо предпринять долгое путешествие на юго-западную окраину Москвы – в Ясенево. Облик этого расположенного вблизи от окружной дороги, но вполне достижимого с помощью метро микрорайона определяют жилые 9-23-этажные панельные дома и лес. Именно в этом окружении и расположился развлекательный комплекс со спортивным и игровым бассейнами, водяными горками, саунами, боулингом, фитнес-залами и роликовыми дорожками. И, естественно, множеством закусочных и кафе. Над облицованным натуральным камнем цоколем расположена стеклянная ракушка аквапарка. Помещение бассейна со структурированным стеклянным фасадом и изогнутой крышей вписалось между сгруппировавшимися под прямым углом постройками спортивного и гастрономического назначения. Сферическая мачта является своего рода указателем, делающим развлекательный комплекс заметным издалека и выделяющим его на фоне многоэтажной застройки. В темноте светящаяся изнутри стеклянная раковина сама по себе становится заметным объектом, привлекающим внимание. Создавая композицию из кирипичных построек и легкой стеклянной ракушки Сергей Киселев реагирует на двойственность расположения комплекса – между городом и ландшафтом: непонятно, принадлежит ли оно еще городу, или является уже частью природы. Кстати, на эту тему уже нет смысла философствовать – после того, как в феврале 2004 года по неизвестным причинам обрушилась крыша аквапарка, развлекательный комплекс больше не функционирует.

Спортивный и теннисный центр в Кунцево
Александр Асадов

Кунцево расположено на западе Москвы – на Рублевском шоссе, на стыке города и пригорода, и более удалено от центра, чем олимпийский комплекс с новым ледовым стадионом и великолепным футбольным стадионом «Локомотив». Тем не менее, и этот теннисный центр является показательным для представленных в этом разделе «органических», экологичных построек. Большая часть площадей из почти 13 000 кв. метров центра находятся под мягких очертаний холмом – по другую сторону от лугов и опушки леса, маркирующих переход от многомиллионного города к зеленой зоне пригорода. Поперечное крыло с теннисными кортами на крыше своим восходящим асимметричным планом явственно противопоставляется мягким естественным формам окружения как нечто искусственное. Тем не менее, озелененная крыша, бирюзового цвета металлические конструкции и кирпичные стены, а так же полукруглый изгиб, обращенный к подъездной дороге способствует тому, что здание органично вписывается в этот пейзаж. Бассейн, сквэш, залы для аэробики, хореографии и бодибилдинга, фитнес-клуб и салон красоты искусно распределены в глубине холма, и в них можно попасть сквозь врезанный в него овальный вход. Отсюда же можно подняться на крышу к теннисным кортам. Три стеклянных фонаря на покрытой травой крышей обеспечивают освещение внутренних залов дневным светом. В подземном и, частично, на первом этаже находятся места для парковки порядка 100 автомобилей. Там же, под землей, располагаются дорожки кегельбана, бильярдный зал с собственным баром и кафе. На первом этаже наряду с парковкой расположены кассы, ресторан, вип-зона, и так же зона сквэша. На первом этаже находятся вестибюль, помещения для фитнесса и проход к теннисным кортам-вип на крыше.

Офисное здание «Пингвин» в Москве
Архитектурное бюро »Остоженка«

Офисное здание маркирует угол одного из самых плотно застроенных участков в центре деловой Москвы. В районе между Белорусским вокзалом и Триумфальной площадью дома становятся все выше, а улицы – все уже. Однако не только на центральных улицах вырастают новые высотные здания, но все чаще и боковые улицы – с их довольно скромного вида старой застройкой – попадают в поле интересов девелоперов. Этот процесс «внутренней урбанизации» имеет два аспекта: либо единичные участки застраиваются с целью максимальной рентабельности – с функциональными, нейтральными в архитектурном отношении зданиями, либо заказчики в союзе с архитекторами делают ставку на индивидуальность здания, не только предлагающего эксклюзивные офисные помещение, но и благодаря своей архитектуре становящегося запоминающимся символом на карте города. Офисное здание на 1-ой Брестской являет собой наглядный тому пример. Задачей было создать здание, выделяющееся на фоне многочисленный помпезных высотных новостроек, выросших в этом районе за последние годы. Выгнутая линия фасада напоминает немного силуэт пингвина – отсюда и сразу закрепившееся название – «дом-пингвин». Однако на самом деле, при рассмотрени этого выпуклого стеклянного фасада скорее возникают ассоциации с минималистским воплощением борочного коммода. Здание выступает своим мягко выгнутым фасадом к улице и создает исключительно за счет эстетических средств запоминающуюся, очень индивидуальную градостроительную ситуацию. Благодаря простым, строго геометризированным фасадам и холодным, гладким материалам, эта постройка обладает ярко выраженным современным, урбанистичным характером.

Жилой дом «Катамаран» в Москве
Владимир Плоткин, ТПО »Резерв«

Участок удален на 250 метров к югу от Можайского шоссе и расположен в квартале, ограниченном улицей Загорского, ул. Вересаева и поймой реки Сетунь. В северной и восточной части этого района доминирует массовая 12-15-этажная жилая застройка. Квартал группируется вокруг заповедной зоны поймы. Жилой комплекс состоит из двух параллельных, расположенных напротив друг друга корпусов, соединенных между собой четырьмя прямоугольными переходами, в центре которых располагаются башни подъездов. Помещения на первом этаже западного корпуса спланированы как общественные зоны, предоставленные для пользования жильцам дома. В этом комплексе предпринята попытка перевести внемасштабные вертикали его окружения в обозримые горизонтали средствами функционального модернизма, когда орнамент в детали переводится в кубатуру здания. Это означает, что если одна часть здания состоит из шести этажей, то расположенные напротив корпуса – в зависимости от расположения – состоят из четырех или пяти этажей. Фасады обоих корпусов ритмично членятся четырьмя выступами и лентами лоджий и балконов. Не смотря на одностворчатые окна, комплекс сильно напоминает о 70-х годах. Он воспринимается слишком холодным и обладает казенным шармом административного здания. Вопреки первоначальным планам лоджии сделали застекленными – это искажает эстетическую основу замысла, согласно которому лоджии создавали пространственную ритмизацию фасадов. Дом выглядит слишком сглаженным и можно только надеяться, что он преобразится с годами – как панельные дома вокруг, приобретшие с возрастом патину романтики.

Жилой комплекс «Татаровская пойма»
Владимир Плоткин/ТПО »Резерв«

Участок размером в 25,5 га, относящийся к Москворецкому природному заповеднику, расположен на западе Москвы – между олимпийским гребным каналом и гольф-клубом. Его кулису составляет великолепный ландшафт, который определяют спортивные постройки и массовое жилье микрорайона Крылатское. Еще в советское время был разработан план застройки, предусматривающий разделить участок в почти 30 гектаров на зону застройки и парк. Теперь здесь возведен город-сад с множеством очевидных стилистических и формальных цитат из архитектурного лексикона 20-х годов. Его композиционным центром является полукруглая площадь, венчающая застроенную блоками домов центральную улицу. В целом комплекс охватывает 12 четырехэтажных многоквартирных домов с нежилыми помещениями на первых этажах, 19 коттеджей, спортивный комплекс, поликлинику, а так же магазины и общественные здания. Дополнительные насыпи и канал придают этому городу-саду совершенно уникальный характер. К реминисценциям 20-х годов можно безусловно отнести П- и Г-образные планы домов, образующих открытые озелененные дворы, обращенные к улице и тем самым размывающие традиционные для городской среды границы между частным и общественным, внутренним и внешним. В архитектурном решении о 20-х годах напоминают белые фасады и их членение горизонтальными рамами окон, ленточное остекление на углах, а так же очень ясная композиция всего комплекса в целом. Здесь нет ничего чрезмерного или лишнего, все редуцировано до состояния гармонизированной функциональности. Даже перголы, объединяющие дома на площади, подчеркивают целостность этого ансамбля.

Центральный вокзал в Самаре
Юрий Храмов

Попав в это здание – с его высокой башней и светящимися зеркальными фасадами, трапециевидными надстройками и трубообразным перекрытием перонов – можно подумать, что ты не на вокзале, а на космодроме, и возникает потребность удостовериться, что ноги еще касаются земли, и сила земного притяжения еще не совсем утрачена. Нет, посетители находятся здесь и сейчас. И здание вокзала стало не только важным пересадочным пунктом железной дороги, но и создало новый облик Комсомольской площади, на которой оно построено. Оно очень эффектно в своей функциональной структуре. Трубообразная конструкция из стекла и стали направляет потоки движения пассажиров к шести перронам. При этом потоки приезжающих, отъезжающих и транзитных пассажиров отделены друг от друга. Вокзал, площадь которого составляет 47 800 кв.м, является не только одним из самых крупных из новых вокзалов Европы, но в нем по-новому осмыслена система пространственной организации и перенята навигационно-ориентирующая система и система разделения потока пассажиров, применяемая в аэропортах. На карте города вокзал стал важнейшим многофункциональным адресом. Кроме гостиницы, офисов, конференц-залов, он объединяет культурные учреждения, магазины, кафе и рестораны и таким образом становится пунктом притяжения общественной жизни города. Трудно представить себе более функционально и экономически продуманный объект.

Центр современного искусства
Михаил Хазанов

Бывшая фабрика по производству театрального и сценического реквизита была перестроена под Центр современного искусства (ГЦСИ) и превращена в современный музейный комплекс с выставочными и исследовательскими помещениями, офисами для кураторов и музейных сотрудников. Наиболее сложной задачей, стоявшей перед архитекторами и конструкторами, было размещение на втором этаже старого фабричного здания просторного выставочного зала, обходящегося без несущих опор. Уже существовавшие колонны были удалены. Это однако создало проблему для позднее спланированного конференц-зала, который проектировался как отдельный объем – для этого не хватало конструктивной основы. Выход нашелся в создании внешней несущей конструкции. На фасаде были смонтированы металлические рамы, обладающие одновременно конструктивной и эстетической функцией. Они придают старому кирпичному зданию современный характер, не привнося кардинальных изменений. За счет этого подчеркивается не только контраст между старым и новым, но и классическая красота старой индустриальной постройки. Здесь не найти чисто декоративных элементов, как нет здесь и завуалированной функциональности. Облик здания сигнализирует о наступлении новых времен. И хотя конструктивные детали, металлические ступени лестниц и поручни демонстрируют классическую индустриальную эстетику, однако яркокрасные поверхности стен и цокольной зоны свидетельствуют об их новом, пост-индустриальном использовании. Ощущение легкости и парения создается благодаря слегка изогнутой, филигранно сконструированной крыше. Мягким изгибом она накрывает тяжеловесные фабричные стены, зрительно уравновешивая их.

Жилой дом «Панорама» в Москве.
Архитектурное бюро »Остоженка«

Внушительный жилой комплекс возведен на территории бывшей индустриальной зоны в центре Москвы. Он вырастает как кристал над крышами своего разношерстного окружения. Его широко раскинувшиеся блестящие фасады отражают свет как водная гладь пруда и заставляют сверкать весь район. Без сомненья, подобное здание – абсолютная новинка для Москвы. Над массивным двухэтажным цоколем нависли стеклянные фасады здания, состоящие из множества стеклянных пластин различной величины. Впечатление легкости и транспарентности создается прежде всего за счет точнейшей обработки стекла и разнообразия визуальных взаимоотношений, возникающих при взгляде вовнутрь, изнутри или насквозь, а также зеркальных отражений. Сложный узор фасада не дает представления о внутренней структуре здания – только равномерные узкие вертикальные ленты маркируют расположение отдельных этажей. Для того, чтобы крупный объем не воспринимался как монолитная масса, здание разделено на две части – малый, простой, куб и более крупный трапециевидный объем. Внутри здания располагаются просторные квартиры, максимально свободные от перегородок – для того, чтобы будущие жильцы смогли оформить их согласно собственному вкусу.

Ладожский вокзал в Санкт-Петербурге
Студия 44

Своим обликом здание апеллирует к эпохе расцвета вокзальной архитектуры, когда вокзалы уподоблялись величественным храмам, вобравшим в себя лучшие инженерные идеи и выражавшие веру в торжество технического прогресса. Эта вера уже немного поистерлась, тем не менее, авторы Ладожского вокзала создали его в рамках той же традиции. Это можно объяснить несколькими причинами. Во-первых, Ладожский вокзал действительно велик. Во-вторых, сегодня сложилась ситуация полной стилистической свободы, когда можно как по каталогу выбрать любой исторический стиль. Так как стальные своды несут в себе исключительно эстетическую функцию и относятся к постмодернистском репертуару, в котором выражают себя архитекторы. Главный архитектор проекта Никита Явейн, говоря о вокзале, вспоминает о римских термах. Таким образом, вокзал не уподоблен ратуше или храму, но в то же время в нем нет ничего непривычного. Потому что архитекторы ориентировались на конкурсный проект Николаевского вокзала, разработанный в 1912 году И.А.Фоминым. Именно отсюда позаимствовала «Студия 44» трехчастную пространственную композицию, фланкированную двумя башнями. Однако классические детали «красной дорики» заменены элементами, выражающими эстетику индустриальности. Тем не менее, в здании есть фрагменты – как, например, шахты эскалаторов, в своей импозантности напоминающие гравюры Пиранези. Здание, с его лестничными башнями, обладает несомненной экспрессией и являет собой важный транспортный пункт на пути Москва-Хельсинки. В то же время, эта архитектура ориентируется прежде всего на саму себя и свое ближайшее окружение.

Жилой комплекс «Триумф-палас» в Москве
Компания «ДОН-Строй»

Реакцией на появление платежеспособного слоя населения и спроса на жилье в центре Москвы стало возведение 270-метрового жилого здания на Ленинградском проспекте, недалеко от станции метро «Аэропорт». Подковообразный комплекс, насчитывающий 1000 квартир считают «нео-сталинистским» и называют восьмой высоткой – в продолжение возведенным при Сталине после войны семи высотным зданиям, маркирующим центр города. Инвесторы же, напротив, подчеркивают его современный комфорт. «Триумф-палас» лишь своим силуэтом может сравниться со сталинскими высотками – символами мощи государственной власти и главного архитектора страны – И.Сталина. Но по своей архитектурной проработке оно не может с ними сравниться – здесь не найти столь хорошо вычерченных фризов, карнизов и капителей. Тем не менее, здание обладает несомненным пафосом. То, что в Москве есть спрос на репрезентативную архитектуру, подтверждает и разработанная мэром Лужковым программа возведения еще 60 высотных зданий подобного рода. Сохранить собственный имидж и одновременно не выпадать из интернационального контекста – вот главный посыл самого высокого жилого здания в Европе. Его стиль – с завершающими композицию белыми балконами и декором – напоминает американские небоскребы предыдущего столетия – такие как Сингер-Билдинг в Сохо в Нью-Йорке. Венчающая шпиль корона напоминает башни баптистских церквей в маленьких американских города. С подножья и до верхушки шпиля этот дом выглядит как собранный из конструктора, как типовой панельный дом, кичево приукрашенный белой штукатуркой, и потому являющийся не более чем карикатурой на достойные восхищения сталинские «дворцы для народа».

Жилой дом «Патриарх» в Москве
Сергей Ткаченко

Жилой дом «Патриарх» расположен недалеко от Тверской – главной улицы города, берущей свое начало от Кремля, застроенной преимущественно домами конца XIX – нач. XX века и нео-классическими постройками сталинского времени, и Садового кольца. Характер архитектурного окружения повлиял на облик этого здания. Возведенное на угловом участке, зажатом со всех сторон существующей застройкой, здание стало важной градостроительной доминантой, просматривающейся с разных точек зрения. Здесь одним, захватывающем дух, художественным жестом объединены современные представления о комфортном жилье – с просторными помещениями, высокими потолками и большими окнами - с классическим декором фасадов, элементами конструктивизма и современными конструкциями. Заслуживают упоминания великолепные лоджии на расчлененных пилястрами фасадах. Обращенная к Садовому кольцу часть здания решена как сужающаяся кверху башня, завершающаяся венком карнизов и увенчанная композицией из нескольких объемов: классической ротонды бельведера, барочного восьмерика и «шпилем» в виде уменьшенной копии «Памятника III. Интернационалу» В.Татлина 1919 года. Находящийся за ним основной объем завершает двухсветная ротонда с колоннадой, увенчанная волнистой шапкой-куполом. Балюстраду украшают скульптурные портреты в рост основных персонажей московской сцены недвижимости, в том числе и главного архитектора города Александра Кузьмина. Цоколь здания облицован натуральным камнем, который используется и в оформлении квартир – наряду с керамикой и паркетом. На первом этаже располагаются охранная служба, предназначенные для жильцов бассейн и сауна, дом оснащен тремя пассажирскими и грузовым лифтом, а так же подземным гаражем.

Жилой комплекс «Монолит» в Москве
Михаил Белов

Если идти по парку Университета им. Ломоносова в восточном направлении, то невольно упрешься в массивное пятиэтажное здание в неоклассическом стиле. Недалеко от изгиба Москва-реки возведен этот эксклюзивный жилой комплекс для семей с достатком – в великолепном и спокойном месте и в то же время – недалеко от главных артерий пульсирующего городского организма. В современной России есть здания, имя которых вынесено над главным входом и несет в себе послание о назначении здания и его эстетике. Без сомнения, к ним относится и этот трехчастный комплекс, величественно открывающийся в парк и огороженный со стороны улицы изящным металлическим забором. Если подойти к зданию с этой стороны, то в глаза бросается величественный портик с мраморными коринфскими колоннами, несущими вполне правда скромный аттиковый этаж с несколькими окнами и монограммой комплекса. Однако за колоннами вопреки ожиданиям обнаруживается не величественный входной портал, который бы соответствовал пафосу портика, а обычная стена с дверью, которая в данном контексте воспринимается как мышиная нора. Недоразумение, трудно поддающееся объяснению или оправданию, тем более на фоне классического фасада с хорошо спропорционированными окнами, карнизами, раскреповками, ионическими пилястрами и рельефами с античными жанровыми сценами. Причина видится в том, что эклектизм – даже при том, что для подражания брались очень качественные образцы – лишен оправданности, и потому легко становится чрезмерным. Ничто в этом криволинейном в плане здании не подходит друг другу. И в то же время оно соответствует своему главному назначению – удовлетворению десятилетиями подавляемой потребности к репрезентативному образу жизни.

«Помпейский дом» в Москве
Михаил Белов

Филипповский переулок – типичный уголок старого Арбата. Все улицы здесь настолько узки, что здания практически невозможно целиком охватить взглядом. Поэтому нет ничего удивительного, что архитектор Михаил Белов в оформлении этого дома сконцентрировался на двух верхних этажах уличного фасада, которые выступают над крышами соседних домов и являются своего рода визитной карточкой дома. На фоне преимущественно сероватой арбатской застройки здание с его ярко-оранжевыми, карминно-красными и синими росписями воспринимается как ренессансный дворец. Вынесенные на фасад колонны несут тяжелый карниз, своими растительными орнаментами и полным набором цитат из лексикона классической архитектуры они являют собой подлинный архитектурный фейерверк. Форму капителей Белов придумал сам, они отлиты из нового синтетического материала, выглядящего как бронза. «Помпейский дом» являет собой яркий архитектурный манифест, заявленный как антитеза модернистской концепции, отрицающей фасадный декор. По словам Михаила Белова, одного из знаменитых архитекторов-бумажников, добившихся международной славы в конце восьмидесятых годов, здание преодолевает так же современную усталость как от деконструктивизма, так и от «органической» архитектуры. Безусловно, такой дом как «Помпейский» - созданный по заказу частного лица - мог быть реализован только в Москве: он абсолютно свободен как от идеологи, так и от контекстуальной традиции. Михаил Белов сам оценивает свое детище вполне прагматично: «Для меня «Помпейский дом» не является воплощением стиля ретро – он не относится ни к историзму, ни к постмодернизму. Он так же не является попыткой удовлетворить заказчика. Это здание представляет современную архитектуру Москвы образца 2005 года.

Жилой дом «Дворянское гнездо» в Москве
Илья Уткин

Этот дом так же расположен в самом центре. В том его районе, где брежневская номенклатура 70-х годов – в то время, как вся страна застраивалась безликими типовыми постройками, - возводила для себя репрезентативные кирпичные дома. Проект в конструктивистском духе для этого места не убедил заказчиков хотя бы потому, что он слишком контрастировал бы с преобладающими в застройке квартала доходными домами и особняками рубежа 19-20 веков. В результате возникло пятиэтажное угловое здание с характерным для этого места скругленным углом, представляющее собой единственное в своем роде смешение классических форм и Ар-Деко. Это здание несет в себе так же и важную градостроительную функцию, создавая эффектный акцент на пересечении М.Левшинского и Пречистенского переулков. Архитектурный рисунок фасада весьма строг. Над отделанным натуральным камнем цоколем возвышается бельэтаж, в отделке которого сочетаются темный клинкер и светлый скульптурный декор. Трехчастная композиция фасадов завершается аттиковым этажом с ротондой на углу. Стена как граница между внутренним и внешним, между общественным и приватным обладает множеством смысловых нагрузок. Она, с одной стороны – оболочка дома, с другой – сама является произведением искусства.

Административное здание в Москве
Сергей Ткаченко

Еще в 1988 году московским городским комитетом был объявлен конкурс на три высотных здания, которые «должны были бы завершить визуальный облик Садового кольца» в юго-восточной его части. Москва окружена несколькими кольцами. Одно из них – кольцо монастырей, в которое входят среди прочих Андроников (1360), Спасский (1420), Симоновский (1379) и Донской (1591) монастыри. Схеме расположения монастырей вторили и указывающие в небо высотки советского государства, возведенные на уровне бывшей городской стены, там, где раньше находились въездные ворота в город. После 1990 года это кольцо мысленных городских ворот подверглось дальнейшей комплектации. Новые высотные здания появились в Оружейном переулке на Краснохолмской (Риверсайд Тауэрс), а так же на площади Павелецкого вокзала, на юге Садового кольца. 26-этажное офисное здание с двумя боковыми крыльями – единственный реализованный проект проводимого 15 лет назад конкурса. Комплекс создает эффектный акцент на этом оживленном участке Садового кольца, где день и ночь бурлит привокзальная жизнь. Задуманная изначально в другом эклектическом ключе башня – как напоминание о Биг Бене в Лондоне – в результате явилась олицетворением двух стилей – московского барокко и сталинского ампира, совмещенных в постмодернистских формах американского нео-урбанизма. Эффектно подсвеченное в темноте, здание несет в себе что-то и от Лас-Вегаса, что современной Москве сегодня очень к лицу.

Жилой дом на улице Машкова в Москве
Сергей Ткаченко

Фантазия архитекторов, протестовавших против монотонности государственно-регулируемого искусства, кажется, не знала границ. Проекты архитекторов-бумажников в советские времена были программно нереализуемы. С распадом Советского Союза эта ситуация изменилась. Как минимум в России. Неожиданно появился спрос на утопии, восстанавливающие вкус к архитектуре, даже если она иногда перенимает на себя роль художественной акции. Одним из этих архитекторов-бумажников был и О.Дубровский. Его объект представляет собой яйцеподобное сооружение, которое изначально планировалось для многих других мест, но в результате было буквально «высижено» на улице Машкова для того, чтобы своим необычным обликом взорвать веками сложившуюся квадратуру квартала и отношения между застройкой и красной линией улицы. Дерзость вдвойне, так как четырехэтажный дом-яйцо с элементами стиля модерн является пристройкой к вполне традиционному многоэтажному жилому дому. Этот протест против главенства консервативных форм в искусстве и противопоставление нового, своего собственного художественного языка были характерны и для авангардного движения рубежа 19-20-х веков. Именно это воплощает собой и дом-яйцо, в котором стилистическое своеобразие деталей переносится на весь объем. Вообще-то предполагалось построить два «яйца» - малое и большое – в «подставке», с палладианской аркой и несомым коринфской колоннадой кольцом, но оно пока осталось нереализованным.

Офисное здание на Долгоруковской улице
Моспроект-2, мастерская 14

Офисное здание расположено в центре города, в квартале с преимущественно старой застройкой, в которую оно органично вписывается, создавая при этом новый градостроительный акцент. Характерно, что дом высотой всего в 14 этажей намного возвышается над другими домами этого района. В то же время, для того, чтобы новостройка высотой более 50 метров вписалась в сложившийся масштаб квартала, была выбрана ступенчатая композиция, при которой здание достигает максимальной высоты, но выглядит так, как будто оно состоит из нескольких примыкающих друг к другу отдельных домов с одинаковыми фасадами, которые завершаются застекленными мансардами и сильно выступающими карнизами. Центральный корпус выделяется стеклянной вертикальной осью, которая завершается наверху верандным остеклением с колоннадой. Фасады выполнены в пропорциональном единстве с непосредственно примыкающей к зданию конструктивистской постройкой Ильи Голосова, с восприятием и развитием его членений и пластики, с использованием карнизов и архитектурного декора.

Паркинг на Якиманке в Москве
Моспроект-2, мастерская 11

Многоэтажная автостоянка на 445 мест, построенная в центре города, на пересечении 1-го и 4-го Голутвинского переулка, является лучшим подтверждением того, что архитектура является прежде всего искусством. В этом квартале между набережной Обводного канала и Большой Якиманкой – с небольшими городскими усадьбами и их романтическими полисадниками, потрепанными временем, однако вполне достойными промышленными и административными постройками конца 19 – начала 20-го вв., а так же гладкими фасадами стилистических экзерсисов последних лет, это здание заявляет прежде всего об одном – о приверженности старине. Все, что находится на его фасадах - карнизы, консоли, раскреповки – можно найти и в облике расположенных рядом старинных усадеб. Гладь же фасада, наоборот, перенимает красный кирпич индустриальной архитектуры. К этому добавляются еще полуциркульные окна различных размеров, иногда даже в форме сдвоенных церковных окон. Однако это здание не является ни учебным заведением, ни церковью, ни предприятием. За его пышно декорированными фасадами скрывается современный паркинг, и потому оно –чистейшая архитектурная иллюзия.

Жилой комплекс в Санкт-Петербурге
Евгений Герасимов

Санкт-Петербург, эта северная Венеция, благодаря своим многочисленным островам предоставляет прекрасные возможности для создания идеальных жилых условий для людей с высокими доходами и запросами. Подобные ниши для элитной жилой застройки можно найти и на Крестовском острове. На Южной аллее 2, непосредственно на стрелке Южного канала – в центре исторического ансамбля Приморского парка, располагается этот современный апарт-отель. Четырехэтажное здание органично вписывается в прекрасный ландшафт и раскрывается П-образно к воде, создавая тем самым эффектную визуальную доминанту. В этом здании все стремится слиться с природой – это артикулируют зеленые стальные конструкции выступающей над фасадом крыши, колонны и торцы боковых флигелей, эркеры и членения оконных рам, придающие облицованному кирпичом и натуральным камнем зданию известную легкость. Филигранная стальная конструкция образует над комплексом легкий покров. Все в целом создает впечатление, что занимающее почти 12 400 кв.м здание вписывается в ландшафт, но не уподобляется ему. Оно обладает суверенностью и в то же время очень гармонично – изогнутая, хороших пропорций, крыша охватывает его целиком, объединяет в единую композицию центральный корпус и боковые флигели и перекрывает комфортабельный внутренний двор, превращая здание в эффектную театральную кулису, на фоне которой у воды могут разыгрываться сцены современной светской жизни его обитателей. Достаточно простора для достойной жизни предоставляют и трех-четырехкомнатные квартиры размерами до 180 кв.м при высоте потолков до четырех метров.

Мечеть Кул-Шариф в Казани
Татинвестгражданпроект

К многочисленным религиозным постройкам, возведенным после распада Советского Союза, относятся не только православные, но и мусульманские храмы. Мечеть Кул-шариф среди них – один из интереснейших примеров. Во-первых, она возведена в окруженном крепостной стеной центре города – средневековом казанском Кремле. Она расположена точно в геометрическом центре Кремля и своими почти 60-метровыми минаретами полностью изменила силуэт его ансамбля, который до этого определялся куполами построенного в 1562 Благовещенского собора, а так же церквей Преображенского монастыря и собора Петра и Павла. Теперь эти символы православия уступили главную роль мусульманской мечети. Это кардинальное изменение, при всей своей непостижимости, в принципе, можно оправдать исторически – Казань в советские времена являлась резиденцией муфтия суннитских мусульман европейской части Советского Союза. Возведение мечети окончательно манифестирует значение Казани как центра мусульманства. Это главенствующее значение предопределило и архитектуру мечети – как ее формы, так и декоративное убранство, вплоть до малейших деталей. Необычным для этого типа построек являетсяе венок окон в барабане купола, напоминающий православные храмы, а так же нетипичные для мечети стрельчатые готические своды. Типичные для ранней готики ланцетные окна с цветными витражами дополняют одновременно отчужденный и возвышенный облик мечети, становясь частью характерных восточных орнаментов. В плане мечеть состоит из двух пересекающихся под углом в 45 градусов квадратов, в углах которых располагаются минареты. Помимо обязательных полумесяцев на минеретах и куполе, характерная ориентальная орнаментика с рельефной вязью сурн корана украшает нижнюю часть здания и фризы стрельчатого портала.

Церковь Св. Георгия-победоносца в Самаре
Юрий Харитонов

Собор был построен к 55-ой годовщине победы в Великой Отечественной Войне. Мемориальный характер этого пятиглавого крестово-купольного храма подчеркивается его расположением на Площади Славы - там, где располагается дом правительства и могила неизвестного солдата с вечным огнем. Таким образом церковь придает этому месту высшую освященность и в то же время становится градостроительной доминантой на верхнем берегу Волги. Издалека видны ее увенчанные крестами, сверкающие на солнце пять позолоченных куполов, обшитых легированным титаном. Подсвеченные в темноте белые фасады церкви излучают «божественное сияние», таким образом визуально выражается сакральное назначение здания. Выразительная сила этого здания значительно превосходит его материальное воплощение. По своим скромным размерам – 200 кв.м площади и 35 метров высоты – оно сравнимо скорее с часовней. Одновременно собор вступает в перекличку с обелиском памятника женщинам-труженицам тыла, с которым их разделяет небольшой сквер. Церковь и мемориал – противопоставление или неразделимое единство? В советское время последнее невозможно было бы представить. К этому стоит добавить, что с 1935 года и до распада Советского Союза Самара носила имя Куйбышева и с 1941 года, когда немецкие войска стояли под Москвой, была альтернативной столицей, в которой были взорваны практически все религиозные постройки. Теперь же здесь построен кирпичный, облицованный мрамором храм с фреской, изображающей Георгия-победоносца, изразцовым алтарем, дубовыми хорами и галереями - что вкупе с романским порталом и другими элементами древнерусской архитектуры, создает впечатление того, что это здание всегда стояло на этом месте, со времен основания Самары в конце 16-го века.

Храм Христа Спасителя в Москве
Моспроект-2, мастерская 12

Как ни трудно в это поверить, но этот собор – возведен в 2000 году. Возведен в архитектурных формах, не оставляющих сомнения в их долгой истории. Все здесь кажется настоящим – и это действительно так, если с изумлением вглядеться в богатый декор купола. В тридцатые годы храм – как и 8 000 других церквей в рамках культурной революции был взорван по указанию Сталина. На месте Храма Христа Спасителя, построенного в 1883 году и при высоте 103 метра являвшегося высотной доминантой города, должен был быть построен Дворец Советов. Уничтожение храма шокировало тогда даже атеистов, так как его проектирование началось в 1839 году архитектором Константином Тоном в честь победы в войне над Наполеоном, он строился на народные пожертвования и был прежде всего памятником народному патриотизму. Хотя его псевдоисторические формы уже тогда у многих вызывали возражения. Сегодня в 177 нишах храма как и раньше располагаются плиты, на которых высечены имена героев, павших в войне 1812 года. На месте собора было спланировано построить Дворец Советов 315 м высотой, увенчанный стометровой фигурой В.Ленина. Перед зданием – аналогично площади перед собором Св.Петра в Риме – должна была располагаться полукруглая колоннада, фланкирующая площадь для народных собраний. Расположенный недалеко от стен Кремля Дворец Советов должен был стать новой композиционной и идеологической доминантой Москвы и самым главным памятником нового режима. Однако реализация проекта осуществилась не дальше фундамента. Пришедший на смену Сталину Н.Хрущев сделал свой выбор в пользу здоровья трудящихся масс, и в вырытом котловане Дворца Советов был создан открытый бассейн с подогревом.

Перевод с немецкого: Ирина Шипова

Don-Stroi: Wohnhochhaus »Triumf Palas«, 265 Meter, Moskau 2006